"I can't think of a more appropriate person than Greg to coauthor a book on the fundamentals of marketing. He not only shares his wisdom and decades of industry experience, he breaks down the essence of the R.E.D. system so that even the greenest of marketing professionals will have the blueprints on which to begin their own career and journey. His R.E.D. system is not a theory. It's not a bunch of charts and graphs. It's proven methodology that for years drove Yum!'s sales to new heights of success, even during some of the most trying times of our economy. Anyone pursuing a career in this industry owes it to themselves and their future to read this book cover to cover. It will be time very well spent."   —**Massimo Ferragamo,**
Chairman, Ferragamo USA, Inc.

"I had the pleasure of doing business with Greg Creed and knowing him personally, and I can tell you that he is one of the most creative, innovative, and customer-focused business leaders I've ever come across. If you want to learn a common-sense, no-nonsense, and effective approach to marketing and business leadership, this is the book for you. In his time as Yum! CEO, Greg demonstrated that the R.E.D. marketing approach translates into tremendous business success. Just look at Yum!'s results under his stewardship!"   —**Dave MacLennan,**
CEO and Chairman, Cargill, Inc.

"I met Greg in 2001, when he joined Taco Bell as the CMO. Although it was a decade before the R.E.D. system of marketing was born, there were elements of the system that were apparent even then. Greg's thought leadership and marketing expertise set the foundation for the success that Taco Bell has enjoyed for the better part of the last decade and will serve the Taco Bell business for years to come. As a franchisee of Taco Bell for more than thirty years, I have seen my fair share of executives; Greg is one of those rare people that leave an indelible mark on what they do."   —**Lee J. Engler,**
CEO, Border Foods

"Often, I get asked what marketing book I can recommend equally to new students to the field and to long-term marketers and advertisers who try to stay on the cutting edge of how to build brands and market products. From now on, I will say *R.E.D. Marketing* because it synthesizes the latest marketing-science learnings into a pragmatic framework that every marketer can apply. A true must-read for any marketer who wants to stay relevant."   —**Michael Fassnacht,**
CMO, City of Chicago

"Filled with simple frameworks and engaging stories, *R.E.D. Marketing* will help everyone in marketing understand what really works for driving sustainable brand growth and business success."   —**John Kenny, PhD,**
Head of Strategic Planning, Intouch Group

"*R.E.D. Marketing* distills all I learned from a decade working alongside Greg and Ken into a quick read that will accelerate any marketer's career."   —**Jeff Jenkins,**
EVP of Global Marketing, Carters Inc.

"In an age of complex and mixed messages, Creed and Muench remind us that consumers want and need straightforward, clear, simple communication. Yum! Brands has consistently created brilliant marketing campaigns for KFC, Taco Bell, and Pizza Hut that break through the clutter and connect with the minds, hearts, and taste buds of their worldwide audience. Read *R.E.D. Marketing*. It is your blueprint for success and will allow your brand to 'Live Más'! It's an effin great book!"
—**Terry J. Lundgren,**
Founder and CEO, TL Advisors, LLC

"Greg has shaped my career, beginning with my first role in marketing as an intern at Taco Bell to the role I am in today. The principles I learned from Greg early in my career have fueled my approach to developing award-winning breakthrough campaigns at every position since then. It's incredible to have that insight and knowledge available in a book for other aspiring marketers to read."   —**Nick Tran,**
Head of Global Marketing, TikTok

"This is a must-read for all brand builders and business leaders! *R.E.D. Marketing* is a simple and powerful blueprint that weaves in captivating stories and lessons. Greg is a proven leader with world-class results and relevant advice that you can apply immediately."   —**Diane Dietz,**
CEO and President, Rodan and Fields

"R.E.D. marketing works! I have witnessed its success over the past decade in more than fifty thousand restaurants in 150 countries around the world. Now Greg and Ken have written a book that translates marketing theories into practical reality that is easy to implement."   —**Robert D. Walter,**
Founder, Former Chairman, and CEO, Cardinal Health,
Former Director and Chairman, Yum! Brands

"Greg was instrumental in taking Taco Bell promotions and advertising from one-hit wonders to a strong succession of winners that built sales quickly but more importantly built the brand over time. He increased the value of Taco Bell and Yum! Brands for franchisees, customers, and shareholders. As an owner with everything invested in my business, I enjoyed the benefits of this powerful partnership between Taco Bell and Collider Lab. As a Taco Bell enthusiast, I enjoyed knowing that my favorite brand was cool, relevant, desired, valuable, and admired."
—**Don Ghareeb,**
Chairman Emeritus, Tacala

"Greg and Ken are deeply respected brand architects and executive leaders. In this book, they have crystalized an actionable framework to help anyone build and optimize brands. After experiences and mistakes building brands around the world . . . if only I had their wisdom in those early days to guide me! Any marketer, operator, or executive will be a better brand steward after reading *R.E.D. Marketing*."

—**Kat Cole,**
COO and President, FOCUS Brands

"I have gotten to know Greg Creed through our work together on the Whirlpool Corporation Board. He is a true marketeer, and this book provides great insights into how he has successfully mastered his craft. I highly recommend it."

—**Sam Allen,**
Retired Chairman and CEO, Deere & Company

"Greg Creed and Ken Muench offer up the philosophy, strategy, and tactics that Greg used as a gifted marketer and CEO to build brands and propel Yum!'s incredible growth. *R.E.D. Marketing* is a welcome lifejacket of practicality in today's increasingly complex—often conflicting—academic marketing research and theory. The best business writers, like the best marketers, have a knack for making complicated ideas easy to digest to inspire their audience and move them to action. Engaging, provocative, yet very practical, this book is a must-read for anyone interested in building—or rebuilding—a marketing and branding strategy."

—**Tanya Domier,**
CEO, Advantage Solutions

"Greg and Ken's take on marketing is a pleasing, frank, and plainspoken wake-up call for marketers to slow down long enough to ensure the lifelines for brand building are moored in relevance, ease, and distinctiveness with their R.E.D. framework. Relevance beats uniqueness over the long haul, ease is the new fast, and distinctiveness beats even excellence. Greg Creed was an early pioneer and marketing legislator of today's immutable law that brands are built on the premise of experience over promise-making and, unfortunately, promise-breaking. I still have gauzy memories of Greg across the battlefield, when I was on a similar journey at Burger King." —**Russ Klein,**
CEO, American Marketing Association

Greg Creed & Ken Muench

R.E.D.
MARKETING

The Three Ingredients of Leading Brands

HarperCollins
LEADERSHIP

An Imprint of HarperCollins

The views and opinions expressed in this book are those of the authors, Greg Creed and Ken Muench, and do not necessarily reflect the views or opinions of Yum! Brands, KFC, Pizza Hut, Taco Bell, or The Habit Burger Grill or any of their employees.

Published by HarperCollins Leadership, an imprint of HarperCollins Focus LLC.

Any internet addresses, phone numbers, or company or product information printed in this book are offered as a resource and are not intended in any way to be or to imply an endorsement by HarperCollins Leadership, nor does HarperCollins Leadership vouch for the existence, content, or services of these sites, phone numbers, companies, or products beyond the life of this book.

ISBN 978-1-4002-2330-5 (eBook)
ISBN 978-1-4002-2329-9 (HC)

Library of Congress Control Number: 2021932201

Printed in the United States of America
21 22 23 LSC 10 9 8 7 6 5 4 3 2 1

Contents

Foreword

by Greg Creed

OVER THE YEARS a lot of people have suggested that I write a book; for all those years I said no. In fact I was so against writing a book that I made the classic error of promising in public on more than one occasion that I would never write one. It also didn't hurt that I am known widely by family, friends, and work colleagues as the world's worst speller. I am very competitive but I have never, ever won a game of Scrabble in my life.

Well, here we are with *R.E.D. Marketing*, so I guess the first thing I should explain is why I decided to write *this* book. Some of my friends suggested I write about the boy who was born and grew up in Brisbane, Australia, yet ended up running a Fortune 200 company when he was appointed CEO of Yum! Brands in January 2015. No thanks. There are too many of those books out there already. Instead, the idea of writing a book about the work, rather than the individuals behind the work, started to slowly feel more appealing as I realized I didn't need to ruminate excessively on my own personal history.

My second reason for changing my mind is that I could cowrite it with my good friend and colleague Ken Muench. Ken is one of the smartest people in consumer behavioral insights that I have ever met in more than forty years of business. We've both been lucky to work at a company like Yum!. Not only it is big, encompassing over 50,000 restaurants (including KFC, Taco Bell, Pizza Hut, and The Habit Burger) in 150 countries, it's a unique creative culture: one that prioritizes courage, conviction, and taking chances in an often staid corporate world. At Yum!, talent and culture are self-perpetuating qualities: great people are drawn to work at a company that supports them taking chances, encourages bold ideas, and recognizes and rewards teams when they have courage and dream big. It's to Yum!'s endless credit that they've embraced the weird, and allowed us to pursue our results in unorthodox ways.

My final reason—and the only condition I had for writing the book—was that if we made any money the profits from the book would all go back to the Yum! Foundation for scholarships for our frontline team members at KFC, Pizza Hut, Taco Bell, and The Habit. Ken and I would never see a penny for ourselves. These frontline employees are working every day to serve our customers under the incredible stress of coronavirus. If we can help some of them achieve their dreams, it will be a small step toward recognizing their efforts.

Ken and I first met in 2007 when I was running Taco Bell and Ken was heading up planning at our creative agency, FCB. The great thing about running Taco Bell was that even though I was serving as the president, I was also the chief concept officer, so I occasionally got to stick my nose in the marketing for the brand. One day, in 2011, Ken was explaining how in consumers' minds food had gone from "*fuel* to an *experience*," driven in part by things like Instagram and other forms of social media. At that moment I realized that "Think Outside the Bun," while the perfect tagline for the early 2000s, when food was fuel, was the absolute wrong one when food was an experience. This was an absolutely seismic shift for Taco Bell, a literal 180-degree turn from how we had been approaching our marketing.

We toyed with "Live a Little Más" as our new tagline for a while. Jeff Fox, who was VP of Marketing at the time, said, very eloquently, that if you can't fit the tagline on the front of a baseball cap it's too long. So with that we made the pivot to "Live Más" (as of now, still our tagline). While we had a new and powerful tagline in "Live Más" the ad agency was struggling to bring it to life, so after much agonizing, we shifted the creative duties to Deutsch LA, a powerhouse agency and one that truly gets the Taco Bell brand. The downside was that leaving FCB would mean losing Ken, Greg Dzurik, and Jeff who had also moved there. So Yum! encouraged and supported them to set up their own marketing consultancy, Collider Lab, promising that Taco Bell would give them enough business to anchor them until they found new clients, which they very quickly did. As Collider Lab developed, so did R.E.D. As you'll read, R.E.D. encompasses the three elements of **relevance**: *cultural relevance, functional relevance,* and *social relevance.* Next comes **ease**: *easy to notice* and *easy to access.* Finally—and crucially—comes **distinctiveness**. Add these elements together and you will have truly effective marketing.

In January of 2020, I officially retired from my position as CEO of Yum!. It's been an absolute blast to run a company that is innovative, brave, and willing to trust its creative teams: Yum! encourages its CMOs to go big, and to be bold. It's even enshrined in our internal mantra, *smart, heart, and courage.* R.E.D. is the *smart* part, our people are the *heart,* and the *courage* is what comes when you believe in both. I had a ton of mixed feelings about leaving, but I knew that I'd get a chance to boil down everything I've learned, and share that wisdom in this book.

All was going to plan, until a global pandemic hit, and the world ended. That's an exaggeration, of course, and the fact that you are reading this book is evidence that life, laughter, and business continue. Still, we have all learned that the world is less predictable, and more volatile, than we might have believed. In our category—the quick-serve restaurant—we had to adapt to a world in which our customers were no longer allowed inside our locations (at least temporarily). Ultimately, we had to scramble to figure out what role KFC, Pizza Hut, Taco Bell, and The Habit Burger played in this new paradigm.

Despite the challenges, something profound emerged out of the mess of late-night Zoom sessions, Teams conferences, and endless Slack threads, humming with uncertainty, anxiety, and confusion. From Shanghai to Sydney, Dubai to Dallas, Louisville, and Irvine, our marketing teams—after a brief period of WTF—knew how to approach the problem. We didn't have an answer right away. What we did have was a team of some of the greatest people I've ever had the good luck to work with. From our head office in Dallas, to Collider Lab in Santa Ana, and to the regional offices around the world, I have been consistently amazed at the sheer talent, ambition, courage, and character of Yum! teams. If I didn't get to shake your hand, and say, "Thank you," before I left, consider this my heartfelt acknowledgment of your ability and all your hard work. Of course, not only did we have great people, we also had a framework and a strategy to address the problem of how to understand and meet our customers' needs in a methodical, rational, uniform, and collaborative way. In other words, we had R.E.D.

Coronavirus was a stress test for R.E.D., and it has proven the underlying brilliance of a framework that enables you to filter, to focus, and to standardize a nomenclature, across dozens of different languages and cultures. This is key. One of my fundamental beliefs is that R.E.D. allows you to operate effectively in different settings and situations (important for a decentralized, global business) or when those settings and situations change (e.g., because of coronavirus). During difficult times, R.E.D. enabled us to create a shared approach, which made us more focused, so we could react more swiftly. By creating a shared set of values and principles *and* then using that framework for thinking about the business and marketing challenges, R.E.D. enabled us to operate at an incredibly high level despite the stress, uncertainty, and all the craziness of 2020.

Hold the Bat Lightly, but Swing for the Fences

I believe that a passion and an ability for marketing can be either inherent, or learned. For me, it was a mixture of both. Marketing was a family business for the Creeds. My dad, who I truly loved and to be honest worshipped, was in the early days of my childhood a sales representative with the Carnation Milk company. Eventually they were taken over by Nestlé, and my dad rose through the ranks to retire as head of supply chain and logistics for Australia after a stellar thirty-five-year career. When he was home from his work travels, we played a game where we would sit in front of our old black-and-white TV set, in the suburbs of Brisbane, and guess what product each of the ads was promoting. My dad was the quintessential Australian: relaxed, humorous, and casual, but also super competitive, and driven to make a mark on the world. Like father, like son. As we played, shouting out, "Pepsi!" or "Colgate toothpaste!" I felt both a sense of love and kinship with my old man, and an awareness of how an effective ad could lodge a product in one's head, sticking there like glue, even when the details of the spot itself faded. Eventually, my mum would call us in for dinner, and the game was over. In hindsight I think that, more than anything else, this experience of identifying brands that were distinctive, and winning in our father and son game, was what encouraged me to become a marketer.

As I learned from watching TV with my dad, being *distinctive* and *easy to notice* were essential to creating a great ad. Another crucial element, however, is to make your product *culturally relevant*. In the mid-seventies, in Australia, I learned my own lesson about the power of a culturally relevant message.

When I started out in marketing at Unilever, I was given the job of reviving an Australian washing powder brand called Softly. For better or worse, the modern Australian landscape has been reshaped and our livelihoods built on the backs of a billion-plus merino sheep, first imported from Spain in the eighteenth century. Wool is central to our understanding of what it means to be Australian. Despite the heat, every Aussie worth their salt knows how to knit. Even me. At one point in my life, I was a dab hand with the knit and purl. Softly was formulated specifically for wool: it was gentle, so it didn't strip out the lanolin from the yarn the way a conventional detergent might. For years, Softly had an 80 percent share of the market, then one day, Australia's beloved Martha Gardener, a radio host who dispensed housekeeping tips on her own show, shared her secret recipe for homemade detergent. Our competitor copied it, and within a few months our share of the detergent market was down to 50 percent. Suddenly this venerable brand was fighting for its life. So what did we do? I realized that there was an opportunity here. Our average customer used two boxes of our product over the winter season, so I had to give her a really, really good reason to go out and buy those boxes. There were plenty of people on our team who reckoned we should just cut our price, or change the formula. But I knew our product was sound, and the price was right. So what to do?

I sat and thought about the problem: Wool. Australia. Winter. Knitting. I thought about all the Australians I knew and loved: tough, pragmatic, full of a deep love for their country, but not prone to saying such emotional stuff out loud. And I realized we had an opportunity. The next day, I spoke to our sales promotion company, Underline, and we decided to produce a knitting pattern booklet, full of iconic Australian images: kangaroos, the Opera House, emus, koalas, Vegemite, and more, created by designer Jenny Kee. The pattern book would be free with two Softly box tops (in an early pursuit of *ease*, you didn't even need scissors to tear the box top off). The promotion was a massive hit, Softly regained its rightful market share, and my career was off to the races.

This early accomplishment has stuck with me over the years, because it symbolizes something bigger about marketing that sometimes gets lost in the shuffle. We didn't change the formula, didn't change the packaging, didn't change the pricing, didn't change anything. What we did was make Softly culturally relevant, and we did so by tapping into something that every Australian felt, but few ever articulated: pride in the simple fact of being Australian.

It's been forty years since Softly, but I still hold true to my belief in taking chances. I believe that R.E.D. can guide even a newbie marketer to breakthrough ideas. All it takes is courage, confidence, and the three components of R.E.D.: *relevance*, *ease*, and *distinctiveness*. I tell my coworkers at Yum! and Collider Lab to "grip the bat lightly, but swing for the fences." By this I mean give me the big idea. Don't be precious about it, swing big. I hope that after reading this book, you'll be inspired to do the same.

Introduction

MARKETERS CAN WEAVE a slick story. It's what they do. They twist and tweak the truth until it's exciting, simple, compelling, and you just can't wait to buy whatever it is they're selling. It's an innate talent and it's a practice as old as humanity. (Surely some caveman somewhere was brilliant at selling moth-eaten pelts for more chunks of meat than they were worth?) The problem comes when you want to *learn* about marketing. For nearly a century we've been listening to these very marketers tell us they have "the amazingly effective and incredibly simple, one-size-fits-all solution to all marketing!" And we've been buying their magical marketing pills for decades. Thousands of books, hundreds of seminars, courses, and degrees. Endless agencies peddling their fail-proof, easy-as-pie methods. And we've bitten, hook, line, and sinker. But now, some adults have gotten involved. More academics, real scientists—and the snake oil business is starting to crash down.

We think that all the instability, change, and rapid evolution in marketing philosophy and science makes this an insanely exciting time in our industry. Pretty much everything that's been written and theorized about our field over the last twenty years is being questioned, refined, or flat out demystified as we speak. Whereas the old-school fundamentals of marketing were often based on anecdotal observations and the authors' belief systems, the new wave of marketing is science-based, backed up by serious evidence, and provable. However, there is still a world of confusion and contradictions. And there is absolutely no definitive, pithy, one-sentence silver bullet idea that guarantees success. Marketing is half science (uncovering human beings' true desires and motivations) and half art (figuring out how to respond to those impulses in a compelling, original, and memorable way). It was never going to be easy or simple. And, as a result, a one- or two-word philosophy, be it *differentiation*, *purpose*, or *brand love*, is never going to cut it in the long term. Those words do sell books, though. They just happen to be mostly BS.

So what do you do, if you don't have endless hours of free time to read the most relevant new ideas on marketing? Maybe you're a CMO, flummoxed by the failure of a recent campaign. Perhaps marketing is so outside of your usual responsibilities that you wouldn't know where to start, even if you did have the hours of downtime to investigate and dig deep on the newest takes on brand building and advertising. Perhaps you've invested millions in creating beautiful ads that—if you are truly honest with yourself—are indistinguishable from your competitors'. Luckily for you, at Collider Lab, Yum!'s global marketing center of excellence, we are passionate about the art, science, and philosophy of all facets of marketing. Over the last nine years, we've taken all the latest academic discoveries in the field, codified a logical and practical marketing system, refined it endlessly, and have proven over and over it delivers real results.

In fact, if you want to understand how we think and process information, have a look at our shelves. We read *everything* that is even somewhat relevant to understanding human decision making, and its relationship to consumer goods and services. At the end of this book, you'll find a reading list with key volumes from the ever-expanding Collider Lab library. We've read the latest research, and devoured the newest ideas about how to reach consumers with effective strategy and messaging. Our desks are covered with books on behavioral economics, evolutionary psychology, marketing strategy, data science, and classics like *Thinking Fast and Slow* or anything by Byron Sharp, which we share around our office in an informal book club. We're perennially on the edge of our seats, waiting for the latest data drop from Peter Field or Les Binet at the Institute of Practitioners of

Advertising in London. We also work directly with more than thirty academics every year and speak directly to over ninety thousand consumers annually in our own studies, decoding how and why they are doing the things they are doing. But what separates us from the theorists is the following: we actually market. We spend billions of dollars a year marketing our own brands, Taco Bell, Pizza Hut, KFC, and The Habit Burger, in over 150 countries around the world. We then see what worked and what didn't, and revise our plan and try again. This allows us to separate the intellectually interesting (but ultimately useless) from the practical and effective.

All of this research, and our years of experience actually marketing in the real world, have led us to create and refine an approach to marketing we know works consistently. We call it R.E.D.: *relevance*, *ease*, and *distinctiveness*. We break relevance down into three components, *cultural, social*, and *functional*. Ease is *easy to access* and *easy to notice*. Finally, distinctiveness is just that: *distinctiveness*. Over the course of this book, we are going to share all we know about how to use elements of R.E.D. to market in ways that work, often for reasons that are strange, surprising, and unexpected.

So, consider us your guide through the convoluted, often contradictory, but also incredibly fun world of innovating, promoting, advertising, and selling in today's crowded marketplace.

Let's recap a few of the ideas that have been floating around the industry for a while. If you've been in marketing—or been on the receiving end of a marketing presentation—over the last decade or so you've heard about the Power of Purpose. Perhaps Jim Stengel's *GROW* inspired you to identify your product with a sense of greater purpose. But is your toaster's purpose radically different from your competitor's toaster's purpose? We're guessing the answer is *no*. (Although we believe Purpose can be a wonderful thing for a company to have, and can be motivating and inspiring for employees, it's a terrible tool for marketing unless it happens to also make your brand distinctive.) Jack Trout's *Differentiate or Die* insists that consumers remain loyal out of appreciation for specific products' superior functionality, come what may. We disagree. Maybe you adored the thought that consumers must connect emotionally to brands (or feel "brand love"), as expressed in *LoveMarks*, but does your customer really feel a sensual and intimate sense of mystery when they think of your brand? The endless books on neuromarketing are fun, but most legitimate neuroscientists cringe in horror at the claims these marketers make. Vague notions about different areas of the brain lighting up with activity after viewing certain communications are not good ways to build a marketing strategy. If you've followed those books to the letter, we're guessing you may not have gotten very far at all. We believe that the evidence supporting all of these competing philosophies is at best ambiguous, and at worst negative, and we will use academic research, practical successes, and decades of personal experience to explain why.

We'll talk about what works (salience), and about what doesn't (emotional connection). We'll talk about the difference between *emotional connection* and *emotional reaction*, and how one hinders, and one helps, your work. Next up will be other wobbly ideas, like reasoned arguments about unique selling propositions, brand love, and brain waves. We'll also demonstrate the futility of only marketing to your heavy users, or buying your media relying entirely on Programmatic Buying (or whatever new miraculous solution the ad tech world is selling you). Perhaps most importantly, we'll offer some solutions to the slow, miserable death of actual brand-building skills in our industry.

Now, as we work through this book, you'll see that elements of these ideas *can* work if they serve to make your product culturally relevant, or easy to access. But if they blend into the ocean of competitive messages, they're sunk, and so are you.

We'll talk about Adam Ferrier's brilliant twist on the old marketing paradigm "change their attitudes to change their behavior." As he points out, it's far more effective to do the opposite: change their behavior and they'll change their attitude. And we'll set you straight about the value—or lack thereof—of highly targeted advertising. We're not doing this in a vacuum. Instead, we are collating and streamlining the work of hundreds of visionary academics and strategic planners who are leading a revolution to purge the quack remedies in our industry. We're leveraging their learnings and putting them into a coherent system that can actually be used—hopefully by you.

To sum up and seriously oversimplify, there have been three theories in advertising for a long time:

1. Convince the consumer in a rational manner, with a rational message. Okay, great, except humans are deeply *irrational,* and for the most part don't know what they want, and can't express it to you anyway. The field of behavioral economics comes from this whole conundrum.
2. Emotional connection. Sure, you may occasionally buy a product because you love it. *But,* trying to build a marketing message off of this? Doomed to fail because the end result is inevitably indistinct, sappy nonsense. (See chapter nine for a more powerful way to use emotion.)
3. Purpose. Only works if it makes you distinctive, and you are the first out of the gate with the message. So, if you aren't Patagonia or Dove, find something else to say.

In the last ten years or so, the Ehrenberg-Bass Institute for Marketing Science (EBI) has ushered in a new era in marketing: one where mental and physical availability rule the day, where creating a functionally relevant and distinctive brand is the marketer's main job. But in the process of igniting this important revolution in the world of marketing, Byron Sharp, the controversial leader of EBI, has completely done away with the notion of giving brands any meaning or cultural cachet. Although we absolutely side with Sharp on the idea that a lot of the emotional mumbo jumbo marketers talk about is not helpful for marketing, we think he may have thrown the baby out with the bathwater by discounting the idea that building a brand's cultural relevance is pivotal to creating a truly powerful brand. Several lessons that Sharp teaches are incredibly important. And a few that he discards are exactly what might've made your brand irresistible today.

We think we have a better way. And, once we've finished burning down the house, and everything in it, and we're standing there looking at the smoking rubble, we'll help you rebuild your marketing and branding strategy with a tried and tested system that has been used—to empirically undeniable success—by Yum! Brands around the world. Together, Greg Creed, Collider Lab, and Yum! have experienced explosive growth. We've gone from 43,000 to 50,000 restaurants, and doubled the share price from $50 to $100 in just five years. Yum! system sales growth (the speed at which sales are growing) has soared from 3 percent in 2014 to 8 percent in 2019. Taco Bell alone has gone from $6 billion a year in sales to an unbelievable $10 billion a year in sales in that same time period. We attribute these incredible numbers to a special culture at Yum!, one where taking chances is rewarded, where intuitive thinking and fast acting is celebrated, where a genuine, people-first group of leaders inspire excellence constantly, and where a massive group of passionate franchisees and team members at the restaurant do an extraordinary job of bringing it all to life. But a big part of that success is also due to the immense power of the brands and a dramatically improved approach to marketing.

Part of what makes R.E.D. work is mixing seemingly incompatible theories to find a happy hybrid with unexpected power. For instance, we subscribe to Sharp's theory of reaching as many consumers as possible with a distinctive brand. But we also believe Douglas Holt is spot on when he says that brands become incredibly powerful icons when they tap into culture and are filled with cultural meaning. These two opposing schools of thought may feel like oil and vinegar, but that's exactly what we're doing with R.E.D.: combining what really works from both sides of the academic world into one coherent system. We'll break down these theories more as we go through the book. Picking and choosing the most relevant academic ideas, then testing and retesting them in the real world, has allowed us to revolutionize the way we build those brands and communicate with, and market to, our customers. It's allowed us to leverage all the latest thinking from the world of marketing academia and make it practical, teachable, and consistently effective. (If you want to dive deeper into any of the ideas we reference in the book, check out the Further Reading section on page 239.)

— 1 —

Why We Needed R.E.D.

W E DEVELOPED R.E.D. because we were in trouble, and no one—not the best authors, nor the most prestigious think tanks, nor the most renowned marketing gurus—had a solution that worked. Taco Bell was slipping in sales. Why? A deep dive revealed some bad news. We were still positioning Taco Bell as a value food, beloved by skateboarding teenagers and extreme value seekers. We poured most of our budget into promoting the lowest cost items with humorous but unsophisticated campaigns: for instance, the classic "Yo Quiero Taco Bell" Chihuahua commercials of the late 1990s to early 2000s, and the "Think Outside the Bun" campaign that followed it. Food back then, in general, was basically all about filling up with something fun for cheap. Funyuns, anyone? Or how about those rad hot dogs at 7-Eleven, slowly rolling under a heat lamp for hours a day?

Here's the problem though: after several years of Chihuahua advertising, transactions declined at Taco Bell. The campaign had helped make the brand ultra-distinctive, but in later years it also made it feel irrelevant to modern food culture. It was a lighthearted, quirky strategy that beseeched young slackers to eat something different today (tacos!). But all people remembered was the dog, who was meant to represent the mentality of the young male of the times: food was about filling up, craveability, and fun. Very little else got in his way on his mission to fill up on some killer grub. That's why the first ad of the Chihuahua campaign shows the hero dog walking right past the cute female chihuahua and ignoring everything until he gets to a guy eating tacos and says, "Yo Quiero Taco Bell." It was an absurdly ridiculous home run in culture. We even sold something like fifty million chihuahua toys. The campaign pegged Taco Bell as the "affordable and filling" option. Unfortunately, transactions continued to go down, and the brand realized it needed to pivot.

Taco Bell launched the "Think Outside the Bun" campaign in September 2001, which focused on portability, with products like the Chicken Quesadilla, the Grilled Stuffed Burrito, and the Crunchwrap. (Today, people remember the "Yo Quiero Taco Bell" catchphrase rather than the actual "Think Outside the Bun" tagline.) For five years sales grew, then that growth started to slow, and by 2009 it was clear we needed to tweak the brand again if we wanted to accelerate growth. As culture continued to shift with the exponential growth of social media, our users continued to grow out of Taco Bell—and worse, the next crop of teenagers and value-driven shoppers were unmoved by the straightforward promise of affordable and tasty food.

Something in culture had shifted and changed our fortunes, and we didn't have the tools to detect the change and adjust the brand. We had done an excellent job of creating a breakthrough, very *distinctive* Taco Bell, and we were incredibly *easy*, with several thousand locations and fast drive-thru, but there was something in the brand that just wasn't clicking. We realized we needed a better measuring stick and a more comprehensive way of managing a brand if we were going to have consistent success. Greg immediately doubled down on a system he had created years ago, called Sales Overnight, Brand Overtime (SOBO), which started to right the ship by balancing out our panicky impulses to slash prices, throw our budget at performance marketing, and focus on LTOs (Limited Time Offers) with a consistent push toward long-term brand building. As revolutionary as SOBO was— especially in its rejection of 1:1 marketing—we needed something more.

We'll tell the story of how we were able to pull Taco Bell back from the edge of irrelevance more fully in chapter five. For now, it's enough to know that this was a pivotal moment in our brand's history, and the birth of R.E.D. Greg Creed, having been president of Taco Bell, had recently been promoted to CEO. Ken Muench was leading the strategy department of Foote, Cone, and Belding, Taco Bell's ad agency, closely working with Jeff Fox and Greg Dzurik. Whatever happened over the next few months would be on us and our teams. Unsurprisingly, we were all deeply motivated to have a happy end result. To get there, though, one thing was clear: we were going to need a far more effective and comprehensive marketing system, one that we would develop ourselves. So, in 2013, Ken founded his own consultancy—Collider Lab—with Jeff Fox, Greg Dzurik, and a few other talented planners and social scientists and grew it to about twenty strategists before it was acquired by Yum!. The consultancy is now a sort of Center of Excellence for Marketing at Yum!. Ken still leads Collider Lab, and is also CMO of Yum!, working with all four brands around the world and helping train the company's nearly two thousand marketers.

Collider Lab

We knew that we wanted every aspect of Collider Lab to embody the three elements of R.E.D.: relevance, ease, and distinctiveness. For starters, we sidestepped more obvious—and fashionable—locations for our office and picked somewhere a little more unique. Instead of Century City, or Abbot-Kinney, or some part of the New York metro area so hip we haven't even heard of it, we opened up shop in Santa Ana. SA was a sleepy town south of Los Angeles, better known for its mix of recent Latinx immigrants, old-school punks, and Orange County Republicans. Santa Ana was a deliberate choice: constantly bump into people who are unlike you and new ideas will flow. (Hence the name, Collider Lab, which reflects how constant collision with different peoples, methodologies, and ideas creates better ideas.) The Surfliner—California's coastal railway—rattles through the graceful Art Deco–ish train station every few hours or so, giving savvy commuters a chance to avoid yet another soul-crushing drive home on the 405. We're a short drive from the best surf spot in town, which explains the fine trails of sand that occasionally track over the office floor after an early morning swell. It all adds up to an enviable quality of life that our employees would lose to hours of traffic every day in LA.

Our office, three stories up on the women's wear floor of the now defunct Rankin's department store, on the historic downtown Broadway, is sandwiched between a Kundalini yoga studio, a barbershop, and a group that is advocating for the normalization of marijuana (perhaps they haven't heard it's been legalized in California?). A recording studio that specializes in late-night hip-hop sessions is wedged in the basement. By late afternoon, the building is alive with muffled beats, burning incense, and tantric chanting adding to the vibe, if not always the productivity.

Our unconventional digs keep us plugged into emerging cultural trends. We may not know who the most relevant Latinx rapper of the hour is, or what the emerging trends in alternative health, like biophotomodulation, are but we're just feet away from people who do. Our neighborhood lunch spot is a former swap-meet-turned-restaurant-incubator, which gives the most innovative and original local food trucks a brick-and-mortar location to experiment with their menus and build their businesses. We've even worked on collaborations with a few of the vendors there. Our walls are covered in yellow stickies—thousands of them—that we use to sort and refine observations and thoughts into coherent strategies and learnings. There *are* a few downsides to our spot, however. The elevator is perennially out of order, something that is endlessly bewildering to Yum!'s Board of Directors (which includes some very bold-name CEOs) when they visit. The air can get a little "hard to breathe" when the aspiring rappers that record in our basement light up for the night, but it's been the perfect location for us, and specifically for the army of brilliant young minds who staff the office.

We knew that for the Yum! strategic nerve center, Collider Lab, to succeed, it would take more than an interesting location. We had to create a work culture that exemplified a tenet of Yum! and Collider Lab, "freedom within a framework." We are blessed to have Greg Creed as our Chairman Emeritus: his brainstorming skills and ongoing work in our company is invaluable. Still, none of us had the time or the inclination to micromanage a team of hardened marketers, set in their ways, and resistant to new ideas. Instead, we sought out newly minted marketers, sociologists, anthropologists, and political scientists. We are huge fans of "PhD dropouts," and many of our cohort have started post-grad programs but walked away once they realized what else was out there. PhD dropouts are smart enough to get into a PhD program and do the coursework, but astute and ambitious enough to realize that they can start having an impact on the world without spending years on a potentially mind-numbing dissertation. One of our senior strategists, Lila Faz, traded her poli-sci dissertation for a job at Collider Lab. Another, Jessika Gomez-Duarte, took a "break" from academia, and she's still here nearly a decade later. We find that full PhDs can speak a different language from other folks, and that disconnection can be hard to cross. But PhD dropouts can hang with the ivory tower folks, and bring it down for the rest of us. So, the dropouts are a Collider Lab gold mine! (No offense to those few Collider Labers that *did* finish. We love you, too!)

The philosophy that went into creating the cultural and physical environment of Collider Lab mirrored the philosophy that went into creating R.E.D. It wasn't enough for us to do one thing well. We needed the skills and the resources to attack every branding and marketing problem from three different angles. We had to be open to discovering truths about our clients and their brands that didn't reflect what they—or we—had previously believed. We had to be nimble enough to reconcile ideas that might seem to be in opposition to each other, and we had to have the intellectual rigor to prove it works or dispense with the bullshit. And it was essential that we figure out new ways of investigating and understanding customers' real impulses and the nuances of their relationships with the products in question.

Between the two of us, we have over sixty years of experience in creating tangible sales results for brands as diverse as KFC, Taco Bell, Pizza Hut, Dove, Nestlé, and on and on. Greg Creed was a CMO at Unilever, and later CMO for KFC in Australia and New Zealand before becoming the CMO of Taco Bell and eventually the CEO of Yum!, globally. Greg is a unique and legendary figure in marketing. Not only is he the kindest and funniest CEO you'll ever meet, but he's one of the bravest. After all, he's the man who okayed billion-dollar ideas like the Crunchwrap and the Doritos Locos Taco on a handshake. He is also the guy who signed off on helicoptering a taco truck to the remote village of Bethel in Alaska, after a couple of teenagers prank-tweeted that Taco Bell was coming to town (a stunt that generated huge amounts of publicity, and a deep and long-lasting connection between Taco Bell employees and the residents of Bethel). Ken has been in marketing for twenty-five years, first as a copywriter and creative director, then as the head of planning of a variety of agencies (where he won a few fancy awards at the—sometimes gratuitous—international ad festivals), and then in 2011 he helped turn Taco Bell around.

Collider Lab's debut task was to develop the first iteration of R.E.D. as we decoded the problem at Taco Bell in 2011. Once it was fully implemented, success was instantaneous. Sales turned immediately positive and have continued growing for eight solid years and counting, beating the industry average nearly every single quarter. Perhaps even more important, thanks to that crisis, Yum! now had a comprehensive marketing methodology that looked at every aspect of the business and could quickly detect and correct issues with a brand before they got critical. The system has been endlessly refined over the years, and many brilliant Yum! marketers have played a direct part in this refinement. Marketers like Catherine Tan-Gillespie, KFC's global CMO, and Christophe Poirier, Pizza Hut's global CMO, have battle-tested the system in 150 countries and made significant improvements to it over the years.

R.E.D. is now the bones of everything we do at Collider Lab and Yum! marketing. If you look at your marketing strategy through the R.E.D. lens and do the work we suggest, you will find a breakthrough strategy that leads to long-term growth and sustained sales. The combination of the R.E.D. system, the team of brilliant marketers across the world, and the intuitive and risk-taking leaders at Yum! (David Novak, Greg Creed, and now David Gibbs) have helped create one of the most exciting marketing environments in the industry. Marketing at Yum! is still thrilling, vital, long term, and brand building, which is why we're writing this book: marketing is awesome when done right. It's powerful, intellectually fascinating, creative, and fun. But more and more, we're seeing the marketing industry at large become short term, small-minded, and full of a mess of technical and jargony tools with no real brand impact. Why? Because marketers get lured by the siren song of whiz-bang digital tools that promise instant success by targeting the right person at the right time with the right message. The mirage of short-term sales is killing what really works: building a powerful brand long term that stands out in consumers' minds and leads to continual sales. In our experience, R.E.D. helps it all make sense again. It also makes it far more effective.

This book takes a very different approach than others out there though. If previous books and marketing theories were touted as one-size-fits-all silver bullets, *R.E.D.* is more like a clear and simple map to guide you through a complicated marketing landscape. If you are fearless and focused as you work through *R.E.D.*, you'll see that many of the most popular theories in marketing over the last decade fall flat in comparison.

We hope you'll also find—as we do—that it is an intellectually stimulating, creatively rewarding, and deeply fun part of your career and responsibilities.

As we go through the book, we'll show you how to revamp your marketing strategy using R.E.D. We'll show you how to make cultural relevance work, get your ease in order, and make your strategy distinctive. We'll explain how all three elements of R.E.D. are an important part of your success, and why all three have to be fine-tuned at some point.

If you're running on only one or two, your brand is still going to struggle. You can be culturally relevant, for instance, but if you're not distinctive then it's just a nondescript public service announcement.

We'll also explain, in the final chapter, how to prioritize each element. Please don't go off running and try to fix all three elements at once. Pick the one that is the most critical, and work your way from there. The final chapter will guide you through a simple process to identify your lead horse.

If you implement R.E.D., you've implemented 95 percent of what a marketer needs to do in today's world. We won't say 100 percent because we're sure there's something we've forgotten, but hey, 95 percent is still a solid A. So long as your brand is distinctive, relevant, and easy to notice, you'll be fine!

All three elements are important to building a powerful brand (see Figure 1.1).

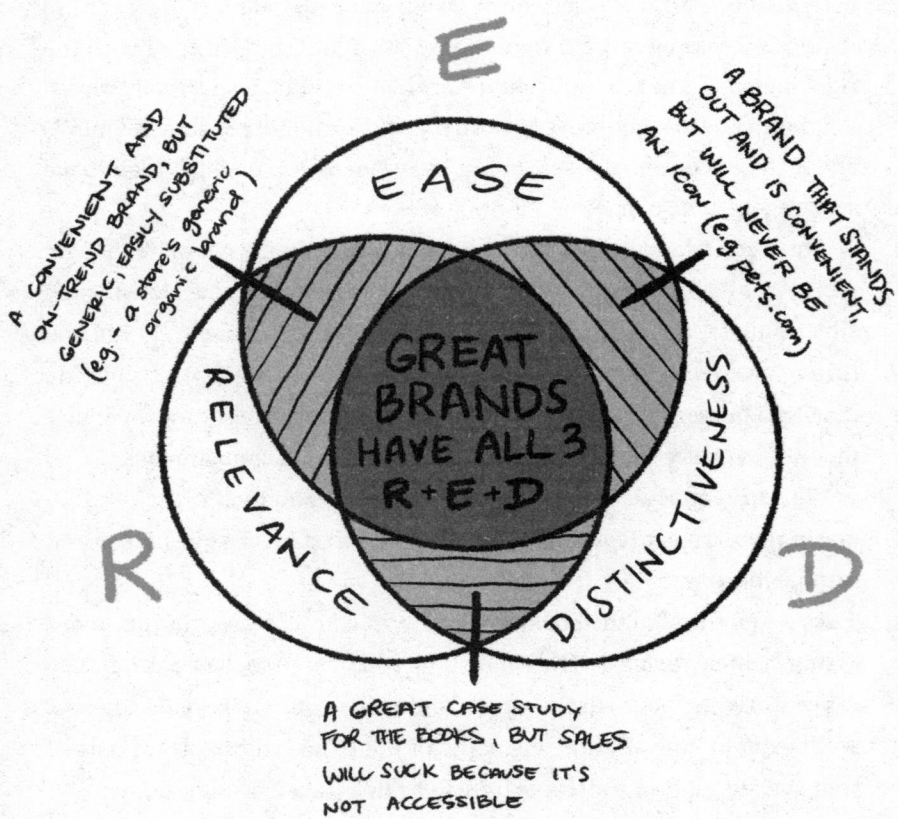

E

EASE

A CONVENIENT AND ON-TREND BRAND, BUT GENERIC, EASILY SUBSTITUTED (e.g.— a store's generic organic brand)

A BRAND THAT STANDS OUT AND IS CONVENIENT, BUT WILL NEVER BE AN ICON (e.g. pets.com)

GREAT BRANDS HAVE ALL 3 R+E+D

R

RELEVANCE

D

DISTINCTIVENESS

A GREAT CASE STUDY FOR THE BOOKS, BUT SALES WILL SUCK BECAUSE IT'S NOT ACCESSIBLE

FIGURE 1.1

2

Change Your Thinking, Change Your Results

A S WE WALKED into the Collider Lab office for the first time, we had three ideas in our heads. They were in our heads because they were so unorthodox for our industry that we worried no one would take us seriously (or hire us) if we articulated them out loud. When it came time to write this book, eight years later, we were still hesitant. We do things differently. We've had great results. We believe in the more legitimate strains of marketing science, the ones that are based in academically accepted psychology and behavioral economics. And we believe in simplifying these complex dynamics to the most basic, understandable, and actionable elements.

But applying those fundamental understandings is a completely different story. That's all about creativity, intuition, big brand thinking, and bold moves. Not really endless focus groups and circular conversations on emotional benefits. It's why Greg Creed; Yum!'s new CEO, David Gibbs; and Collider Lab work so well together. We all believe the exact same thing.

Bold and decisive beats intellectually accurate every time. Our hope is that you will be surprised—maybe even shocked—by how we do things at Collider Lab. If our work was simply mildly unusual, well, would you really need to buy the book? Here's your first provocative idea:

Pebble vs. Wave

We think of our approach to marketing as being a wave, rather than a pebble. Imagine a marketer standing on the shore of a placid pond, holding a pebble in their hand. The pebble is their marketing campaign, and they are determined to make the biggest splash possible. A traditional marketer would have spent huge sums of money, and a considerable amount of time, analyzing their pebble, understanding how the water felt about pebbles, and making sure they picked exactly the right pebble that the water would love.

Our strategy is, don't worry about the pebble, or how the water feels about it. Focus on the wave instead.

You don't need to understand every nuance of the pebble, or have a deep insight into why your pebble is the perfect pebble for the job. You don't need to worry that your pebble might annoy some people, or turn them off completely. All you need to worry about is making the biggest wave possible. When you focus on the pebble rather than the wave, you are getting consumed in the minutiae of making one sale, then another. When you focus on the wave, you are looking at making millions of sales instead. Why? Because the wave is the *reaction* to the initial splash. Meaning, how people start talking (or not) about the campaign or brand. That's real marketing. Not the creative itself, but the reaction that the creative causes among people. The best creatives know this. So, focus on the wave (the reaction the campaign is going to get) and think about how to grow it into a marketing tsunami.

Let's put it back into human language: don't worry too much about understanding a consumer deeply, and don't fret endlessly about what every nuance of their motivation for buying your product might be. It's a red herring. After all, none of us know what we want. Humans are a mess of conflicting desires and shameful longings. We often seethe with resentment at the people we love the most. We are deeply bonded to our spouses, but sometimes long to be free of the constraints of marriage. We would kill for our children, but occasionally question the wisdom of having had them in the first place. We strive for successful careers and material comforts, while longing for the freedom to relax and simply enjoy life. Our outer behaviors and stated beliefs have almost nothing to do with our inner yearnings. What we want is never actually *what we want.* So, forget balance, or any of the usual platitudes. Instead, we're going to make our brands hot in culture and align them with trends our consumers aren't even aware they are drawn to.

The biggest secret of marketing is this: the psychological motivation for why consumers might buy something is often beside the point. You want to understand their cultural world and then rock that world to the core. So, someone can tell you their functional needs, i.e., "I want a car to get my kids to school safely," but that's all they can really give you. The rest is on your team's ability to create something in culture that is so magnetic it becomes irresistible. It's impossible to overestimate the difference this belief system makes. It changes everything. And that takes focus, a strong gut, and courage. Not endless noodling around with charts.

We were determined to pivot away from the old-school techniques of endless qualitative and quantitative research that lead to generic, bland, and forgettable marketing. Call this one branch of a "Y": it's the traditional, safe way that a marketer can go when formulating a strategy. In place of this research, we took the other branch of the "Y" and simply started to talk to anyone in the local markets who could give us some kind of insight into cultural trends. A fem-care brand in Southeast Asia asked us to help them improve their sales, so we spoke to local professors about the evolving language around periods. We interviewed influencers about what motivated their followers and what kind of posts were the most popular and why. We created a WhatsApp group with a bunch of young women and picked their brains for weeks about what was popular. We found cultural figures to explain taboos around menstruation in the region. We never once asked women, "What do you want from this pad?"

Ideas First

At Collider Lab we are massive, 100 percent, believers in the value of instinct. We nearly always start any project with our own personal observations about a brand and its users, then make a hypothesis about what might work in the marketplace, and then test our idea. This is scientifically sound (at least according to one of our aforementioned PhD dropouts, Lila, who compares it to the scientific method). We start with an idea, work backward, and go where the research takes us. Half of the time we are validated. The other 50 percent, we'll try another hypothesis, or, if we are truly stumped, try the more traditional route in marketing, the "blank slate" approach. This is essentially backward from how most marketers do things. If you've worked (or are working) in a more traditional environment, you've probably conducted (or commissioned) multiple research studies, designed to go out and interview your target customer. In the course of your conversations, your goal is to try to uncover some previously unconsidered insight for your product or brand. Why would you do this? Seriously? It's like throwing a random lure in the ocean at a random spot and hoping something will bite.

I can't tell you how many focus groups we sat in in our previous lives, bored out of our minds, hoping we would hear something insightful randomly emerge from the participants. But there was no direction, no hypotheses, so we'd listen to car buffs talk about engines while working on their cars for hours and walk out of the group not one ounce closer to a great campaign. Or worse, further away from greatness because we got caught up in the BS, post-rationalized minutiae the researchers think they heard from the focus groups.

A few years ago we were approached by an unnamed international food brand. They wanted us to conduct a blank slate research study to figure out what American customers wanted from a convenient, portable packaged food. Okay, fine. It was an exciting company full of potential. We can do that. But isn't it obvious? Isn't every single customer going to say they need something on the go, tasty, and somewhat healthy? In the first five minutes of our first company-wide briefing, we identified the appropriate approach. Go talk to cultural makers and figure out what's buzzing in the food space and why. Then talk to food sociologists to understand the latest, emerging food perspectives for further context. Then leverage all that to come up with an exciting angle to make serious waves in the pond. The client looked at us like we were from Mars and kindly requested we keep an open mind instead and conduct some focus groups to understand the emotional connection twenty-year-olds have with convenience food. We were too far along to drop out of the project—although we debated it—and ultimately decided to acquiesce to the client's request. The resulting insights led to some decidedly mediocre creative work, and we vowed to never fall into this trap again.

Here's the issue with blank slate research. For starters, you as the marketer rarely know what you are looking for beyond wanting to hear an opening into a new magical insight that none of your competitors have stumbled into. Often, you're asking customers what they might want from your brand in addition to the products they are already using. True, they can explain what they like about your product now, or how they've liked it in the past. They can speculate that they *might* be interested in various ideas. But it's very, very hard to get a meaningful answer about whether they would embrace a hypothetical product that has yet to appear on the marketplace. Because they simply don't know!

There's a reason that great marketers make a lot of money. A truly brilliant marketing mind has instinctual responses to the questions other marketers are taking out to focus groups and research studies. Sure, great marketers make mistakes and their instincts can fail them (we'll talk about one of Greg's very few misfires with the Drive-Thru Diet for Taco Bell), but for the most part, a marketer with good instincts can catapult you over the process of trying to discover random insights, and just take you straight to making massive waves in the pond.

We have several instinctively brilliant marketers at Yum!. Kevin Hochman and George Felix, who helped develop the world-famous Old Spice turnaround at P&G before coming over and creating the Colonel campaign for us. Catherine Tan-Gillespie, who doubled Same Store Sales Growth across the globe for KFC by using R.E.D., and inspiring marketers to be bold. Christophe Poirier, who made KFC France such a hot destination that lines were still ten deep at 11:00 p.m., by making the brand oh so culturally cool. Yum! is a place that nurtures marketing brilliance because they understand the power of intuition and the pointlessness of endless navel-gazing research.

Greg Creed is an instinctively brilliant marketer. You know this. It's most likely the reason you bought the book. How many other folks have grown a $6 billion business into a $10 billion one in five years? We're guessing that you'd like to see similar, astronomical growth in your own business. Throughout this book, we'll explain how we were able to exponentially grow Taco Bell in such a short period of time. But here's an overview: it takes intuition, bold action, and an uncanny grasp of what really matters in your category. Greg made the brand hot again in cultural relevance (R) and used breakthrough innovations to make it more distinctive (D). This led to more new restaurants to make it easier to notice and access (E). These actions created a sense of excitement around the brand that was palpable. Everyone wanted to work for Taco Bell and have a part in the Taco Rocket propelling sales to the moon. So the people who were involved invested in it, figuratively with their hearts and souls and creative ideas, and literally by opening up new stores. But at the core of the success was momentum, and that momentum was created by the fundamentals of R.E.D.

Let's dig deeper into the concept of intuition. In 2007, Taco Bell was casting around for new growth opportunities. At the same time, the cultural moment was in the midst of the modern health and wellness renaissance. Losing weight, dieting, and counting calories was evolving into the modern health culture, with an emphasis on getting slim and strong and a new focus on ingredients and their nutritional properties. So, several folks at corporate headquarters got an itch for salads. Similarly, sandwiches were exploding in popularity, so those members of the team who weren't advocating pushing leafy greens were promoting the idea of offering a "Mexican-inspired sandwich." Another huge daypart was breakfast: Maybe Taco Bell should push aggressively into that category instead?

Greg said "No thanks" to all those ideas. Instead, he said, "Taco Bell is the voice of rebellion. Rebels don't eat salads, or sandwiches, or breakfast. Let's do something shocking instead." This idea of rebellion was the inspiration for Taco Bell's Fourth Meal (which launched in 2006). The ultra—late night meal was an instant smash hit when we launched. Since then, it has consistently delivered several hundred million dollars a year (and is bigger than McDonald's late-night business). We could have spent months—maybe even years—trying to nail down the single best area to go after. We could have spent millions in research to try and get a customer to convincingly express something they didn't even know they wanted from Taco Bell. Instead, we had the good luck to have a CMO with amazing instincts, and a company that was willing to support that CMO.

I can hear your "But . . ." already. Not everyone has great instincts, and few companies are brave enough to fully support instincts. That's where R.E.D. comes in. If you follow R.E.D., you can develop those instincts and have the fundamental, sound arguments at your fingertips to defend your ideas within the company. Marketing isn't research, it's instinct. So, develop instinct. The first couple times may feel tough, but do it frequently and you'll be able to spot the brand's solution easily, eventually instinctively. Our belief is that by following R.E.D., you'll learn to winnow out bad ideas, and narrow in on the good ones quickly. If you follow our ideas and learn the system well, we reckon you can emulate Collider Lab's "Ideas

First" model. We know this because we've seen it with our own strategists. Most have a hard time when they first get to Collider Lab, but once they've absorbed R.E.D., there's no stopping them.

It's Better to Be Distinctively Off Than Perfectly Right

Finally, here's the scary truth about marketing: you won't be successful all the time. This applies to whichever branch of the "Y" you take, whether you go the plodding old-fashioned route, or try the Collider Lab approach. A few years ago, Ken was having a beer with one of the brand's regional CMOs at Narita airport between flights. They started debating what made a truly great CMO. After some thought, Ken landed on his response: "They have to be smart enough to be right more than 50 percent of the time, but bold enough to execute single-mindedly 100 percent of the time." We still stand by this exchange and this idea. It's more important to fully commit to an idea than noodle away indefinitely trying to come up with the *perfect* idea. Likewise, one of Greg Creed's mantras, that he used to push his marketers to be bolder, is: "You won't always be right, but you always have to be clear." This is a difficult concept for traditionally trained marketers to understand.

At Collider Lab we have a deeply cutting insult that we only pull out in moments of intense stress or disappointment. One of us will review another's concept, turn to them, and say, "That's the correct idea." A correct idea is one that hits all the right notes, that is perfectly good, and that meets the CMO's brief. It's also an idea that excites nobody. When we have a "correct idea," we know that we have something we could potentially share with the CMO, and which they would probably like enough to sign off on, and on which they can base their campaign. It's technically right, but indistinctive, uninspiring, and doomed to mediocrity. We will always choose a strategy that is not exactly right, but tight, distinctive, and exciting over one that is "correct" but nuanced and noodling and just meh.

It's more important to be single-minded and clear in your direction and brand than it is to be right. This is . . . scary stuff? In marketing we invest millions in attempting to nail down a strategy that will succeed. Failure ends careers, terminates agency contracts, and derails billion-dollar companies. Here's the thing. Your odds of success are better with something that is a bit "off" but distinctive than it is with something that is "right" but indistinctive and unmemorable. So, don't hold the bat tightly, and swing for the fences. David Gibbs, the current CEO of Yum!, and one of the principal architects of what the company is today, applies this belief system to business in general: "Having a clear, unequivocal direction is fundamental to success. Nobody ever got anywhere worth going by equivocating and meandering cautiously."

You have to be brave, and you have to be willing to take risks. Have an idea, and commit to it. Greg has perfected the art of making incredibly bold and distinctive decisions seem almost casual. He was, as we mentioned above, under a lot of pressure to expand Taco Bell's offerings to include sandwiches. He immediately said, "No buns, ever." Later, he expanded this philosophy to include, "No salads, ever." This is literally a multi-billion-dollar decision, but it was one he made as casually as he might make a lunch order on a Tuesday afternoon. He stuck with his guns, and it turned out to be the truly correct choice. (Bear in mind, the two biggest-selling items in QSR are hamburgers and chicken sandwiches and Taco Bell has never sold either of them.)

The moment you feel trepidation about something is the moment you lean in. The moment you start feeling that something might be too daring is the moment you should own it and jump on it. But what if it's wrong, you ask? Think of those bizarre mid-nineties Mentos ads in the US that were absurdly off culture and out of tune with the post-grunge era. The clueless announcer would proclaim, "Mentos! The Freshmaker!" after an incredibly cringeworthy, sitcom-like situation played out. I don't think the client ever understood how uncool they were, yet they owned the awkward space fully and completely. They were utterly baffling, but completely distinctive and memorable. I'm guessing you can still sing the jingle. It is more important to completely own an *off* space than to sorta-own the *correct* space. Please do yourself a favor and look up "Mentos. The Freshmaker," on YouTube.

One caveat: you can be wrong, but you can't be completely wrong. Think of the Poo-Pourri brand. Showing an attractive actress on the toilet, describing her bowel movements in vivid detail? So incredibly, ridiculously wrong. And yet, how much more effective than veiled euphemisms, and a "whatever you do, don't mention what the product actually does" strategy. Wrong would have been losing your nerve and pulling back from the acknowledgment that she is, well, pooping. Or, in the other direction, making the spots *too* wrong and vulgar, pushing the ad into even more graphic detail. As it is, the contrast of her absurdly overrefined speech and mannerisms, against the, well, poop, works brilliantly. The spots are perfectly wrong and utterly distinctive.

As you move forward, remember:

- Be the wave, not the pebble.
- Start with an idea, not a blank slate.
- Distinctively off is always better than perfectly correct.

3

R.E.D. Overview

R.E.D., AT ITS very simplest, boils down the basic elements of what you need to make a sale. First, your consumer has to have a need (or you must create that need within them). Then, you must have something that is particularly relevant (R) to that need, that's easy to get (E), and that stands out as distinctive in their mind (D). Suppose you want some running gear for the upcoming winter. That's your need, and what's relevant is something waterproof and warm and not too expensive. It has to be easy to get, so fast delivery and one-click ordering is a plus, and finally, it has to be distinctive to stand out in your mind as an option. In this case, the first brand that pops in your mind is Nike, with its highly distinctive swoosh and progressive brand tonality. Nike just earned $110.

That's an extremely basic example. There are a few important twists and turns we'll cover shortly. But you'd be surprised how many marketers forget about one component or another, even at the basic level. Most folks double down on functional relevance. They'll spend oodles of time

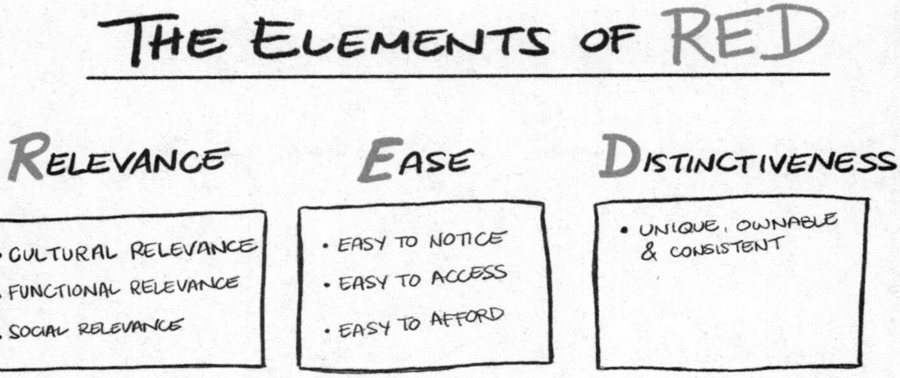

THE ELEMENTS OF RED

RELEVANCE

- CULTURAL RELEVANCE
- FUNCTIONAL RELEVANCE
- SOCIAL RELEVANCE

EASE

- EASY TO NOTICE
- EASY TO ACCESS
- EASY TO AFFORD

DISTINCTIVENESS

- UNIQUE, OWNABLE & CONSISTENT

FIGURE 3.1

figuring out what functional attribute people really want. Waterproof fabric perhaps, or something that will keep you warm in the snow. But they'll gloss over E and D pretty quickly. As far as traditional marketers are concerned, ease is the sales team's problem, or maybe the distribution department. Not my concern. And distinctiveness? Well, isn't that the agency? I don't have to worry about that. Not my job.

But here's the thing. What, ultimately, has the most impact in the sale? Keep in mind humans are deeply lazy creatures. We consistently choose products we like *less* because they are easier to get than the products we prefer. For instance, you might choose the not-so-great supermarket with a parking lot over the better one that requires hunting for a hard-to-find parking spot. In most cases, the most accessible thing wins. Even if it isn't quite what you wanted. Ease, in other words, usually trumps relevance. If you can't find the Nike shoes you were thinking about, you'll switch to Brooks in a nanosecond if your neighborhood running store has a pair. At the same time, if the brand isn't distinctive enough, you couldn't care less about the waterproof attributes because the whole brand will just be invisible. So, although marketers are killing themselves to ensure they have the most relevant attributes, that's most likely not the biggest driver of sales. E and D are: the two points they are glossing over or handing off.

R.E.D. OVERVIEW / 21

Now, R.E.D. is a touch more nuanced than the way we describe it above. We've found that each of the three points has a few different components you really have to nail if you're going to win. Here's the way we outline those components when we train marketers at Yum!. Figure 3.1 (on the previous page) has a quick explanation of each.

The Components of R.E.D.: Relevance

Relevance essentially means that something is appropriate for your wants and needs. Want a cheap and tasty sweet snack? Twinkies are entirely relevant. Need that snack to help you drown your feelings in ooey, gooey, sugary happiness? Again, Twinkies are extraordinarily relevant. But that's basically as far as most marketing definitions of relevance go: a rational and emotional relevance (usually defined as rational and emotional *benefits*). What the vast majority seem to miss is what we call "cultural relevance." Does it align with the cultural values that are becoming important in the category—or, more importantly, in your cultural group? So yeah, sure, rationally you want that sweet snack, and okay, emotionally you want to drown your feelings, but culturally, you're going to feel pretty guilty about eating that box of Twinkies, aren't you? Not likely something you'll throw up on Instagram, is it? You would've been fine with it in the 1990s, but not today. Today it's got to have some sort of redeeming virtue. Is it organic? Plant based? Is it about energy and per-formance? Maybe it's manufactured by a socially responsible, woman-owned company? Perhaps its authentic origin story makes it culturally relevant? And so you end up choosing Onnit Protein Bites: just as tasty as a Twinkie, but packed with plant-based goodness and the energy required to defeat your cultural guilt (and yes, you'll still get to drown your sor-rows in sugary happiness).

This is why we break relevance down into three main categories: *cultural relevance*, *functional relevance*, and *social relevance*.

1.
Cultural Relevance:
Be in Sync with Culture

Does your product reflect the world your customer *wants* to live in?

Ken wears Adriano Goldschmied, or AG, khakis. So do a bunch of the Gen X C-suite leaders at any semi-creative company from Toronto to Los Angeles. There's no particular reason. Sure, they're comfortable and look flattering. But in all regards they're not dramatically better fitting, higher quality, or more functional than the khakis you could get at Gap. The problem is most creative leaders find the idea of shopping at Gap unlikely. It may have represented them in the 1990s, but they haven't stepped foot in Gap stores since AOL dial-up was cutting-edge technology. When was the last time *you* bought your jeans at Gap? There's nothing inherently bad about Gap trousers or jeans. They fit well. They have multiple washes and fades, low rises and high rises, and boot cuts, flares, and skinnies. You can get them in literally any mall in America. They're cheaper than Everlane or AG, and way more accessible than prestige brands. So why aren't you wearing them? More importantly, why does the idea of buying them seem so improbable to many?

Gap has floundered for two reasons: it's indistinct (which we'll discuss in chapter eleven) and it's become culturally irrelevant. In fact, Gap hasn't embodied the cultural code of a moment since its classic Khakis Swing ad perfectly encapsulated the joyful post-grunge era of the mid-nineties. At that moment, Gap represented a herd that many of us wanted to belong to. Gap, along with other 1990s brands like OK Cola and CKOne, nailed, or even defined, the cultural code of being young at that specific time: democratic, uninterested in overt status symbols (while coveting more subtle ones, such as unisex designer scent), and rejecting the traditional trappings of adulthood, gender codes, and success. Today, however, there are numerous newer brands like Madewell and Everlane that operate in the same Gap space, but in a more relevant way. Despite a constant churn of designers, new design philosophies, and designer collaborations, Gap has never been able to reclaim a piece of the contemporary zeitgeist. Their latest collaboration is with Kanye West's line, Yeezy. It will be interesting to see if this high-profile name can resuscitate the brand's fortunes.

Why Cultural Relevance Matters

AG khakis matter. Citizens of Humanity jeans matter. The right trousers matter because they—like any consumer good—signal whether you are ahead of or behind the cultural moment, and what cultural group you belong to. Greg wore Gap jeans for years. One day, he was at a meeting where the attendees were discussing the idea of allowing jeans at the upcoming Taco Bell Franchisee Convention *if* the wearer donated $50 toward the Taco Bell Foundation. One of the marketers jokingly said that if Greg paid $50, it would be more than he had spent on his Gap jeans. These small moments are happening *all the time.* Despite being a decades-long customer, Greg realized his denim choice had dated him. It said he was no longer in tune with the cultural codes he was claiming to intuitively understand. (To his credit, he laughed it off and couldn't care less, but his wife was swift to pick up on the significance and rather quickly bought him a few AGs.) If your brand is so far behind the cultural code that your loyal customers are being laughed at for using them and, worse, losing credibility for wearing them . . . well, you're in trouble.

It remains to be seen what will happen to premium denim brands and Gap in the post-coronavirus world. Their fortunes—once seemingly permanently altered by fashion trends—could once again reverse. It may be that an economic downturn makes Gap more culturally and functionally relevant, while pricing premium denim firmly out of the reach of most buyers. There may even be an opportunity for Gap in aligning themselves with a Dorothea Lange–style spirit of survival and persistence. Or maybe they tap into the inevitable resurgence of democratic values, and Yeezy will lead the charge against the bourgeoisie in their AG pants. Time will tell. So will the agility and cultural awareness of their brand team.

Unpacking and exploring cultural relevance is the beating heart of what we do at Collider Lab. It's the reason we've spent days shadowing young people as they go about their lives in Mexico City, or passed hours as a fly-on-the-wall in a JolliBee in Manila. Cultural relevance is why Collider Lab dispatches anthropologists and sociologists to sit and drink coffee with folks in Changshu. It's why half our staff seem to be on a plane, rather than in the office, at any one time. It's why our data science team crunches numbers to find emerging signals in culture. You might not have the time, resources, or need to explore cultural relevance on this scale, but what you do need to understand is the cultural relevance—or lack thereof—of your own product, in your specific market.

If your brand is international, understanding the differences in culture— and what is relevant to that culture—on a global scale becomes even more important. For instance, one pillar of cultural relevance in America is about insisting that you're an individual, rather than a member of a herd. I may have spent the last thirty minutes of rush hour on a suburban exit ramp idling behind a mid-range SUV identical to mine. No matter, in my heart I am still a unique individual, unquantifiable or categorizable (sidenote: definitely not true). This is radically different from how other cultures place themselves within their bigger community. In many Asian countries, working toward the common good of the larger group is vastly more im- portant than individual desires. So, a marketing message that works for America might fail in Japan, and vice versa, despite the fact that ultimately an American consumer is just as much a member of a herd as a Japanese consumer (albeit a herd that defines itself by its shared perception of inde- pendence). The cold medicine category is an easy place to see this in action. Messages in Japan tend to be more along the lines of, "Get better so you can support those around you," while in the US they tend to skew toward the more self-centered, "Get rid of your symptoms so you don't look like hell."

In this chapter we'll get you thinking about questions like:

- Does our team understand the cultural codes that are relevant to our customers?
- Does our product reflect a cultural moment that customers want to be part of, and that they will be proud and happy to be aligned with?
- Am I part of an emerging cultural moment, or am I holding onto something that worked in the past, but is no longer relevant?
- Do I understand the deeper category code of my brand and how *that* might be changing?

There's a reason we talked about the aesthetics and the vibe of the Collider Lab office. Being in the center of an emerging neighborhood, surrounded by new businesses with innovative financial models, is essential to our ability to observe, understand, and share emerging cultural codes. You might not be able to drop out of your regular life to determine whether Travis Scott, Lil Nas X, EXO, Lana Del Rey, or Billie Eilish is the more relevant expression of an emerging cultural code in your customers' lives. What you *can* do is work through our process to identify, unpack, understand, and respond to those cultural codes. This is a multi-step process that involves acknowledging your past, understanding your present, and anticipating your future cultural relevance.

The cultural relevance chapter (chapter five) will guide you through the heavy lifting of asking the right questions, executing the right type of research, and choosing a cultural path that is both true to the brand and the times you find yourself in.

Imagine being a brand that is still selling sex in the era of #MeToo and Harvey Weinstein, or *Maxim*-style laddish-ness in the age when politicians seem to be outed on a daily basis for their sexual transgressions? You might be a distinctive brand. You might even be an easy brand, but your cultural relevance tone-deafness will act as an anchor to your brand, and potentially sink you. If you're not culturally relevant, nothing else is going to feel right. Why would a consumer trust you to sell them a product that is relevant for the contemporary world, if you are openly out of touch with the moment we are living in?

2.
Functional Relevance:
Be Useful

Does this product offer something that a customer needs or wants?

As marketers, operations officers, sales managers, or product developers, we're all familiar with the idea of fulfilling customer needs such as:

- Your customer needs a late-afternoon pick-me-up, so coffee shops sell coffee and individually sized afternoon treats.
- They need to get from Atlanta to Denver, so airlines start to fly that route.
- Their kids are bored, so streaming services offer enhanced streaming options.

Success! You've made a sale, and earned a customer—for now, at least. Here's where brands are in danger of stalling out: it's not enough to meet one customer needstate. In order to thrive, you have to offer multiple *category use occasions*, or CUOs. A CUO is a need a consumer is trying to fulfill by engaging in the category. And there are dozens or even hundreds of CUOs in any given category. Take Twinkies, for instance. The three CUOs we describe above for Twinkies are: 1) A cheap snack, 2) A sweet snack, and 3) A snack that helps me drown my sorrows. But there are other ones, too. Something to fill me up, for instance. Or something to give to my kids. Or something I can eat while driving, and so on. Brands that are successful will methodically own as many CUOs as possible in consumers' minds. In chapter six we'll talk you through the process of methodically building new

CUOs to broaden the appeal of your brands and your products. We'll explain why you want to be Toyota, not Mini Cooper, or Nike rather than Brooks. And we'll detail a logical, structured plan to ensure that your emerging CUOs build upon your existing CUOs in a way that makes sense to your consumer, and doesn't stray too far from your brand's core identity.

In chapter six we'll challenge you to answer the following questions:

- What category use occasions does your brand fulfill? Do your competitors fulfill more?
- Which CUOs are the lowest hanging fruit for your business to grow sales?
- What are the logical, stepping-stone by stepping-stone, extensions of those CUOs?

3.
Social Relevance:
Be the Pop Culture Moment

Pop culture tells us what to do, how to behave, and why.

In R.E.D., we use the concept of social relevance (see Figure 3.2) to leverage our very human desire to share and discuss moments that are briefly hot and buzzy in culture. Social relevance is less about being part of the "herd" and more about being "heard." By creating stunts or activations that are funny, strange, or remarkable, we give our consumers something to talk about, and a chance to engage or connect with each other. Think of the last time you saw something truly quirky and random or amazingly interesting—I'm guessing your first instinct was to pick up your phone and text a friend about it. Successful social relevance activation is based on this impulse. It has nothing to do with helping your consumers identify with a herd, and everything to do with making them click-to-share or forward-to-a-friend in the line for Starbucks, their 9:30

a.m. staff meeting, or wherever they were when they happened to see your activation. These shares and forwards are invaluable, as consumers end up using brands more often when they see that their friends are using (or, at the very least, talking about) them.

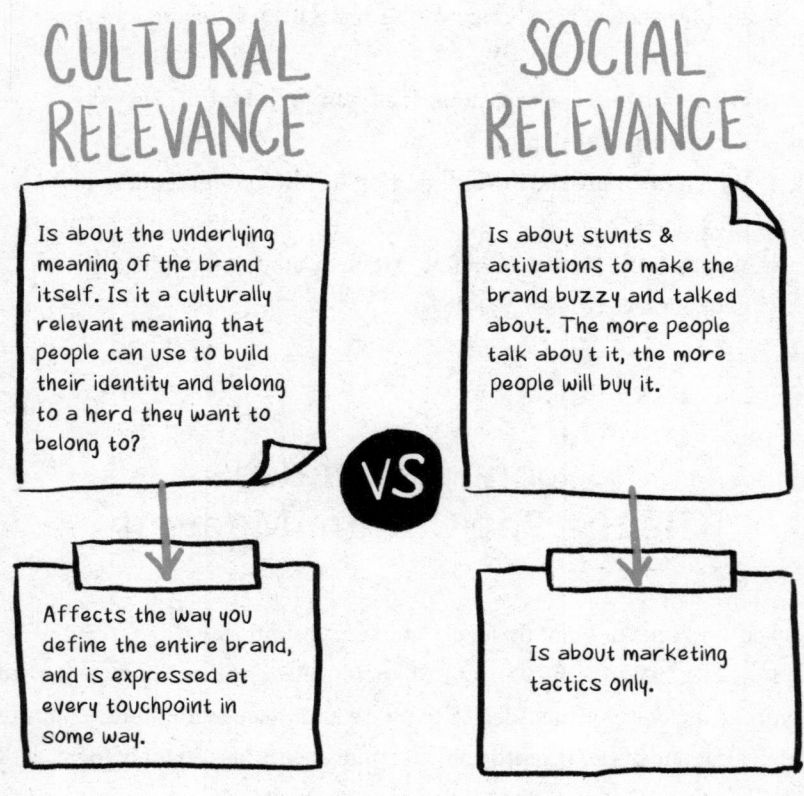

FIGURE 3.2

In 2019, we unveiled the Taco Bell Hotel and Resort in Palm Springs. It sold out two minutes after going online, and created a genuinely brilliant social media moment. KFC Spain was able to take a −10 percent sales trend to a +15 percent with a bizarre, but much-talked-about and end-lessly imitated, TV campaign depicting people singing about "Chicken

Chicken!" Why did the numbers jump? Because consumers use brands that they see and hear other people talking about. Our consumer may think himself immune to conventional advertising, but he is almost guaranteed to absorb and share a pop culture moment that feels relevant to his life, interests, and needs, and that is being shared and commented on by people around him.

Social relevance requires reacting quickly and thoughtfully to the cultural shifts happening in that moment. During the early days of the coronavirus crisis, David Timm, the CMO of KFC Germany, and his team created a pretty hilarious social relevance activation on TikTok, where they invited people to do "the Colonel Dance." "It's now well past five hundred million views," David explains, "and more importantly achieved more than half the total media impressions from the prior year in *two* weeks. A big part of its success was timing: it was released over Easter weekend, when locked-down people were bored, and eager for ways to entertain themselves, feel aligned with their herd, and express themselves to the outside world."

There's another reason that social relevance moments are so important, and, if done right, can be a powerful way to shift consumer attitudes about brands. The more people talk about your brand, the more people will automatically assume it, or your product, are important, good, and current. This is partly something called the *mere exposure effect*, where we have a preference for something simply by having more exposure to it. For instance, people who repeatedly see impressions of a celebrity will grow to have a more favorable impression of that individual, simply because they are more familiar with them. It's as simple as that.

The effect is also linked to what behavioral economists call the "availability heuristic." This is a fancy name for a type of shortcut your brain takes when trying to make a decision. Essentially, it means that the more easily you recall something, a brand in this case, the more importance you automatically give it. So, if people are talking about your brand all the time, it means you're probably pretty important. It's why you think that one show everyone is talking about is probably pretty good. That's the effect we're trying to achieve with social relevance: get people to talk about your brand, and it'll raise its status in everyone's mind. Remember Lady Gaga's meat dress? It was the only thing anyone talked about the day after the 2010 MTV music awards. Over ten years later, a joke built around the dress still needs no explanation or description—it is that iconic. Now imagine doing the same for your brand.

How to Craft the Perfect Socially Relevant Moment

Creating social relevance is much harder than it sounds. Poorly conceived social relevance stunts are massive wastes of time and resources. Uber, for instance, dressed up a bunch of cars in Paris like toy cars, with blocky edges and the iconic Lego-brick look. It created a bit of a stir, but our bet is that a couple days later few people could remember if it had been Uber or one of its competitors, BlaBla Car, LeCab, or Bolt. More than likely, the only thing consumers remembered and talked about was Lego—the real winner of this stunt. I hope they sent Uber a nice thank-you note and maybe a basket of fruit for all the free buzz?

On the other hand, when Taco Bell announced that it had bought the Liberty Bell in Philadelphia and renamed it the Taco Liberty Bell, people lost their mind. Thousands called the National Park Service and Taco Bell headquarters to complain. On the very next day, April 1, 1996, Taco Bell announced that it was an April Fool's joke. Twenty-five years later, people still remember the prank—*and* the brand that did it. Why was Taco Bell's outcome so much better than Uber's in Paris?

The Taco Liberty Bell was a winner because it was intrinsically linked to the brand, with virtually zero chance of misattribution. And, more importantly, it reaffirmed Taco Bell's role in culture as the rebel, the prankster, the brand that refuses to play like the burger boys. In chapter seven we'll explain the importance of defining a "role in culture" for your brand. This role will help guide you in creating the right type of cultural moments and social moments that support your brand's distinctive positioning.

Pop culture moments can be emotional, funny, thoughtful, or even political. Think of the NFL's Colin Kaepernick, fresh off of his kneeling-during-the-National-Anthem controversy, whose Nike ad was released on Labor Day, 2018. It created a pop culture moment that worked in multiple different ways: It got his fans to love him more, haters riled up, and Nike sales went up 31 percent that weekend, almost doubling the previous Labor Day's increase of 17 percent.[1] All the while allowing Nike to align itself with a powerful and progressive message about race in America. Sure, they came under intense criticism from some very prominent people, including the president of the United States, who attacked the brand mercilessly. But making that statement was unquestionably the right thing to do. Fast-forward two years to the murder of George Floyd at the hands of the police and the ensuing global protests. In the wake of this massive awakening of conscience, the NFL meekly apologized and officially allowed players to kneel if they so chose.[2]

Clearly, not all social relevance activations have to be so profound. But they all absolutely must be "party-talk worthy." The annals of marketing history are full of embarrassing social relevance flops—activations that only the most out-of-touch brand director could think are good. We remember a certain toilet paper brand trying to create controversy about which way to hang your toilet paper: flap in front or flap in the back. They plastered Chicago with earnest posters asking people to vote on social media with a hashtag. Ouch. For a social moment to win, it must give your consumers a bit of social capital: something they'd be proud to share at a party, because only someone as dialed-in as them would know about these cool things. "Did you hear Taco Bell bought the Liberty Bell?" does a far better job at that than, "Hey, guys, let's talk about which way you hang your toilet paper roll!"

Ease

HAVE IT YOUR WAY

Ease Is Everything

Ease is everything. In fact, ease is everything to the point where R.E.D. was originally called EDR, until Lluis Ruiz Ribot, KFC's CMO in India, pointed out that R.E.D. was infinitely more distinctive (and sounded less like the music your kids are stream-ripping as we speak). So, R.E.D. it is.

Remember in the introduction when we said that one of Collider Lab's core philosophies is, "Behavior Changes Attitudes"? This is a radical shift from the more traditional marketing belief that, "Attitudes Change Behaviors." Let's unpack that—and how it relates to ease—for a minute. A conventional approach to marketing says that in order to successfully market your product you need to create a relevant piece of advertising, and make it so ubiquitous that your customer views it over and over again. Eventually your customer will have absorbed your message so completely that their belief system shifts in favor of your product, and they are convinced enough of its value to purchase whatever you are selling.

It makes sense. After all, we humans are deeply rational creatures, and our purchasing decisions, like all our other life choices, evolve in a logical, analytical, and deliberate way as we absorb more information about our various options, and make our educated pick from among them, correct?

Of course not.

We humans (or, more accurately, our brains and the way they function) are actually deeply *lazy* creatures. Our choices, in almost everything, are determined more by what is easiest and least painful than what is actually in our best interests, or reflects our true desires. Every afternoon, Ken goes to the office candy drawer, rummages around, finds a Snickers mini-size bar, and eats it. He loathes Snickers. The texture of the chocolate is too smooth and oily, the caramel too viscous and cloying. He once read that there are small particles of insects in each piece of mass-produced chocolate. Nauseating. And yet, he eats the Snickers. Why? Because the chocolates he does love—Vosges, a small-batch, organic, and artisanally produced bar—is only sold in a grocery store a ten-minute drive from the office. Ken could make the effort and have what he really wants, or, he could make zero effort and have something he loathes, but which nonetheless fulfills his needstate and satiates his sweet tooth. The crumpled-up Snickers wrappers on Ken's desk are all the evidence we need to prove that we humans will choose ease over just about any other motivation.

So, where does "Behaviors Change Attitudes" come in? Ken's afternoon Snickers bar leaves him feeling vaguely unsettled. Fitness, organic food, and positive health choices are a big part of his life. He talks a big game about taking care of himself. So why did he just eat that Snickers bar? This feeling—cognitive dissonance—is uncomfortable, so, to get rid of it, Ken starts to justify his choice to himself. "The Vosges is $8.00 a bar, and I'm meant to be saving for retirement. The Snickers is free. So, choosing the Snickers is actually a fiscally wise choice." His brain embraces this justification, and he feels peaceful and serene about his selection. He relaxes into it and thinks to himself, "Well, they're really not that bad . . . maybe they're even quite good?" Now he can move forward, happily eating Snickers, because his brain is satisfied that he made an active decision out of love for his family, and an awareness of the importance of saving for their future.

It is your job to make experiencing, recalling, and purchasing your product as easy as possible for your customer. For those of us in the Quick Service Restaurant (QSR) category, that means prioritizing speed over just about anything else. For those of you in Consumer Packaged Goods (CPG), this means distribution in as many stores as possible, as well as placing in the store. If you're a nonprofit seeking a donation, this means text to donate vs. a multi-stage sign-up that involves finding your wallet, getting out your credit card, and filling in multiple forms. So, in the Ease chapters, you'll learn how to make your product:

EASY TO ACCESS (CHAPTER EIGHT)

A product that is easily available, and removes as many friction points as possible along the purchasing journey, both psychologically and physically.

And

EASY TO NOTICE (CHAPTER NINE)

A broad advertising strategy that reaches both heavy and light users across the category with a breakthrough message that causes an emotional reaction.

This section is similar to the concept of mental and physical availability.[3] Win with ease and you'll be way ahead of the game.

Distinctiveness

"I'M ON A HORSE."

The personal care category can be a messy battleground. Massive brands battle back and forth with millions of dollars in marketing for shelf-space dominance. So much comes down to that final moment when you reach out your hand to pick your deodorant. By the late 2000s, Procter & Gamble's Old Spice had been a declining brand for years, and was continuing to lose shelf space everywhere. They had lost relevance compared to P&G's arch rival Unilever, which launched the Axe Body Spray Brand in the United States in 2002. In six years, Axe had grown dramatically in the male deodorant and body wash category. Axe was targeted at young adults promising "sex in a can," which immediately depositioned P&G's Old Spice male grooming brand as, well . . . old. Compared to Axe, Old Spice was the stuff your dad or grandpa used. The solution was obvious: make the brand appeal to a new, younger consumer base. However, instead of owning the core distinctive assets of the brand, the prior teams had blindly chased relevance, leaving Old Spice indistinct and standing for nothing. A review of older Old Spice ads that focused on a blander vision of sexuality can attest to those misguided times.

The P&G team, which Kevin and George were part of, tapped Wieden+Kennedy, out of Portland, Oregon, to reboot the brand. The brief? Restore the Old Spice brand to its original luster and relevance. W+K embraced the quixotic nature of their mission. Instead of tweaking here, or refining there, they galloped straight for the windmills, rediscovering what the brand meant from the floor up, starting with the brand's DNA that 1) Old Spice made you smell musky and manly and 2) Being older could also be viewed as being experienced, everything the Axe brand couldn't claim.

W+K brought back key distinctive assets from the brand's heyday. These included the original Old Spice clipper ship logo, the iconic Old Spice whistle jingle, and the red and beige color scheme, which separated it from a sea of black and silver brands on the male shelf. Most importantly, they returned to and fully embraced the ownable positioning of smelling like a man.

Two years into the rebranding campaign, another Unilever personal care brand launched in the United States, Dove for Men. The brief to defend Old Spice? Why would you want to wear a women's scented body wash, which would make you smell like wildflowers, when you could "Smell Like a Man, Man" (the tagline for what insiders call the "SLAMM" Campaign). This brief led to one of the most iconic advertising characters in the history of branding. Isaiah Mustafa, the former NFL player turned actor, embodied the "man your man could smell like": a shirtless Adonis who rode horses, played the harp, and dove off waterfalls among varied adventures. While the spot never actually aired during the Super Bowl, instead showing the weekend of the 2010 Super Bowl, it still is remembered as one of the greatest Super Bowl ads of all time. The ten-year-old campaign has evolved over the years, but the core concept is still going strong. In January 2020, Old Spice celebrated a decade of success with a reboot of the original campaign, featuring the original Old Spice Man, Isaiah

Mustafa, and actor Keith Powers, as Old Spice Man's mildly embarrassed, but ultimately understanding, son.

Old Spice, whether you like it or not, owns a tiny little piece of your consciousness. We call this ownership "salience," and it's the core quality of any successful marketing campaign. The Old Spice campaign is memorable because it is bizarrely, weirdly, and ridiculously distinctive. In fact, I'm betting if you rewatch that first "The Man Your Man Could Smell Like" spot you'll find you remember many of the visual gags and much of the dialogue (including the iconic closing line).

Your ability to a) remember the Old Spice campaign, and b) correctly attribute it to Old Spice, is priceless. Why? Because more than 50 percent of advertising is attributed to the wrong brand. If you can create a campaign that is so distinctive that it takes up space in consumers' brains, and they can correctly remember both the ad, and what and who it is advertising a decade later, that's salience, that's distinctiveness, and most importantly, it's powerful, effective marketing.

Unlike ease or relevance, distinctiveness is based solely on being memorable. In order to *be* memorable, a campaign needs to be three things:

1. Unique
2. Ownable
3. Consistent

Old Spice nailed it by dramatically modernizing the essence of the brand, and how it relates to the modern man, standing out boldly in an incredibly distinctive way. In less dramatic ways, brands that stick with a visual code or message for decades can also be distinctive: Coca-Cola, Target, and Starbucks are classic American examples. Further afield, Guinness or After Eight Mints in England, or Absolut Vodka, Perrier, Hello Kitty, and Orangina internationally. In chapter eleven, we'll look at brands like Virgin Atlantic, and consider how they've created an instantly and utterly distinctive brand identity that stands out in an ocean of homogenized airline branding. We call this Mirror vs. Magnet marketing.

Brands that mirror are simply reflecting what they believe their would-be customers want to see: usually reflecting back their customers' lives in a desperate attempt to create emotional connection. How many cool party scenes have you seen in beer ads? How about sweet family moments in frozen food ads?

Brands that are magnetic are giving would-be customers a reason to look at them instead. Most iconic, beloved brands are magnetic: Apple creates a super-cool, creative, modern world that is incredibly magnetic. Nike's progressive, cutting-edge athletic world is nearly as irresistible and magnetic. Neither of those brands simply reflect the consumer's life back to them. They are magnets, not mirrors.

The Old Spice vs. Axe saga is also an example of how distinctiveness can wax and wane as cultural codes evolve: no element of R.E.D. exists in isolation. Old Spice was almost obliterated by Axe when the younger brand's salacious and hyper-sexual ads blew away Old Spice's old-world decency and conventional masculinity by expressing the boyish culture of the era. Axe ads from South Africa to the United Kingdom to Argentina focused on a simple sexual equation: spray, conquer, repeat. It worked. Until it didn't. Sometime around the dawning of the #MeToo era, Axe went from charmingly laddish, to threateningly inappropriate. Men might still secretly enjoy watching the old ads, but they now felt embarrassed to openly view them. The ads felt predatory, rather than joyfully part of a boyish clique getting an innocent thrill out of the mostly naked female bodies. In 2016, Axe renounced their distinctive, hyper-sexualized marketing, found an approach that was more culturally relevant, and debuted their "Find Your Magic" campaign that celebrated masculinity in all its varied forms, genders, desires, and complexities.

Distinctiveness is a particularly important quality for QSR brands to nail, precisely because our category can often be murky and nondistinctive. One pizza brand can easily blend into another. Ditto with burgers or chicken. So, if you want to make a lasting impact with consumers, you have to stand out.

Conclusion

So far, so simple, right? We've created a streamlined, rational system (see Figure 3.3) that allows you to analyze individual elements of your marketing program, identify weaknesses, and uncover areas of opportunity to communicate more effectively with your customers. There is another aspect to R.E.D., though, and that's how relevance, ease, and distinctiveness work together, and how you or your marketing team prioritizes the three elements in developing a marketing strategy and the final campaign.

As you work through the next three chapters, you'll be guided through the process of uncovering relevance, ease, and distinctiveness as it applies to your product. There will be smaller personal exercises, larger group exercises, and finally, strategies that require outside assistance with qualitative studies, outside experts, and focus groups.

As you go through these next twelve chapters, read everything, but keep an eye open for the exercises that fit your ambitions, budget, and time frame best.

THE MAIN IDEAS OF EACH RED POINT

RELEVANCE

Cultural Relevance

People value brands that let them feel like they belong to a culturally relevant herd. Imbue your brand with an emerging cultural code in a distinctive way.

Functional Relevance

Growing your brand means growing your category Use Occasions. Measure CUOs carefully in your category and understand which are lower-hanging fruit and right for your brand.

Social Relevance

If people talk about your brand, they'll be more likely to buy your brand. Do things in culture that are party-talk worthy and leverage your distinctive brand assets.

EASE

Easy to Notice

Advertising works by creating memory structures about your brand with lots of people, so don't target niches. Buy low-cost media that targets everyone in your category and make your creative memorable by ensuring it causes an emotional reactio n.

Easy to Access

Brands that are easy to access and buy ultimately win. Look for both physical and psychological friction in the buying process and remove or reduce it.

DISTINCTIVENESS

Unique, Ownable & Consistent

Brands that create and defend unique & ownable distinctive brand assets are far more mentally available. Brands that are consistent in creative beat brands that prioritize change. As a marketer, this may be your #1 job; find your DBAs and be consistent, consistent & consistent.

FIGURE 3.3

4

Relevance Mythbusting

The Demise of Brand Love as a Marketing Strategy

In order to understand relevance, it's helpful to understand the ideas that this concept has replaced. The concept of *brand love*, or creating a desire for your brand or product, is number one on this list. For our purposes, think of desire as a pretty close synonym with relevance. Why? Because if something is highly relevant to you, then it's also highly desirable. If something isn't terribly relevant, then it's not terribly desirable. Once you understand that, then you can see that when we say, "How do you create desire?" we're also saying, "How do you create relevance?"

At its most basic level, desire is created by making something *relevant* to the consumer's needs. If something is relevant to your needs, then you desire it. I'm running out of gas and I see a gas station: that gas station is extremely relevant. I just finished lunch and I'm full: that restaurant across the street isn't relevant at the moment. I want to feel I belong to the CMO set: I buy AG pants. I want to feel like I'm on the cutting edge of culture (and have a lot of money): I buy Nike's Travis Scott shoes.

A successful marketing strategy either creates or fulfills a need or desire (and can sometimes do both). However (you knew there was a "however" coming . . .), creating desire isn't as simple as it seems. In fact, we argue that marketers have fundamentally misunderstood what desire means. Desire is a potent idea, because it is such an elemental part of being human. It makes sense that if a marketer can turn a product pitch into a visceral, emotional experience then that pitch will be more impactful and more likely to affect a shopper's behavior. However, everything that we've experienced over the course of our careers, and all the research we've done at Collider Lab, says that this take on how to create and implement desire as a marketing strategy isn't effective. There are two points to take away from this:

- Yes, desire is the fundamental force that motivates a consumer.
- But right now you might be doing desire all wrong.

When we talk about desire, we do so through a R.E.D. perspective. For the last decade or so, the marketing community has been obsessed with "creating emotional connections" with their consumers. The idea is that this emotional connection creates some sort of desire. Like love. You desire your partner. So, in the same way, you'll desire your brand. What BS. For us, desire is less about rational choices, or emotional connection, and more to do with functional or cultural relevance. If you want to create that sense of desire, you have to do it through these lenses. Making something functionally useful, and ensuring it helps consumers feel part of culture, is what makes a brand truly desirable.

The Irrational Argument, or Reason to Believe

Another old idea that needs to go away for good is a decades-long, now-dated approach to marketing: the Reason to Believe, or RTB. This theory says that if you differentiated your product with a strong RTB, you would create relevance by giving people a logical and rational product they would buy. Kudos to Byron Sharp for his valiant personal mission to vanquish the notion of differentiation, even as it still persists to this day.[1]

One of Ken's early jobs was writing copy for a beer account. Now, this wasn't some artisanal, locally micro-brewed IPA. It wasn't a Hefeweizen, or a Porter, or a Belgian Stout. Heck, it wasn't even Sam Adams. Ken's account was the kind of beer that is close enough to H2O that you could probably water your plants with it. But, he needed a compelling reason for an all-American beer lover, propping up the bar on a Friday night, cold one in hand, to defend his mainstream choice against other beers in the same category *and* the burgeoning craft beer trends. Back then the marketing industry called this a reason to believe. Whether our guy believed that his particular beer was beechwood aged, frost-brewed, or cold filtered, the idea was to give him a logical reason to believe the beer was better than its competitors.

RTBs come from an era when marketers thought you needed to convince people logically to buy your product. With hindsight it seems pretty obvious that your pitch to your customer should never be a defensive gesture ("Hey, I have my reasons for drinking this lousy beer!"), or something to fall back on when you are vaguely aware that your choice (in this case, beer) is dating you, or exposing you as being old-fashioned, set in your ways, or otherwise out of touch with other people in your immediate social group ("herd," in R.E.D. marketing parlance). Unfortunately, life isn't simple, nor is desire.

The RTB approach has largely been discredited. Humans are simply not rational creatures, and while we are majestically awesome at post rationalizing with reasonable-sounding arguments, these rarely have any impact in our actual decision making. We'll come back to this idea in a few pages. Looking back at this campaign from a R.E.D. perspective, we now realize that the real value of "beechwood aged" or "frost-brewed" is simply the creation of a "distinctive brand asset." That is, an asset that is used consistently and over time and becomes a shorthand for the brand itself. Using distinctive brand assets in your advertising is what makes the advertising distinctive, and this distinctiveness helps the brand become more salient and hence purchased more often.

Emotional Connection

So, if you can't create desire through a rational argument (my beer is colder than yours), how do you create it? The next big idea that marketers devised was emotional connection.[2] However, the theory that consumers can be persuaded to fall in love with household products holds little water with us. As a matter of fact, there is a whole cadre of modern marketers who fight against this idea daily. The more you analyze the notion of loving your brand, the flimsier the whole thing gets. After all, do you feel love when you think of the brand of your toaster? What about the gas in your car? Do you get teary eyed when you think of the awesome brand that stands behind it? Certainly you love the brand of the convenience store you visit every day? No?

There will always be some consumer products that an individual person genuinely does have a special affection for. We see this love as a happy side effect, rather than a singular selling point. For instance: You may love your Nike running shoes because they allow you to run faster, and give you a sense of entrance into an elite circle of runners. Your sister loves Patagonia because it allows her to feel more connected with the outdoors. Your best friend may adore her Instant Pot because it makes her a better cook, and gives her an hour of her life back each night. Hydro Flask had a moment as the only water bottle the weekend adventurer could be seen out with. However, setting out to "connect emotionally" with consumers sends marketers down the wrong path. Of course we all like, or even really like, a certain product or brand. But those feelings arise because a brand or product is so functionally or culturally relevant that it has become integral to our lives.

The fact that marketers have been chasing "emotional connection" as a goal has led most people astray from this less dramatic but more accurate revelation: what marketers think of as emotional connection is more accurately defined as functional or cultural relevance. In other words, it's not intimate love for a brand that makes you desire the product, it's the functionality of the product and the membership it affords you into a cultural group. Functionally, fans love that Teslas can drive themselves. Culturally, Tesla gives them membership into a select aspirational class of wealthy and eco-aware trendsetters. And it's not just $90,000 purchases that have this dynamic. Products in any category where the idea of brand is important demonstrate it. Fifteen-dollar Stance socks are highly coveted for their functional comfort *and* the fact that wearing them makes you part of the young, surfer-minded cool crowd. Breville toasters nail that perfect brown crunchiness every time (functional relevance) and they also help you feel like you belong to the foodie sect (cultural relevance). The exact same dynamic applies to lower-priced products as well. Teens in the US love $29.99 Dickies pants because they're functionally perfect for skating, but they also signal an edgier and more rebellious identity. It's why the word "brand" is so perfect. Brands not only serve to identify the maker of the product. They also help give an identity to the end user.

Desire as emotional connection as legit marketing strategy has long and tenacious tentacles. However, if all the logical reasoning above still fails to convince you that emotional connection is an absurd notion, here's another, more practical reason to dump the idea: it creates sloppy, generic, and deeply forgettable advertising.

Pointless Purpose

"Thinking is to humans as swimming is to cats: they can do it, but they'd prefer not to."[3]
— DANIEL KAHNEMAN

Another great myth that has (in our eyes, at least) derailed marketers is *brand purpose*.

Now, we are all in favor of brands elevating themselves, and the impact they have on the world, with a sense of internal purpose that pushes them to act with integrity and high ethical standards. Brand behavior like this actively makes the world a better place and we do everything we can to encourage it within Yum!. *However,* making this behavior the cornerstone of your marketing strategy doesn't work. Furthermore, this isn't actually how purpose, at least in marketing, was initially conceived. Purpose was something closer to a more traditional brand messaging strategy. If you bought an Apple computer it would make you more productive and creative than that poor "I'm a PC" schlub. It's not a "make-the-world-a-better-place"-type purpose, but it is, quite literally, a clear and defined *purpose*. If you bought a Subaru, you'd get outdoors more. Simple. These products had purpose, but this purpose represented essentially pretty straightforward ways in which they'd add some tangible benefit to your life.

It wasn't until around 2012 that purpose evolved into Purpose. Now it's not enough that your computer helps a user be more creative; it also has to connect with them on an altruistic level to save humanity. Or else they'll never buy your product. This new Purpose claims that if you want your brand of jeans to resonate with Millennials (or Gen Z) or whatever supposed-altruistic generation is just on the horizon, then those jeans must not only be comfortable and cool, distinctive and easily accessible, they must also have a central Purpose to reduce carbon emissions on the planet. Or else those jeans will just sit on the shelves and rot. But this just isn't how consumers make decisions, and even if it were, "greenwashing" (brands pretending to be good for the environment) is so rampant that consumers no longer believe/care/want brands that claim to care about environmental issues.

This desire for brands to be about purpose has resulted in what we think of as Patagonia Purpose: using your platform and your customer base to spread a socially responsible message and take positive actions toward your particular "mission"—in this case, saving the environment. When done sincerely, this is an honorable and noble goal, and we applaud it. It's worked wonders for Patagonia. Their products allow their wearers to transmit a clear message about who they are, and how they see themselves. "My body may be in my third meeting of the day, but my heart is totally free soloing the Cap to raise funds to save Yosemite." Because Patagonia was first out of the gate with this philosophy, and they are unwaveringly committed to it, it works for them. This purpose not only makes them culturally relevant, it makes them distinctive.

But.

It probably won't work for you.

Why?

First off, this isn't how customers make decisions about what product to buy. If Purpose were truly compelling, who would shop at Amazon? Just the amount of packaging alone is everything Generation Z and Millennials are supposed to be deeply, passionately opposed to, right? Well, yes, but Amazon is also Millennials' overwhelmingly favorite brand. It doesn't matter that Amazon can make it hard for the small, indie businesses that sell their products on the website. Millennials, and all American consumers, are okay with this. If it is cheaper and easier, they are going to buy it on Amazon. Easy beats purpose, every time.[4]

The second reason to refrain from using Purpose as your central tool for branding is a simple one: unless you are first out of the gate, like Patagonia, you're going to blend into a crowd of your competitors, each with similar heartfelt, socially or environmentally conscious senses of purpose. You may think you can create a purpose so thoughtful, so singular, so unique that it will stand out—but it won't. Consumers just don't care enough to think through your statement of purpose and distinguish it from your competitors. Daniel Kahneman argues that we have two systems of thought that we use throughout the day: System 1 is fast, intuitive, and emotional. System 2 is slow, rational, and deliberate.[5] His research uncovered that we make the vast majority of our decisions with System 1. Why? Because thinking through all our options with System 2 is extremely taxing, and we're deeply lazy. Which is a pretty solid argument that explains why nobody is researching their toothpaste's purpose to ensure that it aligns with their ideals. Being second to a compelling purpose can also backfire against you. As we'll discuss, misattribution is a huge problem in our industry. If you're copying a better known brand's strategy, your work may well end up being attributed to them.

So, Purpose, while noble, is rarely a viable strategy to sell your product and connect with your customer. In the rare occasions that Purpose does work, it works because it is distinctive (TOMS was the first to offer a one-for-one donation for each pair of shoes sold, or Dove's Real Beauty campaign, which made the brand stand out in a sea of overly glossy and photoshopped competitors) rather than because of emotional relevance. Here at Collider Lab, we *do* like purpose for internal purposes. It forces the company to make socially responsible decisions quickly and it helps inspire employees. But trying to use purpose as a marketing strategy doesn't move the needle in the vast majority of purchasing decisions. So, what's left? If using rational arguments doesn't actually create desire, and emotional connection is a fallacy, and purpose isn't a viable way to make an authentic connection . . . then what is it?

What's Really Relevant

We think that the more obvious way to make the brand desirable—or relevant—to the consumer is twofold:

1. **Fulfill a need.** When brands are clearly connected to clear category use occasions in consumers' minds, they become more desired. It's an obvious point, but an important one not to gloss over. Make your brand known for the right CUOs and desire for your brand will grow. This is why functional relevance is one of our three relevance categories.

2. **Be culturally relevant.** Figure out a way to allow your customer to identify themselves as a member of a herd, and express their membership in their herd through your product. Why does every fintech bro on either coast covet a Nano Puff? Because it identifies them as members of an influential and desirable subset of the business community: powerful enough to shrug off coat and ties, but insider-y enough to have earned that coveted corporate logo, ideally next to that all-access SXSW laminate. The Patagonia "herd" is rich and sustainability-aware. Kind of like a Tesla driver. It says, "I'm wealthy and can afford a $60,000 car (or $200+ for a light jacket), but I also understand that sustainability is a required bit of cultural capital to be allowed into today's aspirational class."

Before we go any further, here's a quick crash course in what we mean by *herd mentality*, and how it can affect you, your brand, and your business.

Herd Mentality: What's Everyone Else Doing?

Herd mentality is explained well by Yuval Noah Harari.[6] He shows why Homo sapiens dominated life on the planet over all other species of humans. The theory goes that when Homo sapiens reached the Middle East and Europe, they encountered the Neanderthals. These humans had more muscular physiques than Homo sapiens, and larger brains. They were better adapted to cold climates. So why did Homo sapiens win? Why are there no more Neanderthals (or why do they only make up 1–4 percent of our genes today)?

The answer may be a small tweak in behavior. Unlike Neanderthals, Homo sapiens could organize themselves into larger tribes, and those groups gave the individual members of the group safety, social bonds, and a better chance of survival. We are social animals. And that's the key to our success: Neanderthals couldn't organize into larger social groups, but Homo sapiens could.

The question is, why could Homo sapiens organize into large groups? The key is that they created a new way of communicating that fostered a sense of a shared history and a shared future. They did this with stories. Harari explains that Homo sapiens' ability to create and share stories allowed strangers to believe a shared myth about themselves, cooperate with each other, and thus to build ever greater communities of thousands, and eventually millions, of individuals. Not only are we a herd species above all else, we are highly attuned to social cues and behaviors. And all of us, on some level, still instinctively want that safety, companionship, and sense of being part of an ongoing, multigenerational story above all else.

Brands that understand this have an edge. After all, brands are what we use to tell the world who we are. Brands are part of our collective fiction. Picture a guy in his late twenties wearing a shirt from The Hundreds, Nike joggers, and red and black Air Jordan 1 sneakers. The brands he wears tell us part of his story, and send signals that other tribe members will recognize and respond to. Perhaps even more importantly, it *tells you who you are.* This collective storytelling is what binds us as herds. Like our Homo sapiens ancestors telling the first myths about their origins and their ancestors, we want a shortcut to communication, which will help us gain access to a herd, which will lead to the big, overarching benefit: safety and success together. Think of the kid with the wrong sneaks and the bad jeans: He's on the outside of the socially accepted, teenage "cool" herd, mocked by his peers. He isn't safe, at least until he gains membership into another herd, perhaps the rebels, outsiders, or geeks. Ultimately we are all seeking to bond tightly into a herd because we are vulnerable outside of it, and more successful within it.

As you move through the book, remember this connection between our natural desire to hear and tell stories, our herding instincts, and how brands can use cultural relevance to become storytellers themselves.

Herds are important. This gives you, the marketer, product designer, or operations guru, an opportunity. Reframe how you think of your product. It's no longer solely a consumer good, but now also an opportunity for a group of people to express the things that unite them, allow them to feel a sense of connection, and help them recognize like-minded souls. This is what we mean by cultural relevance. What story is your brand telling and what herd does it serve to unite? More importantly, how is your herd changing and evolving?

In the food category, people loved eating Ding-Dongs in the eighties, and were happy to be placed in the herd of comfort and convenience eaters. Now, no way! No one wants to be in that herd, when vegan, flexitarian, and ethical eaters are the ascending herd. Look at cars and fuel efficiency. Why have Hummers died out? Because almost no one wants to be in the herd of people who don't care about gas mileage or the environment anymore. Those herd values are what you are looking for when you're building or defining a brand, or creating a new set of values that the herd will react to.

If you don't understand what herds were hot in the past, how can you understand the ascendant herds that are emerging now? We don't usually recommend narrowly targeting your marketing to small herds (unless of course you are in a small, niche category), but we think it's essential to understand them because they are signifiers of how the macro herd is evolving. If you understand the small, growing herds, you can start to find and understand those emerging values that will inevitably spread to the macro herd you actually want to market to.

— 5 —

Cultural Relevance

I N THE LAST chapter we demystified two of the most tenacious, "well, it *feels* true," marketing myths that have plagued our industry since an early hunter-gatherer woke up, realized he had gathered an extra bushel of seeds and berries, and decided to figure out a way to talk his neighbor into a mutually beneficial exchange of goods.

One last time:

Purpose, as a tool for marketing, is a mirage. Focus instead on helping build your customers' self-identity and enable them to align themselves with the herds they most aspire to belong to.

Emotional connection for a product or brand can occasionally be a by-product of your product's functional or cultural relevance. However, this kind of "love" is almost impossible to create. So, don't waste time trying to spark a love affair with whatever it is you're selling. Instead, focus on maximizing the functional or cultural relevance of your product, and accept any resulting emotional connection as a happy, if unexpected, bonus.

In many countries, the brand that has the most history there also has the most family memories and sweet, warm, and fuzzy emotional connections— because you remember going there with your mom or dad when you were a kid. But rarely is that brand our top performer. Emotional connection just doesn't translate to sales.

It's easy to debunk old, bad ideas, and can be harder to create good, new ones. In this chapter we will take on that tricky task, and show you how to utilize *cultural relevance* to create that elusive connection that purpose and emotional connection have failed to do in the past.

So, What Exactly Is Cultural Relevance?

IT'S THE REAL THING

Cultural relevance (see Figure 5.1) is a more sophisticated and modern take on the old trope of emotional connection. Instead of trying to create an artificial sense of love or affection for your brand, you are giving your user a *reason* to feel connected to your brand. You are doing this by finding a symbol that offers your user a sense of belonging to a particular herd that they believe they are a member of, or would like to join.

This is where Collider Lab differs from a few modern marketing academics we otherwise respect. These folks are adamant that the only thing that matters is mental and physical availability. The only type of relevance that is worth a damn is functional relevance. In other words, create a product that suffices for people's functional needs, make it top of mind

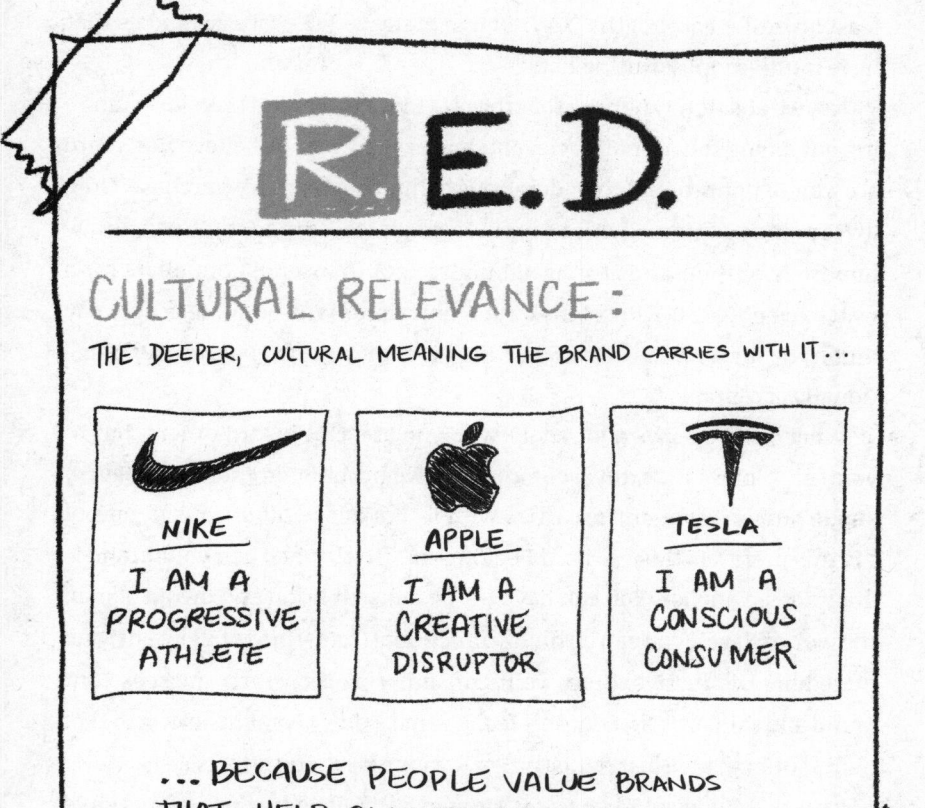

R.E.D.

CULTURAL RELEVANCE:

THE DEEPER, CULTURAL MEANING THE BRAND CARRIES WITH IT...

NIKE
I AM A PROGRESSIVE ATHLETE

APPLE
I AM A CREATIVE DISRUPTOR

TESLA
I AM A CONSCIOUS CONSUMER

... BECAUSE PEOPLE VALUE BRANDS THAT HELP GIVE THEM AN IDENTITY AND HELP THEM FEEL LIKE THEY BELONG TO A HERD.

FIGURE 5.1

through your media and distinctiveness, and make it easy to get. Everything else is useless mumbo jumbo. We beg to differ. Their approach radically discounts Nike's "cool" brand aura or Tesla's sense of futuristic aspiration. If their worldview were right, the coolest skater kids in town should be fine wearing Gap jeans. Everyone would be pining for a sensible

Toyota Prius or Nissan Leaf or the Chevy Bolts that are readily available (at least on either coast of the US), not one of the S-3-X-Y Tesla models that have multi-month waiting lists.

No, we absolutely believe that there is more to a brand than just standing out, being functionally relevant, and easy to get. We believe that there are a lot of nonrational considerations behind nearly every purchase. Greg loves pointing this out with a couple of examples. Why do some people pay hundreds or thousands (or even hundreds of thousands) of dollars for a watch, when a $40 Timex tells impeccable time? Why do some people pay hundreds for a haircut when an $18 clip at Supercuts is perfectly, functionally acceptable?

What you buy says a lot about who you are. Not just to others, but to yourself. Unless it's truly a commodity, we have found that nearly every single purchase you make carries with it that added bit of consideration: "Is this me?" "Is this the herd I belong to?" If it's not, then your brand is dragging an anchor. You can have the best distribution and media plan in the world (Ease); you can be highly functional (one-third of Relevant) and incredibly Distinctive. But if your consumer pauses when she sees your brand and thinks, "That doesn't feel like me. I don't want to belong to that herd," then you've just hamstrung all your marketing efforts.

This is a nuanced idea, so let's unpack it a little further. "Emotional connection," as defined by believers in that approach, means your customer feels some sort of love for the brand itself. In this situation, a marketer might believe, "I've created enough goodwill with consumers that they now love me, and will, therefore, buy me." On the surface, this idea seems reasonable. But it doesn't translate to sales because—in part—of the sappy, mirror-like creative it invariably produces. On the other hand, cultural relevance done right *does* lead to sales and a stronger brand long term. It's the difference between "I feel emotionally connected to this brand" and "this brand gives me some cultural cachet that adds to my identity." This is the key point. We're saying brands *are* more than just distinctive and functional, but that "more" is not "emotionally connected to my consumer." That "more" is actually, "this product is a standard-bearer of a cultural identity that I as a consumer can use to build my identity and belong to a herd."

Michelob Ultra learned this lesson and dominated the US beer market in what has become one of the greatest modern marketing stories in the industry. They went from the number eight beer in the category, to the number three, easily blowing away long established brands like Heineken and Corona. How? We spoke to John Kenny, all around marketing genius and the Chief Strategy Officer of FCB. He was part of the team that masterminded the effort.

"Michelob Ultra was the first beer to embrace the 'active is the new premium' trend, where fitness was the new status symbol." Beer drinkers everywhere wanted to join that herd. John's advice for brands that want to imitate their success? "Don't follow the conventions of your category, follow the innovations in your culture. It makes you both incredibly culturally relevant and incredibly distinctive in your category."

The Oatly Effect

We believe in cultural relevance, because we have seen huge amounts of evidence that it works in how our brands, and in how brands around the world, perform. At the same time, there are serious academics that have done outstanding research to show the very real effect of a brand's cultural relevance.

Douglas Holt, who was a professor at the Harvard Business School and L'Oréal Chair in Marketing at Oxford, has explored the phenomenon of what he calls a brand's "symbolic load" (and what we would consider cultural relevance) in depth. He calls brands that have a powerful symbolic load *brand icons*.

Icons come to represent a particular kind of story—an identity myth—that their consumers use to address identity desires and anxieties. Icons have extraordinary value because they carry a heavy symbolic load for their most enthusiastic consumers.[1]

That "symbolic load," or cultural relevance, is a tool that consumers use both to build upon their own identity *and* attempt to belong to a certain herd. Take Oatly Milk, for example. Sure, it's a wonderful milk alternative that most anyone would find quite tasty. But why on earth would a milk alternative have branded merchandise—T-shirts, track suits, sweat-shirts—that seems to be constantly out of stock? Do a little sleuthing on-line for Oatly and you'll discover a ridiculously passionate group of users. When the product briefly ran out in 2018, twelve-packs went for four times their regular price on Amazon. That's right, consumers were paying resellers $200 for a twelve-pack of oat milk, while endless quarts of its milk-alternative competitors gathered dust on store shelves. That's the difference between a brand that understands the power of cultural rele-vance and one that thinks it's only about mental and physical availability.[2]

Holt goes on to explain what he calls the "identity value" that certain brands carry with them.

Customers value some products as much for what they symbolize as for what they do. For brands like Coke, Budweiser, Nike, and Jack Daniel's, customers value the brands' stories largely for their identity value. Acting as vessels of self-expression, the brands are imbued with stories that consumers find valuable in constructing their identities. Consumers flock to brands that embody the ideals they admire, brands that help them express who they want to be.[3]

Another one of our favorite collaborators is Elizabeth Currid-Halkett, professor of public policy at the University of Southern California. Her research has taken her further down the path of understanding how consumers use brands not merely as a form of self-identity and belonging, but as a way of seeing themselves in a *better* light, or belonging to a more *aspirational* herd. Over the last few years, she has found that the defining elements of that more aspirational herd tend to be related to ethical behaviors of a brand. We spoke to her recently and she explained,

> The aspirational class is not simply interested in what a product looks like, even just what it tastes like. Aspirational consumers seek products and services that allow them to be better humans, to "aspire," as it were, to a better place. That's why where a product comes from, that it's sourced ethically, that the production process is transparent, that it "does no harm" informs how members of the aspirational class consume. Part of this type of consumption involves the story of the product—whether we are talking pasture-raised chickens and their eggs or a Barbour jacket and its English heritage story. For members of the aspirational class, part of the product's value is derived from deeper social and cultural meanings and stories.[4]

Oatly proves Currid-Halkett's theory nicely. We'd argue that the group that is drawn to the brand the most is the aspirational class. And a big reason for that attraction is that the "social good" story of the brand creates a herd that they want to belong to. We reached out to John Schoolcraft, the Global Chief Creative Officer of Oatly, and floated the idea of cultural relevance by him, and asked him if it was an important part of the brand's success.

> Neither Toni [Oatly's CEO] or I have really been interested in selling oatmilk but rather using oatmilk as a means to create positive societal change. Every carton of sold oatmilk is roughly a 70 percent carbon footprint savings for the planet compared to cows' milk. We have been pretty good at making this culturally relevant by highlighting its societal benefits and turning that into power statements on T-shirts and pins and posters and wall paints, whatever. We've created an oatmilk cult, but in a nondestructive, for-the-greater-good sort of way.

Wearing an Oatly T-shirt, in other words, helps the aspirational consumer "construct their identity," as Holt would say, and belong to a progressive, culturally relevant herd. Understanding that helps us comprehend why people would feel the need to pay $200 for a case of oatmilk. That intense desire for the brand clearly does not just come from its functional relevance and distinctiveness. There's meaning in that brand. Meaning that consumers find extremely valuable. Here's an important sidenote: the difference between emotional connection and cultural relevance. Oatly users don't feel emotionally connected to the brand as in, "I love this brand because they are good for the environment and will therefore buy them." Instead, they find the brand's cultural meaning incredibly important for their own identity: "I will go far out of my way to buy this brand because it makes me feel on trend, and part of the cool crowd." This is not some silly academic distinction we are making. If you brief your creatives with the goal of "make an emotional connection with the consumer," you'll get a radically different output than if you say "make it so cool that consumers will want to wear a T-shirt of our brand." Emotional connection is nothing compared to cultural relevance.

As we've talked about before, we also dislike the idea of "purpose" as a tool for marketing. Unless it happens to be absolutely true, you're the first brand in the space to make the specific claim of "purpose," and the purpose makes your product distinctive at the same time. Oatly is one of those rare cases where their social good purpose is genuine and also helps them stand out as distinctive, especially because of the totally unique, ownable, and consistent way they express it: irreverent, funny, unexpected. They were also the first product in that category to try this approach. But since Oatly's wild success, a pile of other milk alternative brands have jumped into the market with the same "we're about a bigger purpose" idea. Naturally, many will fail miserably because it will not be distinctive to them (brands like Good Karma Flaxmilk, Planet Oat Oatmilk, Silk Oat Yeah Oatmilk, and store brand generics might struggle for this reason).

Regardless, to become an iconic, highly desired brand, marketers must clearly imbue their brand with culturally relevant meaning. Most traditional marketers will readily agree that there is more power to a brand than its mere functionality. But this is the point at which they'll make one of two fatal mistakes. Many, like the Oatly imitators above, will desperately chase after a bigger sense of global purpose as a tool for marketing. Many others will go down the emotional connection rabbit hole, trying desperately to overtly establish some sort of "love" with their customer (most often by mirroring back how beautifully the product fits into their lives). But a new breed of marketers are beginning to reject the concept altogether. These folks will mistakenly believe that by simply making a functionally useful product readily available and highly distinctive they'll be able to create this sort of illogical brand passion. We've heard marketers jokingly refer to this approach as the "brand's logo, efficiently deployed" strategy. We agree with the criticism. It's an approach that is sorely lacking.

We discussed this recent phenomenon in marketing with Dr. Holt, and asked him why marketers are starting to divide into two philosophical camps:

1. Marketers that understand you can make your brand more valuable by making it culturally relevant
2. Marketers that feel you simply have to stand out as distinctive, end of story

He explained that academics that support the *distinctiveness-is-the-whole-story* approach are using "data from very pedestrian brands and so [are] modeling brand mediocrity. My model," Holt explains, "is based upon the top 1 percent [of brands], which either require building culturally [what we would call cultural relevance] or simply a phenomenal world-beating product (which is rare)." Holt, in other words, is arguing that if you want to create an iconic brand with lasting power, then distinctiveness alone is not enough.

This is the core of why we found it necessary to build R.E.D. We needed a system that combined the idea of cultural relevance with the powerful notion of mental and physical availability. One of the founding tenets of Collider Lab is that a simple black-and-white marketing strategy is never going to work. If you're culturally relevant but not distinctive, you'll fail. And if you're incredibly distinctive, but not culturally relevant, you'll also fail. And it goes without saying that if you're not easy you should probably just hang up your marketer's hat and go home. All three elements are important, and when you deploy them simultaneously you get the Oatly effect: the very real potential of massive share gains. So massive, in fact, that Oprah and Jay-Z (among other investors) purchased 10 percent of the brand in 2020 for $200 million, thereby effectively valuing the company at $2 billion.[5] The next stage in the oatmilk battle, though, will be interesting to watch. Oatly has done an amazing job with relevance and distinctiveness, but is struggling with ease. They simply can't open plants quickly enough to satisfy demand, so distribution is spotty—it's not easy to find. As copycat brands flood the market, it's quite possible that one or more of them "out-eases" Oatly and ends up winning, especially if they do at least a decent job with R & D.

At this point, we hope we're being clear with cultural relevance: We don't think our consumer stands at the shelf and feels his heart pitter patter with a sensual attraction when he sees our brand. We don't believe she's buying us because she feels emotionally connected. We believe he buys us (or doesn't buy us) because of what that brand says about him, and more to the point, what herd that brand says he belongs to.

It may seem like a small nuance, but it's one that results in radically different marketing campaigns. Send your marketing team off on a quest to "build brand love" and expect to get some pretty sappy "mirror" creative, lots of heartfelt messaging, and an overall tone of "please love me!" Send your team on a mission to make your brand relevant in culture and you'll get something else entirely. The first thing they'll want to figure out is, "Where is culture heading?" And immediately thereafter they'll ask themselves, "Now how do I make my brand an exciting and distinctive part of that culture?" No sappy ads. Just dialed-in, "magnet" work that people will talk about. That's the difference between emotional connection and cultural relevance.

The key learning about cultural relevance is this: *Consumers move in herds. When you think of your end user, understand that they—like most people—are consciously or unconsciously looking to gain access to herds where they belong—or want to belong. Your on culture product or brand creates an opportunity for them to identify as a member of a herd. Your success at cultural relevance hinges on your ability to see when those herds are changing and evolve your brand meaning—ideally before your customers realize their needs and desires are changing themselves.*

Understand Your Cultural Codes

We call these *on culture* symbols cultural codes, inspired by Clotaire Rapaille's theories. Think of category codes as a shorthand for understanding the reasons why consumers either engage with, or are repelled by, your brand in any given category. Fast food, or QSRs, is a fascinating category because the same brand can have wildly different cultural relevance around the world. In the US, the foundation of fast-food culture is a Puritan ideal of functional, efficient caloric intake. This comes both from the German meat and potatoes culture, and the British culture of not particularly prioritizing food. In Mexico, the purpose of fast food is socialization. In France, as Rapaille points out, it's enjoyment and pleasure. In the Philippines, we've found that fast food is about escapism and fantasy. In Russia, it's about exploration and trying something Western and new. But in the US, it's always been a functional experience and recently shifted to be more about what we came to call the "Fast Foodie." Bear in mind we are talking about the *same brands* in all these different countries: KFC, McDonald's, Burger King, and so on. So what works for KFC in Jakarta may just fail miserably in France, and vice versa. (In chapter six we'll talk about a Taco Bell innovation, the Crunchwrap, that was specifically designed to be functionally relevant for an American audience.) We're not kidding about culture! You need to understand the culture of your consumer base, and accept that what works brilliantly in one country could flame out in another.

This sounds complicated, we know. Luckily, we've developed a system to help you uncover and understand how cultural relevance and cultural codes apply to your brand and products on a local and a global level. We'll get to the nuts and bolts in a moment, but first, let's show cultural relevance in action with an example out of KFC South Africa.

Uncovering Cultural Relevance

In the post-Apartheid era, KFC South Africa promoted itself with a joyful, "Rainbow Nation" brand identity that worked brilliantly for years. It was a mindset people were proud to be associated with. But starting in about 2012, the brand went into decline. By 2015, we'd had three years of shrinking sales, and our iconic "togetherness brand" was clearly out of place with the shifting cultural trends of the new millennium. Our main competitor's stores were decked out in black walls and golden chandeliers, and pumped house music through the dining area. By comparison, we suddenly felt old, stodgy, and somehow out of date.

So what had changed? Collider Lab launched a major investigation of South African culture. We identified a couple of brilliant professors of anthropology and sociology in Johannesburg, and with their help developed some hypotheses of what ailed the brand. We then bounced our ideas off some of the coolest South African poets and cultural commentators of the time. These few weeks of collaboration were foundational. Walking into the next phase of research with a broad, modern understanding of culture *and* some fresh hypotheses in hand made all the difference. Finally, Ken and Jessika Gomez-Duarte flew to Johannesburg. They spent twelve hours a day meeting customers, touring the stores and neighborhoods, and getting to the bottom of why our brand was in free fall. They then did something very Collider Lab: they went to Soweto and spent days just sitting with families, talking with them, and absorbing and observing their lives. They consistently heard the themes our professors and cultural collaborators had briefed Collider Lab about: The old people would say, "Kids today, they don't understand the dream. The dream is, we lived through this horrible moment. There comes a time to come together and to be to-gether." The young people . . . well, they were the opposite. They had no interest in being part of a post-Apartheid Rainbow Nation. They were am-bitious, driven, and desperate for the chance to succeed on their own terms. One of the interviewees was an eighteen-year-old college student. Ken and Jessika were in his tiny apartment, piled with books all over the floor. Nothing else was attended to. The fridge had a few moldy fast-food sandwiches and his bed didn't have sheets. After a couple of hours of quiz-zing him on every aspect of his life and vision for his future, he looked up at them, and said, "My father says I'm a fool. My grandfather says I'm an idiot because I don't believe in his dream. You know what I believe in? I believe it's me, and just me that is going to get me to where I want to go. And I'm *going* to get there." That moment is frozen in Ken's mind, and he says he'll always remember it. He can still see every detail of his stark, dark room and the awe-inspiring intensity in his jaw. It's been a few years since that interview, but Ken and Jessika have no doubt he got to where he wanted to go.

South Africa was in the midst of a monumental cultural shift. KFC was tanking because it was still telling a story of post-Apartheid racial har-mony and community that had literally nothing to do with the experience of living in South Africa at that moment. When our driven student stood in Maponya mall in Soweto, trying to decide where to eat, he had two choices. On his left, the KFC of his forefathers, whose logo alone made dozens of warm, togetherness memory structures light up in his mind. On his right, our competitor with their deep black walls, their massive golden chandelier tinkling to the insistent, rhythmic bass and a line of young people snaking out the door, wearing the latest kicks. It wasn't a hard decision.

A few days later, the Collider Lab team boarded a plane for the thirty-one-hour trip home. When they got back, they followed up their hunches and instincts about their observations, contacting South African professors, poets, bloggers, writers, and anyone who seemed like they could either debunk or verify what the team had found. The young people of South Africa were hungry for self-actualization and independent achievement. The Apartheid era felt like ancient history. If anything, they were cynical about the dreams of their parents, and had little interest in sitting around a metaphorical campfire, sharing their feelings. This is powerful, radical stuff. What Jessika and Ken had discovered was that the brand had been operating on an outdated set of cultural codes. Our "Kumbaya" campaign was offering them an identity they didn't want and membership in a herd that they didn't want to join. Other brands were noticing the shift, too: Guinness has had success with their *Made of Black* campaign, which celebrates a more empowered African spirit.[6]

Interestingly enough, KFC Japan is grappling with a similar shift away from community and togetherness. For the last forty years, KFC Japan has been the unofficial Christmas dinner brand, something families buy and share with each other around the holidays. As in South Africa, young people in Japan are rejecting these old ideas of togetherness and family. Single households are growing (and are projected to make up 34.5 percent of the country in 2020). These young professionals see food as being a precious and peaceful break from obligation. So, the Christmas tradition of KFC bringing together large social groups was starting to feel seriously off code. As a result, Yuko Nakajima, the brilliant and understated CMO of KFC Japan, is having to reinvent a marketing tentpole that has worked beautifully for decades. Her team is finding surprising ways to bring the brand back into alignment with the emerging culture. One of our favorite tactical executions is surreptitiously placing random Colonel statues on park benches overnight.

The Three Cultural Codes

In R.E.D. we refer to the kind of evolution we saw in South Africa and Japan as an emerging cultural code: a shift in consumer trends that is in the early stages of development, but which heralds a major change in how customers think and feel about a category code. The Rainbow Nation cultural code was slowly slipping into obsolescence as the young people of the country reframed the culture to reflect their hopes, lives, reality, and dreams. There are three stages of a category's cultural code as we see them:

1. **Residual code.** What worked in the past
2. **Dominant code.** What works now
3. **Emerging code.** What will work in the future

It's important to be aware of this ongoing evolution. Consumers' tastes, interests, and belief systems are always in flux, and as a result cultural codes never stop moving and evolving. As you move through this chapter, and the book, ask yourself the following questions:

1. What cultural codes have worked for my category in the past?
2. What is working now?
3. And what is going to work in the future?

Meanwhile, back at Taco Bell . . .

The Survival of the Crunchiest

FOOD AS FUEL
TO FOOD AS EXPERIENCE

First, some backstory: Remember Taco Bell in the 1990s? If you were a teenager, you probably spent your fair share of time there, wolfing down sixty-nine-cent tacos, and filling yourself up on bean burritos and Nachos BellGrande. If you *had* teenagers, you probably felt that palpable sense of relief that comes from getting them fully fueled and ready to go, with change out of a five. The Taco Bell cultural code—*food as fuel*—worked for years. It worked because it was in perfect sync with the early grunge, *Slackers*-style ethos of the 1990s. The nineties was the Big Gulp era, and food, especially fast food, was something a person consumed to allow them to do the actual interesting and meaningful stuff in their lives, be it work, skateboarding, soccer, or goofing off. Our customers responded to us because Taco Bell was culturally relevant. We were perfectly aligned with what our customers needed and wanted: affordable food, super craveable, slightly rebellious.

We were still fully invested in our dominant code: keeping the young-at-heart and value-oriented eaters of America powered up on chalupas and nachos. Sales were okay, and our customers loved the Taco Bell Chihuahua, introduced in 1997.[7] As the campaign continued, however, management noticed something disconcerting: the public loved the dog, but it no longer seemed to love the food. Sales were slipping, and they continued to slip into the 2000s. In hindsight we were missing the very urgent, flashing red sign that said *emerging code ahead*. Our old code—food as fuel—still felt good to *us*, so what the heck were we missing about our customers' changing tastes?

Here's the thing about changing cultural codes: If you're not out in culture, you're not going to see them. If you're not placed to see—and more importantly, *realize that you are seeing*—an emerging cultural code, you won't be able to make the necessary changes to your understanding of your product and the strategy you use to sell it. If you do nothing else, you need to be out in the world, absorbing what people both like and *unlike* yourself are finding fascinating. Here's a perfect example of just how important this is:

Find Your Changing
Cultural Code in Culture

Ken and his wife, Fabiana, lived in Chicago in the late 2000s. Let's set the scene: Chicago is a huge food town. *Huge.* And at that period in time, it had the most riveting, exciting food scene in the country. Monday morning, the conversation wasn't, "What movie did you see?" or, "What club did you hit?" Every Monday, your coworkers wanted to know where you'd eaten that weekend, what you'd eaten, and what you'd thought about it. Chicago, and specifically the experimental, controversial restaurants of the moment, was changing what fine dining meant. Alinea had a six-month wait list, and a prix fixe of hundreds of dollars per person. Moto, in Chicago's meatpacking district, used a laser, centrifuge, and a particle ion gun in the creation of their dishes. The chefs were tattooed rock stars in the Anthony Bourdain model. Dinner was pretty much whatever the chef felt inspired to create in that moment, be it molecular dining, rarefied vapors, or foie gras hot dogs. Even more traditional restaurants were experimenting with what food could be. Ken's favorite casual place on the North Side was Hot Doug's, a restaurant that served $10 brats made out of alligator or duck, venison or veggies. The limits of what people were willing to try were being pushed ever further, in part because the culture around food, and what it was, was evolving. This is a huge change in what fine dining, and indeed the experience of food, meant to people.

Of course, it's one thing to be excited by a burgeoning restaurant scene, another to be able to afford it. In 2009, Ken and Fabiana decided that they would forgo their annual vacation, and have dinner at Alinea instead. This was approaching a thousand-dollar night, so it wasn't an easy choice. But eventually they decided that the experience was worth the sacrifice.

The dinner was, of course, astonishing. Eighteen unique courses, each one more surreal than the next. Edible apple balloons filled with helium, a deconstructed peanut butter and jelly sandwich made from a single grape dipped in peanut puree and wrapped in a brioche, hanging from a wire dish. Eventually, it was time for desert. The chef, Grant Achatz, came to the table and spread out a rubber mat. Another chef walked up with a subzero brick of nougat, fogging in the warm air. The chef then hit the brick with a hammer and it shattered all over the table. Next, he took three different chocolate sauces and started dripping them all over the table. Finally, when he was satisfied with the surrealist canvas-that-was-a-table, he grabbed this piece of nougat and demonstrated how to smear the chocolate and the nougat together. It was delicious, and dinner was finally over.

For years after that dinner, Ken felt vaguely guilty about it. That was a huge amount of money for a public school history teacher and an ad agency planner to spend. They'd sacrificed a much anticipated trip to Oaxaca to experience it. Yet, that one night was a revelation, because it crystalized multiple different experiences into one overarching insight: Fine dining was no longer about overstuffed red leather banquettes, supercilious sommeliers, and slabs of beef so big you grew weary of eating them halfway through the dinner. Fine dining was now an adventure, an unpredictable experience. Sitting down at that table in Alinea was electric: What was going to happen? Would diners be pushed to experience something on the edge of what they would consider food? Would they taste things that challenged and pushed them beyond their usual comfort level? Today, Fabi still tells Ken that that dinner was the best rent check they ever spent. Because that one dinner gave him clarity over a vast new emerging cultural code. It gave him the insights that would turn into "Food as Experience." Most Taco Bell customers (most people, really) are not in the position to spend four figures on dinner. However, they still want to be part of that

Foodie Herd. They want an entrance into this new world, where food is exciting, different, provocative. That old "food as fuel" herd was receding into the past, and Taco Bell's fortunes were going to go with it if they didn't change.

Trust the Emerging Cultural Code

By the time Greg was made CEO in 2011, Taco Bell sales were heading toward the free-fall category. Greg initially followed the traditional protocol for fast-food turmoil: lower prices and offer crazy deals, in this case the "Summer of Savings" featuring comedian Aziz Ansari.[8] Greg is the first to admit that these kinds of sales may scare up some additional revenue, but they can look—quite frankly—desperate. Doubly so in Taco Bell's case, because, in a bout of exceptionally bad timing, we were also dealing with a nonsense lawsuit alleging that our beef wasn't really beef. This lawsuit a) proved that some publicity really is bad and b) it's possible to swat that bad publicity right back at your adversary, in our case by erecting billboards around the lawyers' golf club, pointing out the similarities between their tactics and those of Somali pirates. The case was dismissed, but not before cementing the idea that our beef was a low-grade product in the public's mind. We needed a radical evolution in how we talked about our product, and we needed it fast.

The year 2011 was big for another reason, one unrelated to Taco Bell. In January, the newborn Instagram enabled hashtags for its million-odd users. By June of that year, the app had five million regular users. By September, it had ten million. The exponential increase in users, and the functionality of the hashtags, meant that by the close of 2011 Instagram had gone from an outlier app that savvy twenty-somethings used mostly as a visual diary, to being a significant way to develop an online persona. This persona could be an unexaggerated extension of an individual's offline self, or a distinct entity with its own set of attitudes and a unique voice, often unrelated to the day-to-day reality of the individual's actual life. Instagram users were now, quite literally, the stars of their own show, and everything they did or experienced was now potential "content." Naturally, Insta users loved to document their dining experiences, and, as the app grew, so did foodie snaps of melting ice-cream cones, kimchi tacos, and BBQ dripping with sauce.

Taco Bell was in a perfect storm of uncertainty. Our dominant code (food as fuel) was sinking like the *Titanic*. Our emerging code was clearly linked to the exponentially growing foodie and Instagram culture, but no one was completely clear on what that code was.

Back at the agency, we were doing further research to back up Ken's observations. We logged in, refreshed, and scrolled down Instagram and social media culture. What we saw backed up what Ken had seen in Chicago: Food was no longer fuel. Food—like all elements of life—was now an experience that served two functions, satiating your needstate (in this case, hunger) *and* giving you content that would allow you to belong in the emerging cool club. We were witnessing the birth of mainstream foodieism. To be shareable, the food you ate suddenly needed to be exploratory, exotic, new, quirky, interesting, and worthy of eyeballs among all the other Insta content, jostling for #attention. Taco Bell was none of those things. As a result, our cultural relevance was slipping. People weren't as thrilled to be connected to us as they once were. Now we just needed to sell Greg and the team at Taco Bell on this idea.

Cultural Relevance: How We Did It

At the time, Ken was heading up strategy at the advertising agency FCB. The FCB team met with the Taco Bell group to discuss possible solutions: they wanted change fast, but, more importantly, they wanted the *right* change. Our thinking was in sync from the start, but compatibility alone wasn't going to fix the problem. What were we actually going to do to save Taco Bell?

From the start, we agreed that Taco Bell's prices weren't the real problem. The food was very affordable and always had been. Consumers were eating elsewhere, even paying more to do so, because something in the culture had changed. But what? Ken's experience at Alinea, and the burgeoning food truck culture, gave us a pretty strong hypothesis about how food culture was evolving into more than just a functional experience. The next thing to do was explore this hypothesis with research. The problem was, if you straight-out asked someone why they no longer ate at Taco Bell as much, they'd give you explanations, not *reasons*. They'd say the food cost too much, or that the ingredients weren't high quality, or offer some other pragmatic-sounding excuse. But we already knew from our research that these were rationalizations, not true motives.

Think back to chapter three, and Ken's ability to justify his choice of Snickers over the higher quality chocolate that he *actually* wanted. He still does this every day, and he's a person who is literally paid to get to the bottom of people's real motivations and desires. So, it takes work to understand what consumers really want but are either genuinely unaware of, or too embarrassed or proud to admit to wanting, as opposed to what they think is socially acceptable to want.

Step One: We worked with psychologists to create a new set of subconscious, qualitative methodologies that would help us figure out what our customers really believed about the brand. (An important note: We're not trying to find some psychological reason why people are buying or not buying the brand. We're trying to understand how they view the brand. It's critical to have a clear view of how your brand is perceived. You need to know what you're working with in order to see if it fits the cultural world your consumer aspires to.) These questions allowed our consumers to express their subconscious feelings toward the brand while filtering out their post-rationalizations. In one study, for example, we asked participants to choose from among hundreds of images to metaphorically represent the brand's positive and negative traits. To our surprise, the images they chose were dull, sleepy, even "basic." How could the only Mexican-inspired brand in the QSR category be boring?

That's the thing about consumer research: if you're doing it properly, the findings can surprise you, even if you have a strong ingoing hypotheses. Remember our regressive, dominant, and emerging codes. These codes are constantly evolving. The dominant code is always slowly fading, while the emerging value is in a constant process of slowly entering the mainstream.

Our research gave us insight into the real reasons for Taco Bell's downward trajectory. Underneath justifications like price and quality, consumers saw Taco Bell as "food made by the stoner in the back of the classroom." If the brand were a person, it would be, as one woman eloquently put it, "the guy peeing off the porch at a frat party." That image became a pivot point for the brand. Did it make sense to be the porch guy anymore? Drunk frat culture might have been cool in the 1990s, but in 2010? All of Taco Bell's ads were about cracking jokes. Taken together, they gave consumers the impression that Taco Bell was funny, silly, stupid, and cheap. That had worked for Gen X, but Millennials weren't buying it. They wanted food with a sense of cool or interesting or new to it. Food wasn't just fuel anymore. To satisfy this new cultural need, a brand had to offer a memorable, shareable experience.

By this stage, the team at FCB was convinced that Taco Bell needed to pivot from *fuel* to *experience*, and pivot fast. They set up a meeting with Greg, sat down, synched up a laptop to the conference room's big screen, and pressed "play." Up came old footage of Julia Child painstakingly, slowly preparing a roast chicken, intercut with an Iron Chef contestant flipping sizzling octopus in a pan. Back to Julia, adjusting her pearls. Back to the Iron Chef, smoke filling the screen as the cephalopod seared. Julia, musing on the benefits of French butter. Iron Chef, collapsing in emotion as the judges praise his bizarre yet weirdly delicious creation. The message was clear: food could no longer capture people's attention if it was simply delicious and available. It had to be *on culture*. It had to fill a third need: to be exciting, experiential, and unexpected.

All of this was a far cry from the microwave-burrito-and-go mentality of the 1990s. The culture had changed more radically than anyone who *hadn't* done this level of research would have guessed.

From Research to Revolution

As Ken and Greg worked further in understanding this evolution, they came up with a name for their customer: The Fast Foodie. Now, The Fast Foodie isn't an individual. The Fast Foodie is a collective of millions of like-minded people (in this case, young-at-heart, adventurous, social, and slightly rebellious). In other words, The Fast Foodie was a new herd, quickly evolving to replace the herd Taco Bell used to rely on: the rebellious punk-at-heart who loves craveable food. In order to reach our Fast Foodies, we were going to need to offer them something worthy of putting up on their feed. Like the Iron Chef, it had to be unexpected, spectacular, and somewhat amusing.

As it turned out, Greg had been nursing along an innovation that now proved timely: the Doritos Locos Taco. His innovation team had been working on a nacho-chip taco shell for years, but what they'd really wanted to do was make a legitimate Doritos shell: genuine texture, genuine flavor. (The cult of Doritos would know the difference.) In light of our findings, we saw our chance. We'd speed up development of the taco and use it to springboard the brand back into alignment with the culture. Greg's motto as CEO became "from fuel to experience." He had it printed up and put on everyone's desks. In addition to being affordable, delicious, and convenient, Taco Bell would become surprising, exciting, and shareable.

Now that these kinds of crossovers are commonplace, it may seem obvious, but in 2011, the idea of combining two crave-worthy household-name brands in one product was an electrifying feat of alchemy, a new experience that millions of Millennials would consider Instagram-worthy. We changed everything about the marketing to complement the product. For example, every taco came with a QR code you could use to post a picture to a digital billboard in Times Square. Once we launched the product, social media lit up and, as we'd anticipated, people weren't talking about the taste as much as the social experience of eating it together. More proof that cultural relevance drives sales, not emotional connection.

Our advertising had to adapt, too. It was time to leave the frat jokes behind if we were going to stay relevant. We could no longer trumpet only how convenient and delicious the food was—those aspects were no longer relevant by themselves. This was the origin of our wildly successful "Live Más" campaign, designed to present Taco Bell as an experience. The first ad featured a man returning to his apartment and emptying his pockets of the relics of a wild night out: a ticket stub to a concert, a strip of photo-booth images with a beautiful girl, and, of course, a packet of Taco Bell hot sauce. From food to experience.

The Doritos Locos Taco was a home run. Taco Bell sold almost one billion tacos in the first two years, making it—at the time—the fastest-selling product in Taco Bell's history. From that point forward, it became the brand's mission to make each and every new product memorable, sticky, and *shareable*. Over the next few years, we launched a slew of successes, from the Naked Chicken Chalupa (it had a chicken-breast shell, instead of a tortilla) to the Quesalupa, a giant quesadilla with cheese *inside* the actual tortilla shell. If it wasn't worth talking about, it wasn't worth adding to the menu.

Likewise, the brand itself became a bigger player in culture. Tracee Larrocca, Taco Bell's longtime VP of Marketing and general caretaker of the soul of the brand, authored a series of activations to dial up social relevance (she calls this "giving the brand cultural topspin") that were constantly buzzed about, from a Taco Bell speakeasy to an insanely popular annual promotion called Steal a Base, Steal a Taco, where everyone in America got a free Taco if someone stole a base during the World Series. Her team's efforts helped land Taco Bell on *Fast Company*'s coveted list of the fifty most creative companies in America, only a few spots after companies like Apple, Alphabet (Google), and Uber.[9] Marisa Thalberg, Taco Bell's CMO during several of these years, took the brand to even more dizzying heights in culture. She launched a line of Taco Bell clothes with Forever 21, opened the aforementioned Taco Bell Hotel, and started offering weddings in a chapel inside a Taco Bell in Las Vegas.

Taco Bell was inordinately successful under Greg's leadership because it was the first to jump on the emerging value of foodie-ism. That's the power of cultural relevance. Brands willing to take risks and stay on the leading edge of the category will occasionally strike out, but the wins will more than make up for the losses.

We took a two-pronged approach to cultural relevance: say it ("Live Más") and prove it ("Doritos Locos Taco"). Everything was aligned and it all said one thing: Taco Bell matters again. Consumers agreed to an unprecedented degree. Taco Bell's sales have increased consistently every single year for the eight years since then, as of this writing.

Due to the extraordinary success of his effort to turn Taco Bell around, Greg was asked to apply this approach to Yum!'s other brands as CEO of the organization. He leveraged Ken, Jeff, and Greg Dzurik, who broke off from the advertising agency and created their own brand consultancy to lead the global charge. Within two years, Collider Lab had proved its worth by helping increase sales around the world, and, as one of Greg's first official acts as Yum! CEO, he acquired Collider Lab, making Ken the CMO of Yum! and Greg Dzurik the VP of Marketing and Innovation. Jeff became the Chief Brand Officer of Pizza Hut, until he retired a few years later. He now serves on multiple boards. The mission at Collider Lab since then has been to stay on top of cultural relevance, from brand to brand and around the world.

Now It's Your Turn

Apply the lessons of cultural relevance to your own brand.

Research Done Right Starts with an Idea

When it comes to effective qualitative research, methods vary. Each culture has its own nuances. The gold standard, however, is to conduct a series of in-depth, one-on-one interviews with consumers run by a moderator trained in psychological questioning designed to reveal subconscious preferences and biases. At Collider Lab, we run these interviews ourselves. Many traditional marketing researchers are out of their comfort zone doing anything but direct, factual questioning that misses the subtext entirely. Others, adept at real, academically sound research, are just too disconnected from the brand or the world of marketing to understand the significance of what they may start uncovering with consumers. It's important to find people capable of conducting subconscious research, or what is sometimes called System 1 research, as coined by Daniel Kahneman.[10] Otherwise, you're just going to hear rationalizations, not reasons.

In our own research, we have found great success using projective techniques. For instance, we might ask consumers to select images that represent fast-food restaurants versus fast-casual and then carefully discuss the thoughts and observations that led them to choose those specific images. Other projective methodologies include personification, storytelling, or basic projecting.

- If Taco Bell were a car, what make and model would it be?
- Pretend you're having a dream. You're one of the people in the dream and Taco Bell personified is another. What happens? And what happens when the McDonald's person comes into the dream?

- What did people think of Taco Bell in the 1990s? What do people think about Taco Bell today? Not you. Others. What's changed?

We found that asking which celebrity different KFC products would be unlocked the idea of Extra Crispy chicken for us. Our research subjects told us that Extra Crispy was RuPaul, whereas the Original Recipe was Jennifer Aniston. This insight helped us unlock that Extra Crispy had an extra energy around it because it was crunchier and more of an experience for your mouth (no offense to Jennifer Aniston who is clearly lovely and a perfectly good sandwich). This "extra"ness was much more relevant for today's cultural codes. You can see the resulting brilliant creative campaign on YouTube by typing in, "The Extra Crispy Colonel."

One note: We find that asking why a person chose a particular brand or image over another triggers their rational side. It is more effective to explore the "why" without asking it overtly. Try digging further into their answers and drawing out the stories, without doing what researchers are always tempted to, and say, "But *why* did you choose that?" Remember that for the most part no one knows why we make a choice or what we really want. Asking "why" can throw your research subjects into confusion, and make them feel they have to justify their choice. All they really know is that their choice feels right. It's up to you to guide them and yourself toward a more nuanced and layered understanding about that choice. Interestingly, we've often found that the metaphors our interviewees come up with, such as, "Jennifer Aniston is like Original Recipe," are far more memorable than data. Years later, people still remember that line, while no one remembers the hard data we also gave them at the same time. We think that's another reason metaphors are useful, because they bring insights to life in a way that no amount of perfectly rational data can.

These hypotheticals may sound silly, but it's amazing what you can learn when you let consumers project metaphorically instead of asking them to articulate their beliefs directly. The ultimate point of all our questioning is to understand the cultural codes of the category and how brands stack up against it. Metaphors are a powerful tool for unearthing those underlying sentiments.

When it comes to understanding culture, you have two jobs as a marketer. You need to know where the culture is and, crucially, you have to know where it's going. To stay on top of the emerging value in your category, you need to talk to cultural experts: authors, professors, influencers. This may sound intimidating, but it's actually easier than it sounds, even for smaller companies or individuals. Just go to Google Scholar and do a little research on your topic. You'll quickly find several professors who have written academic pieces on it. Do another Google search on the professor and their email will usually be readily available, often on their university department's page. Shoot them an email and offer to pay them their standard hourly rate for a few hours on the phone to pick their brain (but download and read their papers first, they love that!). One of our favorite such chats was with a professor who studied telenovelas in the Philippines. Over the course of one conversation, he helped us decode why KFC was no longer in sync with the emerging culture in that country. A few hours spent talking to the right expert can offer dramatic insights into your brand's blind spots, even if you're not ready to conduct a full-scale qualitative consumer research study. We'd actually recommend spreading your experts out across the length of the project. Interview a few up front, to establish some hypotheses. Then chat with some during the project, to get them to help you contextualize what you're hearing. Finally, once you think you have it all figured out, talk to a few more experts and see what they say.

Cultural experts could include,

- Authors of books or research relevant to your category
- Professors who specialize in a specific discipline related to your work, such as professors of gender studies, and women's rights activists if you're talking feminine care and beauty standards
- Influencers, micro or macro, people who other people look to in order to be on the cutting edge of culture

Beyond experts and formal studies, culture is visible everywhere, most prominently in the arts. If you simply watch some of the shows and movies your younger consumers are watching and listen to the music they love, you'll already be ahead of the game. (And perhaps have a whole new hobby: Lila Faz, the aforementioned PhD-dropout-turned-Collider Lab strategist, watched "just a few" episodes of the Japanese reality show *Terrace House*, while doing a project in Tokyo. Three years later, and she's still watching it.) Every emerging theme and trend is visible if you know where to look. Ask yourself: What do the heroes of these shows and songs want? Chances are, your customers want that, too. Be deliberate and at least somewhat scientific about analyzing these themes, though. Categorize the themes of songs, for instance, and then quantify the change over the years.

To learn about food culture, create your own discussion groups. Through friends and friends of friends, put out the word that you're offering a quick forty bucks for a couple hours of time. You can make this recruitment process even easier by creating a free online survey at a site like SurveyMonkey. Email or text that link to people you know and post it on social media. If people are interested and meet your criteria, they're in the group. Abby Batcheller, one of our cultural strategists, loves setting up WhatsApp groups and inviting opinion leaders or micro influencers from the category to form part of that group for the entire duration of the project. For up to twelve weeks she'll ping them with questions, thoughts, even mock-ups of products we develop to get their instant feedback. Working with Abby when she's got one of these groups going is like working with six dialed-in experts on a daily basis. Her tip, though: pay them well and make them feel valued. If you do, their insights will get better and better.

Don't do any of this alone. Enlist a brainstorming partner or two to help you run the session. We've found the ideal number to be three, because it breaks stalemates, but two will do in a pinch. Conduct the group over coffee and donuts. During the discussion, ask: What are these people buying when they buy your category? Why did they select these images to metaphorically describe your brand? What were the verbs they used?

After the group discussion is over, start putting sticky notes up on the wall with your partners. At the top, put the product or service. For example, let's say you make "creative socks." In this case you are trying to crack the old category culture code of socks and figure out the emerging one. You might ask why were your group members buying certain socks five years ago, and why are they choosing certain socks right now? In which case the answer might be something like, five years ago they were buying socks to fit into corporate America: now they are buying socks to feel like the next Silicon Valley rulebreaker. Write the answers in a row of notes immediately below it. Maybe you heard "to feel fun" and "to be a rebel," and so on. Write them all down, and stick them up on the wall. Next, dig into those reasons again. *Why* do they need to be fun? Because work is boring. *Why* do they want to be a rebel? Because work forces them to follow the rules.

Ask why again and again until it feels like you're getting to the heart of the matter. Wearing creative socks to work is their way of breaking rules, for instance. Look for articles in the mainstream media—newspapers, magazines, websites—that touch on this underlying value of rule-breaking and nonconformity. In this case, you're exploring the idea of how rebellion is changing. You might discover that the emerging value is about rebelling to find better solutions than the status quo can provide, not simply rebelling for rebellion's sake. Maybe you discover that the old code of socks was "Fitting into Corporate America" and the emerging code is "Standing Out in Entrepreneurial America."

Be Smart, But Don't Be Precious

Now, here's a little warning for you to keep in the back of your mind. You're looking for insights into culture, and specifically where culture in your category *may* be headed. Strive to get it right, but don't grip the bat too tightly. As Greg loves to say, "You want to be 'right' enough so that you understand the general direction of culture, but if you strive for perfection and left-brain this analysis to death, you'll end in paralysis."

Get a good sense of where culture is headed and then take the big next step. Lay your brand's bold, distinctive flag in that general direction. Make the space unique and new. Make it so that it can only really belong to your brand. The result should feel like you're creating culture, more than just reflecting it. We'll talk about this more in chapter eleven, but remember that in marketing it's always better to be distinctively off (if only by a few degrees) than perfectly right and meh.

6

Functional Relevance

What Is Functional Relevance?

Hopefully by now you are starting to realize that the three core elements of R.E.D., relevance, ease, and distinctiveness, are interwoven. None of these elements exists in isolation. So while you're thinking about social relevance (for instance), you have to be thinking about it in terms of distinctiveness as well. Likewise, when you are thinking about distinctiveness, you have to ensure your distinctive asset is culturally relevant. This is especially important when we look at functional relevance (see Figure 6.1), because it can be tempting to assume that any new functional benefit is a good thing for your brand. Well, no. If your new functional benefit is indistinct, or radically out of step with the existing distinctive assets of your brand, it's either going to make no impact, or make the wrong kind of impact.

R.E.D.

FUNCTIONAL RELEVANCE:

THE ABILITY OF A BRAND TO BE IMMEDIATELY
THOUGHT OF FOR KEY FUNCTIONAL NEEDS AND BENEFITS
(aka CATEGORY USE OCCASIONS)...

NEW!

Doritos
LOCOS TACOS

TACO BELL
LATE NIGHT MEALS + PORTABLE LUNCH
+ SOMETHING EXCITING AND INNOVATIVE

... BECAUSE THE MORE CUOs A BRAND IS
KNOWN FOR, THE MORE OFTEN IT WILL
BE USED, AND THE MORE IT WILL GROW.

FIGURE 6.1

If you remember from chapter three, we make brands functionally relevant by owning what we call CUOs, category use occasions. Essentially, we establish clear connections between the brand and a given usage occasion in the category. Nike, for instance, has clear connections in consumers' minds with a variety of usage occasions, like shoes for basketball, shirts for athleisure, cool clothes for kids, technical clothing for athletes, and so on. The trick is that Nike is able to do this in a very distinctive way. This delicate balance between expanding your category use occasions while maintaining the core distinctiveness of your brand is the primary tension of this chapter. Over the next twenty-nine pages, we'll share some examples of how Greg and Collider Lab have succeeded and failed at this. Then we'll share our strategies for you and your organization to proactively and effectively create distinctive functional relevance.

We define functional relevance as a consumer's basic need to find a product that provides a function they are looking for. In our category this might be, "Does Taco Bell provide a food that will feed my family affordably?" Or, "Does KFC provide a tasty lunch offering to keep me full through a long afternoon at work?" Outside of QSR, a consumer might ask, "Does Honda have a car that can seat my whole family?" Or, "Does Maybelline offer a lipstick that is non-allergenic?"

Over the years, we've found that expanding your CUOs is the primary way in which you grow your brand. The more you are known for, the more often your brand will be used, and the more it will grow. Your long-term goal, therefore, should be to own as many CUOs as possible in consumers' minds. Every time there is a mental connection between your brand and a CUO, it gives a customer another reason to consider your brand for their purchase.

We've studied this phenomenon in detail, and measure CUOs quite carefully around the world. We've done dedicated category use occasion growth studies in over 30 countries for several categories, and the pattern is quite clear. In Figure 6.2, we've taken 130 brands in 14 countries, and plotted them out based on their share in the market (y axis) and the number of CUOs consumers think of them for (x axis). As you can see, it's nearly a 1:1 relationship. The more CUOs you're known for, the more share you have in the marketplace.

Let's use the athletic wear category as an example. Nike was started in the sixties by Bill Bowerman and Phil Knight selling innovative running shoes out of a car on college campuses. But once they got a strong foothold

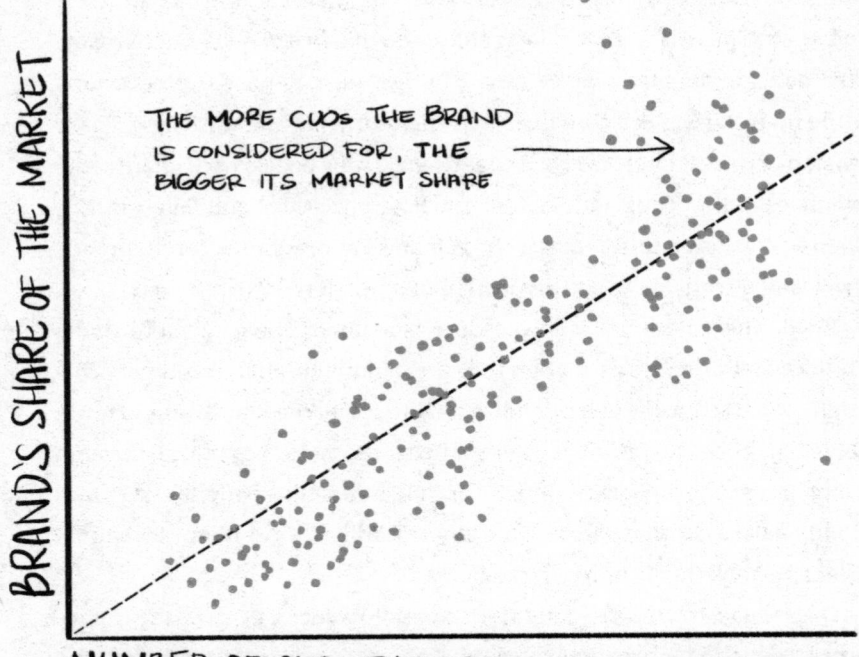

FIGURE 6.2

(sorry!) in that CUO, they eventually expanded into basketball shoes with Michael Jordan's famous Air Jordans. From there, the world was Nike's oyster and the brand began dominating more and more CUOs: soccer, tennis, cool clothing for hanging out, and on and on (except surfing, many independent-minded surfers will proudly tell you!). The Brooks Running company, on the other hand, took the opposite tack. They were founded in 1914, fifty years *before* Nike. Originally, they developed shoes for a variety of sports and activities (bathing shoes were a thing!), and eventually, they narrowed their CUOs to only running. Today, many consider theirs the best running shoes in the world. Their annual sales? Just under $750 million.[1] Nike's annual sales? Just under $40 billion. The way we see it, that's a pretty powerful endorsement for the idea of growing your CUOs. Now, of course, Nike did it while nailing every single R.E.D. point beautifully.

They've been masters of cultural and social relevance, and their brand is powerfully easy to notice with all their well-placed distinctive advertising. It's also incredibly easy to access with a bunch of innovative digital and physical storefronts. But none of that would've mattered had it not been for the fact that they are well known for nearly every CUO in the athletic wear world. We'd argue that Brooks made a mistake in narrowing all the way down to one CUO (running). They also never really made their brand culturally relevant outside of the running circle, and never had a Michael Jordan moment to make it culturally relevant. But the main point is simply this: that they chose to own one CUO and one CUO only.

Achieving a level of success like Nike requires a different mindset, one that invests in R&D and is okay with failing as you try to expand. Nike not only failed at surfing, they also failed at expanding into skating several times until they finally unlocked it with the Nike SB brand and Paul Rodriguez sponsorship.[2] Investing in R&D and being okay with failures are both critical components to expanding your CUOs. Both of these elements should be nurtured and celebrated at the corporate level. (Yes, we actually mean celebrating failures! If your marketers and innovation teams are afraid of failure, they won't get very far in this journey!)

Finding category use occasions for your brands is vital. But it's important you go about this in the right way. One thing you *don't* want to do is artificially create segmented customer groups. Why? We'll explain.

The Folly of Segmentation

There are lots of productive and useful ways to ensure your product is functionally relevant to different people. There are also some dubious ones. In the modern marketing era, one ridiculously popular take is *segmentation*. And that's fair, because it makes sense on the surface. If you're struggling to give your product more uses for more people, fracturing consumers into multiple smaller groups might seem like a logical way to do that. Perhaps your car is only known for its sporty, exhilarating ride. If you segment the market, maybe you can make your car mean sporty to young men, and also an escape to older women. Maybe you can even make it mean youth to older men! Voila! Your product now meets different needs for different segments! This fails almost every single time.

Why Segmentation Fails

Segmentation is the process whereby a larger group of potential customers, let's say, "women who buy financial services," is broken up into subcategories defined by their demographics and psychographics—or beliefs and attitudes. For instance, let's assume our marketer is selling laundry detergent. She knows through research that 78 percent of laundry soap is purchased by women between the ages of twenty-eight and sixty-five. But segmentation theory hypothesizes (correctly) that these women are not a homogenous group. Instead, our marketer uses large quantitative studies and statistical techniques to identify different categories that these women fit into.

- Perhaps one group prioritizes ultra-cleanliness, washing their families' clothes after one wear, no matter what. She might name these women the "Driven Cleaners."
- Another group prefers organic, and insists on sodium borate–free products: she'll call them the "Organic Suddsers."
- A third is ambivalent about brand name laundry soap, choosing the cheapest product. Let's call them "Budget Washers."
- And finally we might have the "Lax Launderers," who only wash clothes after multiple wears, and are okay with small stains if it means time away from the washer and dryer.

Our pro-segmentation marketer will now recommend one of two directions: either pick a segment or two and market exclusively to them, or create different campaigns for each group she has identified. At Collider Lab, we often debate which is the worst sin.

Segmentation makes sense on the surface. Humans aren't homogenous, and we all have different motivations and desires, no matter how similar we might be demographically. The problem is that while we aren't homogenous, we aren't consistent either. Suppose you decide to solely focus on Driven Cleaners with a product that promises a sparkling clean result, but requires careful application to tough stains—because, after all, that's what Driven Cleaners find so gratifying! But sometimes our Driven Cleaner is going to have had a terrible month at work and no longer has time to worry quite so much about household chores. Her employer offers her "work from home" flexibility and she doesn't need to look clean and pressed for work every day (or is wearing the same Zoom sweatpants with her best blazer). Suddenly she's a Lax Launderer, and all she cares about is getting her laundry done fast, with as little effort on her part as possible. Another month and she might be suddenly anxious about the tumbling stock market. All of a sudden she's looking to cut her grocery bills, and is heading toward Budget Washer territory. Your advertising, which you thought would be a slam dunk because it was so finely tuned to that particular consumer, is now irrelevant to her. More worryingly, you've made yourself completely irrelevant for the other 87 percent of the consumers out there who weren't Driven Cleaners to begin with. Here is another dirty little secret about segmentation: even when it works as planned, it's all based mostly on slight skews in the data! For instance, in our hypothetical example, 35 percent of our Driven Cleaners will agree with the statement "Scrubbing is always an important part of cleaning." But overall, 25 percent of consumers said that to begin with! So, because of "cluster analysis" (the statistical methodology usually implemented to create consumer segments), this relatively small difference in opinion (35 percent vs. 25 percent) results in a new segment that is supposed to be radically different from the rest of the group. It's a questionable assumption, because in 65 percent of the cases, "Driven Cleaners" are not into scrubbing at all!

Perhaps you decided to go after all four segments. For each, you create highly targeted advertising that just talks about their particular needs. We've encountered several digital-first marketers who love this approach. Maybe you do Facebook ads about the joy of scrubbing for "Driven Cleaners," but then for "Lax Launderers" you target them with ads that talk about watching a movie while their clothes basically wash themselves. Because of course you want to appear like a more chill brand for Lax Launderers and a more intense brand for Driven Cleaners. Well, what you've done is taken your one Big Brand and made it into four Mini Brands instead, each with a different tone. Ehrenberg's law of double jeopardy states that bigger brands have both a larger base *and* stronger loyalty, meaning that big brands get the double benefit of a wider reach and higher frequency. If you cut your brand into four small brands, each with a different look and feel, each targeting a different group, then you've wasted the benefit of double jeopardy. You've also prioritized relevance over distinctiveness and that is almost always a fail. So suddenly, you're not distinctive, not consistent, double jeopardy is working against you, and your whole department is anxiously updating resumes.

Remember, *everyone* is *everything* at some point or another. Humans are inconsistent, and our needs are ever-fluctuating and influenced by hundreds of different variables. (Consider the Myers–Briggs personality test: at least 50 percent of individuals get different results when they repeat the test after five weeks.)[3] None of us fit neatly and permanently into any psychographic or behavioral segment, at least not for long. If you rely on segmentation, you are going to sacrifice your best and most important asset—your distinctiveness—and lose your opportunity to stand out in an impactful way.

Why We Say "No" to Segmentation

Yum! learned all this the hard way, with KFC in South Africa, in 2015. In chapter five we talked about how we eventually came to understand the KFC South Africa conundrum. However, there was another problem with the brand's strategy, and this one had more to do with the marketing approach the South African team chose to take: segmentation. KFC is one of the best-known brands in South Africa: we have almost a thousand restaurants and three times as many outlets as McDonald's.[4] But as we discussed in chapter five, sales had slipped by a few points every year, for three years running. Part of the problem was that few young people wanted to be associated with a Rainbow Nation–Era brand. In a well-intentioned bid to elevate KFC's success in South Africa even further, the brand team decided to segment their customer base into six groups, and create a distinctive mini-campaign for each. As far as segmentations go, it was the most sophisticated one we'd ever seen. They used a massive sample size, surveyed every corner of the country, and even created a VR experience where you'd insert your phone into cardboard goggles to experience how each segment lived. As wannabe anthropologists, we loved it! But as marketers, we had a harder time with it. Taking your one big brand and dividing it up into six small brands, each with its own look and feel, was not likely to end up garnering more attention, regardless of how correct or impressive the segmentation may be.

Dhruv Kaul took over the marketing helm in South Africa, and with the help of his extremely talented team, turned around the business and returned to positive sales in short order. Their first order of business? Dismantle the segmentation approach and rediscover that one big brand full of distinctiveness. "The mistake wasn't really the segmentation," Dhruv explained recently. "It was how the brand acted upon that segmentation. We shouldn't have actually targeted those segments individually, and much less with six unique approaches." Dhruv proved that distinctiveness is king—but we'll hold off for now; that's for another chapter.

In their defense, and to Dhruv's point, South Africa is one of the most complex countries in the world, with at least eleven official languages— each with its accompanying culture. Understanding your consumer deeply is never a mistake. It's what allows you to create the right category use occasions to grow your business. But using segmentation as the actual mechanism to direct the marketing is almost always a mistake. In fact, if you're in the US, you probably think Taco Bell is targeted to young males. If so, you'd be wrong. Sales at Taco Bell depend on women over the age of forty just as much as McDonald's does. According to our own extensive studies, there really is no big difference between the shoppers of Taco Bell, McDonald's, and Burger King. And that's true for every category we've ever studied. Segmenting and targeting young males would mean instant sales collapse for Taco Bell. (Greg loves surprising people with this fact.)

We believe segmentation is a weak approach for most marketing tasks. If you are tempted to segment, ask yourself these questions: Are real-life consumers in my category actually that distinct from one another, and consistently so? Or are they sometimes one thing and sometimes another? Will my brand really be stronger by being different things for different people? Or will my brand truly be able to grow long term if I'm so narrowly focused on one target and one need? The ultimate challenge that comes from targeting and segmentation is that you end up achieving a reach below your means. You sacrifice your budget getting niche consumers when that money could be used going for a bigger mass reach. Based on the argument of everyone being everything, spend the money on *reach* and you will get who you want and more. It also makes the job harder for your media teams to be efficient and effective. Chasing around make-believe targets and trying desperately to find enough of them is an arduous, pointless job.

One caveat: It's okay to have a "design target" or "brand muse," a consumer segment that you identify, name, and use as a muse to define your brand around. Taco Bell's muse is a twenty-five-year-old male. Our brand is built around this character and we look at everything we do through the lens of "what would our muse think?" Note: We're not actually targeting our muse with our advertising. Instead we make sure that everything we do is something that is in alignment with who our muse is and how he sees the world. This keeps the work unique, ownable, and consistent—the core attributes of distinctiveness. It may seem counterintuitive, but it's at the core of the distinctiveness philosophy. In the end, it's more important to stand out as distinctive than it is to seem perfectly relevant to my life. This is the mirror/magnet argument we've mentioned before, and will look at more deeply in chapter eleven. Above all else, stand out as unique. That will help people recall your brand. And a clearly defined muse can help you do that (as long as you don't then try to actually target that muse!). One thing that was done well in South Africa was identifying a brand muse in David, a young man emblematic of the emerging trends in his country. Alas, rather than focusing on their muse, they were distracted by other segmented groups and "David's" impact was too diluted to be useful.

CUOs:
A Better Mousetrap to Catch
Yourself Some Functional Relevance

Our recommendation is simple. Instead of spending your time needlessly and questionably segmenting the marketplace, spend that time cataloging all the different use occasions in the category and devising a plan to own as many as you can. Forget about the consumer for a moment, and just focus on the use occasions. If you do that with the laundry detergent example above, for instance, you might discover that 40 percent of occasions are driven by "the easiest solution," while another 15 percent are all about "the brightest colors," and another 12 percent are about "the whitest whites," and so on. Who cares what Scrubbing Sam finds emotionally relevant in the rest of his life. Instead, just devise the most culturally relevant and distinctive way to own "bright colors" and as many other CUOs as you can. Chasing a fickle (and, quite frankly, fictitious) consumer segment around with your marketing is a massive waste of time, energy, and money.

Remember back in chapter five when we talked about Oatly and their awesome R.E.D. brand? If there ever was a brand that you'd imagine would do a segmentation it would be Oatly. After all, how many people are even interested in milk-alternative products? And then, if they are, it must be for very different reasons, like lactose intolerance or anxiety over the carbon footprint of cows or taste preference. Those are some really differ-ent groups! You can easily see how a marketer could feel like segmenting the market would be a good idea. That way they could fine-tune the mes-saging to each segment and target them differently. But, of course, noth-ing could be further from the truth. Again, John Schoolcraft, of Oatly:

> We don't do any target group analysis studies at all. Why? Because I am not interested in segmenting things into some sort of fake marketing terminol-ogy graph diagram thingy to find an answer. Our target group is everyone who is interested in what they put into their body and everyone that is interested in having a planet to live on in the future. So what, roughly 80 percent of the population. Pretty broad.

What if Oatly had gone down a different path? What, if instead of find-ing the one thing they wanted to own and just nailing it distinctively, they had segmented the market? Our bet: Their (brilliantly segmented and tar-geted) product would be up on the shelf right now, gathering dust with all the other milk alternatives in the category. It's difficult to overstate how different of an approach Oatly took vs. a more traditional, global CPG com-pany—which would've almost certainly taken the path of spending sev-eral months segmenting the market. Instead, Oatly spent their time deciding what CUOs they wanted to own (the health of the planet and body) and bringing that to life in the most distinctive way possible. We cringe to imagine what Oatly would look like today if they had decided to go after "Lactose Larry," "Balancing Life Betty," and "Healthy Hilda."

If you'd just spent all that time coming up with a cool way to own the attribute or need instead, you might've already stumbled onto something like Old Spice's "Swagger" scented underarm deodorant. It's a brilliant way to fulfill the CUO of "I want something that makes me feel confident." Can you imagine what they would've come up with if they'd been trying to innovate something for the "Tony the Teenager" segment? Probably the exact same thing their competitor had: nothing inspiring. Instead, their laser focus on "make them feel confident" gave them their top-selling product that today is used by both Ken, clocking in at nearly fifty years old, and his thirteen- and fifteen-year-old sons. No two segments were ever more unalike.

Want to know just how important it is to redirect your energy from the complicated task of segmentation to the creative task of distinctively owning a CUO? Well, go back about twelve years to when Old Spice was struggling. Old Spice's worst performing product was a scent called Glacial Falls. Yum!'s very own George Felix (now CMO of Pizza Hut) and Kevin Hochman (CEO of KFC) were on the brand. They told us how Glacial Falls was failing and retailers wanted it off their shelves. That space was des- tined for the way cooler Axe brand, which promised sex to every clueless boy in America. I suppose P&G could've done another segmentation and tried in vain to appeal to another customer base, but instead, their agency, Wieden+Kennedy, stepped in and did something magical—they simply refocused everything on owning *one* CUO: confidence.[5] The brilliant solu- tion? Rename the product Swagger. That's it. Just rename the exact same product and tweak the packaging. No other change. In no time at all, it went from their worst-selling scent to their top-selling one. That's the power of owning a CUO in a distinctive and culturally relevant way. And it's a far better use of time than endless meetings with a segmentation com- pany trying to decide what the psychographic profile of the "Tony the Teenager" segment is telling you.

How to Win at CUOs

1. Measure all the CUOs in your category. For instance, if you're selling breakfast cereal these could be "something healthy" or "something fun," "something for my kids," or "something for adults," "something with fiber" or "something natural," and so on. You can measure this by doing a last occasion quantitative study. With a very large sample size of at least three thousand people you can field a study that asks them what need they were trying to fulfill the last time they used

breakfast cereal in their household. In the same survey you'll want to ask what brand they chose, and finally, what CUOs would they consider your brand for. This will give you a chart like the one on the following page. The size of the bubble shows the size of the CUO. The horizontal position defines how often your brand is used for that CUO, while the vertical position defines how likely consumers are to consider your brand for that CUO. Your lowest-hanging fruit are the ones in the upper left quadrant: high consideration for your brand, but low usage.

2. Next, go through the lower-hanging CUOs and decide which ones have the most potential for your brand to distinctively play with, given the memory structures your brand already owns in consumers' minds.

3. Come up with the most culturally relevant and distinctive way to fulfill that CUO.

A CUO Growth Study for Old Spice might've looked like Figure 6.3.

Expand Your Mind to Expand Your CUOs

One of Greg's biggest innovations was five words long. Back in the early nineties, Greg was Category Director of Bar Soap at Unilever in the US. His core brand was Dove, the iconic bar soap that, for fifty years, had promoted the fact that it was one-quarter moisturizing lotion, and promised women it would give them softer skin. It was a perfectly distinctive brand, so much so that the advertising agency who handled Dove had a head of accounts who had been on the job for three decades, and who repeatedly told Greg, "I'm here to make sure you don't mess this up!"

One day, one of the younger people in a creative meeting made an off-hand comment in a brainstorming session: "My mother doesn't use bar soap anymore; she only washes with liquid soap." This was a pin-drop moment. Liquid soap was not being tracked by the Dove team, and as a result the bar soap group had been in the dark about the explosive growth

A CUO GROWTH STUDY FOR OLD SPICE MIGHT'VE LOOKED LIKE THIS:

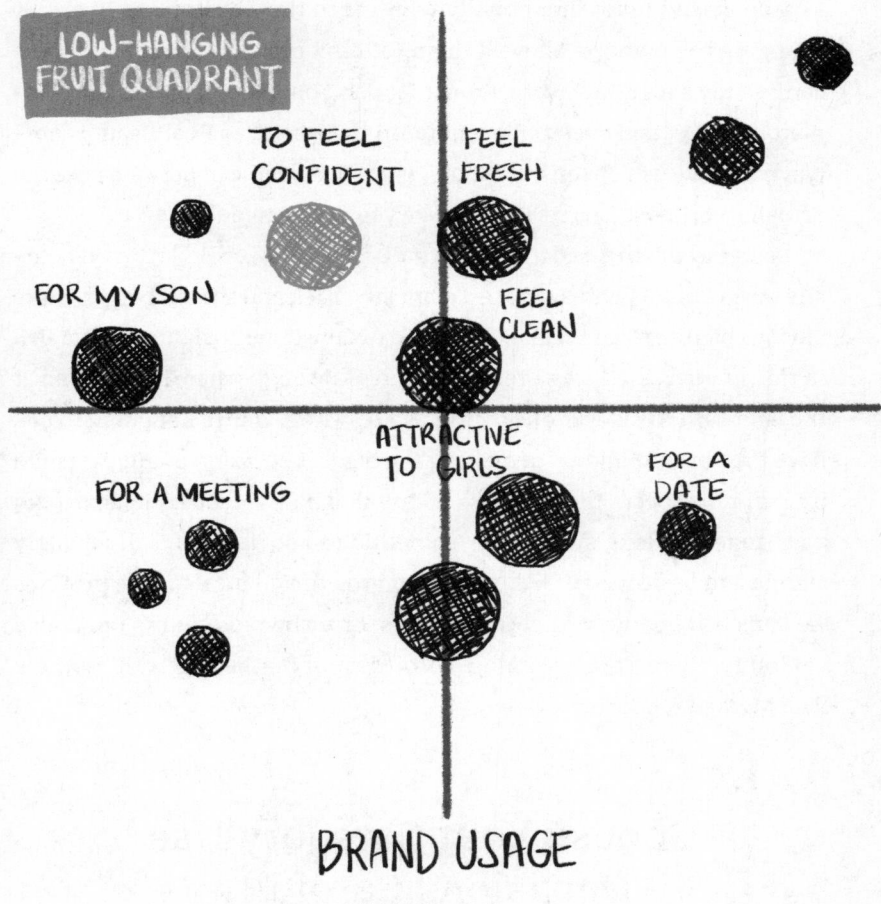

FIGURE 6.3

in liquid soap in their category. Greg realized that something very basic had to change: the name of the division he ran.

That day he put out a memo. The bar soap group was dead; long live the personal washing group instead. Sometimes the biggest impediment to CUO breakthroughs is how you see and define what you do. Until that morning, Greg's team saw themselves in the bar soap division. Even as they were looking for ways to expand what they offered, and even as they discussed liquid soap and different formulations, there were invisible parameters around them, limiting their ability to envision something more expansive and more functionally relevant to their customers' lives. By changing the name, it allowed them to think more creatively and more confidently about their work. From that point on, Dove expanded into numerous CUOs, and eventually embraced their beloved Real Beauty campaign in 2004, which, on a side note, is a rare example of how purpose *can* actually work: if it also serves to make you distinctive.

Don't be embarrassed to realize you've missed an obvious CUO. It actually takes a bit of genius to take a giant step back and see the bigger, more obvious picture. Tom Wagner, the Head of Consumer Insights at Taco Bell in the nineties, and Greg Creed had a breakthrough when Tom looked at the data with fresh eyes one day and said, "Greg. You're not going to believe this, but I think we're missing the biggest occasion of all: portability." In retrospect, it is a little shocking that a fast-food company could have gone that long overlooking something so obvious. This deceivingly simple and basic insight led to years of growth and incalculable profit as we launched highly portable quesadillas, Crunchwraps, and so on. It also led indirectly to Tom becoming a professor of marketing at UC Irvine's Paul Merage School of Business.

Choose Your Category Use Occasions Carefully

As we move through this chapter, we will be exploring ways that Yum! and other brands have developed CUOs that are functionally relevant to their users. The ones that have worked were either naturally distinctive to the brands or were *executed* in a way that was distinctive to the brands. I want you to ask yourself these two questions about your brand, and what you hope to accomplish with functional relevance:

- What category use occasions do we want to own?
- How do we do this distinctively?

Some CUOs are just wrong for your brand. Think Harley-Davidson Wine Coolers. Seriously, they tried. Yes, it would be awesome to add a whole new occasion to your brand experience. But it has to make sense. You'll shortly read about our efforts to pivot Taco Bell to being diet food, something that made *no sense.* We were essentially copying Subway, without making our pitch in a way that was truly distinctive, or brought any of Taco Bell's distinctive assets into play. It flopped, not because the product was bad, but because it was such a long shot for the consumer to connect weight loss to our brand that it led to an awkward brand overstretch.

The reality is that most successful innovations are going to come by fulfilling CUOs that are a lot closer to home. KFC in Australia, for instance, found that snacking was an underdeveloped part of their sales, but one that wasn't a long shot for most consumers to connect to the brand. It would probably land in that upper left quadrant of the CUO Growth Map. The brilliance, though, was just how incredibly distinctive they made the offering. Catherine Tan-Gillespie, the then CMO, explained, "We took one of our most iconic assets, the bucket, and shrunk it down to fit in a cup holder. We called it the Go Bucket and it doubled our snacking sales overnight." That's the magical formula: pick a CUO that makes sense for your brand, and make the offering as distinctive as you can. Remember that when we say distinctive, we mean distinctive to *your* brand and *only* your brand.

Not all long shots are a fail, though. Sometimes you just have to dig deeper to find the unlock. There's a reason that our strategists at Collider Lab devour books and papers about culture, economics, human behavior, and marketing. They give us insights into what forces shape the human decision-making process, often giving us those invaluable unlocks.

In 2012, we were assigned the job of creating a winning strategy for Taco Bell Breakfast. Now, Taco Bell had already taken *seven* swings at this. It was a big, fat, juicy bubble in the lower left quadrant. Lots of potential sales, in other words, but breakfast at Taco Bell just didn't make sense to America yet. To overcome this, they'd tried strategies that were too bold, emphasizing spiciness and flavor over blander breakfast options (a valid attempt at doing breakfast distinctively, just not terribly relevant to most Americans). They'd been too timid, offering stability and predictability with a Jimmy Dean cross-promotion breakfast sandwich (a great attempt at making breakfast relevant, but not terribly distinctive). Neither marketing campaign—the first: shouty, spicy, "get out of bed," or the second: safe, familiar, and inoffensive—worked. What was worse, there didn't seem to be an obvious entryway to look at this problem creatively. That is, until our informal office book club found a paper from an ego psychologist that talked about disrupting habits. It posited that habits are incredibly hard to break, and in order to break them, you have to disrupt them, and make your habit feel a little uncomfortable. In marketing terms, think of the wildly successful Truth anti-smoking campaign—including spots such as "Body Bag," which saw 1,200 body bags dumped outside of Philip Morris to signify the daily death toll of cigarettes.[6] An uncomfortable image helped the habit *feel* uncomfortable by reframing it as "not cool" to a teen cohort who had traditionally embraced smoking as a symbol of rebellion.

Our discussion of the paper led us to ask, "What if people don't actually *love* our main breakfast competitor, McDonald's? What if it's less about the taste of their breakfast products, such as the McMuffin, and more about decades of habit? And if it is, how do we break it?"

So, first functional relevance insight: *Find your question, then ask it.*

We now had a viable entryway to looking at the problem of cracking the breakfast code. First, we did basic brand personifications with our target audience (revisit the end of the cultural relevance chapter for our tips on how to do this effectively). As we did in the Taco Bell survey, we asked them to imagine a McDonald's breakfast being magically transformed into a person, and they told us that McDonald's breakfast was George Costanza: safe, comfortable, but no one was proud to be seen out with him. Taco Bell was this rebellious kid in the back of the classroom—but do rebellious kids even eat breakfast?

We took one big lesson from this initial work: mornings were indeed driven by habit. You got your George Costanza Egg McMuffin, even if it was not terribly exciting. It was comfortable, no surprises, and this is what our consumers wanted, at least during the breakfast rush. This evolved into a second observation: people want boring in the morning. As the day goes on, they slowly become more adventurous and more willing to experiment with their food.

Our second insight was: *Dig a little deeper to understand your customers' underlying motivations and the culture that surrounds them.*

It's not enough to have a superficial insight like, "Our customers are comfortable with their routine." You have to push a little further and this generally takes expert help. At Collider Lab we've found that the most relevant help is from sociologists or psychologists: if you don't understand either your customers' social or subconscious motivations, you'll struggle to devise a product or a message that resonates with them. For your business it might be different. Whatever the most relevant course of action, this is one place where it pays to invest in a professional study.

So, our next step was to dig in and understand our consumers' habits on a deeper level—hopefully one that would give us an insight into how we can break that habit and give our potential customer a reason to start eating Taco Bell breakfasts instead.

We worked with an ego psychologist to do in-depth interviews with frequent McMuffin consumers. What he found was fascinating. Morning, on a deep, primal level, is about separation anxiety. For many people, the experience of morning is that you are being pulled out of your bed, out of your home, away from your children, and away from everything that symbolizes happiness and safety. People respond to this separation anxiety in one of two ways: They find other comforting things to bolster them on the transition to their workday (the McMuffin, or a steaming hot, flavored, and sweetened latte, or something as simple as plugging into a comforting podcast on their commute). Or they experience a kind of performance anxiety, leading them to get "pumped up," by talking themselves into having the confidence and energy and enthusiasm to attack their day with vigor.

Now here's the important part. By analyzing the culture of the moment, we found an emerging cultural code we called "the hustle." Basically, young folks at the time were all about waking up and kicking ass, finding their own unique way in the world. It certainly had something to do with the fact that they had been living through some grim economic times since the global recession had started. And perhaps it was also a pushback against the slacker mindset of their Gen X parents in the nineties. Regardless, it was an emerging code. Nobody wanted to be George Costanza, puttering along. They wanted to hustle. And that was a cultural code Taco Bell could work with.

This led us to our third insight: *Your new CUOs have to be a logical extension of your brand.*

We did a lot of work to uncover a psychologically and culturally sound reason for why a fast-food breakfast customer might give Taco Bell's offerings a shot. We'll explain a little of the process that went into developing our breakfast menu, specifically the AM Crunchwrap, in a few paragraphs, but first remember that uncovering new CUOs isn't about invention, it's more about finding a logical extension, or "stretch," to what is already working for you. We tried to invent a new CUO for Taco Bell with the Drive-Thru Diet. The fact that we had to work so hard to try and shoehorn the concept into the Taco Bell universe should have alerted us to what a bad idea it was in the first place.

We now had a way to approach Taco Bell Breakfast. We knew that we had a sound motivation for our prospective breakfast eaters to give Taco Bell a shot. Our food is tasty, stimulating, and packed with interestingness—in other words ideal stuff to get the morning crowd pumped up for the day. Now we needed a product that was distinctive enough to break through.

The Journey to the Breakfast Crunchwrap

A few pages ago we touched on how fast food means different things in different markets. In America, our food habits are still shaped by our Puritan values and work ethic. That's a big part of why fast food was born in the US: we like and need portable food because it's traditionally been seen as fuel, rather than an experience. (One urban legend has it that as American drivers switched from manual to automatic cars, they began to gain weight, since it was easier for them to hold a snack in their non-driving hand.) This paradigm shifted with the dawn of Instagram. Food is now absolutely an experience—however, it is still an experience shaped by our need for functionality and portability. We may never morph into a Malaysian food culture ("a liberating escape" that allowed people to go from a life of moderation to a moment of freedom) or Mexican food culture (socialize, linger, and chat). So, our functional relevance also has to be culturally relevant and vice versa. We want our food to be 'gram worthy, but it still needs to be super-functional: something that allows us to multitask and doesn't require utensils or our full attention to enjoy.

This need—food that is portable, contained, and can be eaten in a messless, easy way—is a priority at Taco Bell (and most fast-food restaurants). In the early 2000s, Greg was leading a push to innovate more functionally relevant items on the menu. TacoHeads loved our food, but it could be messy. An overstuffed, or poorly assembled, taco could spill its contents out the side. A badly wrapped burrito was prone to guac and sour cream explosions. Not good. The one rule that our developers had to adhere to was simple: "You can change either the taste or the form, but you can't change the taste *and* the form." This is a distinctiveness rule. No matter what you do to develop a new product, it has to be recognizably in line with the existing assets of the brand. You'll learn more about this in the distinctive chapters (chapters ten through fourteen), but for now understand that in our case it meant a new product either had to have the classic taco taste in a wildly new form, or an innovative new taste in a classic taco presentation.

One morning Greg was at a product food showing in the Taco Bell food lab. A product designer named Lois Carson had an idea she was excited about and that she thought might solve some of our portability questions. Her invention was the Crunchwrap: a flour tortilla, folded in a hexagon shape around traditional taco fillings, and grilled shut so that it held its shape and didn't spill any contents as the consumer ate lunch. Greg looked at this invention, and said, "I love it. Let's do it." Now, Greg was the *fifth* CMO who had seen Lois's Crunchwrap presentation. Every other CMO had seen the careful, origami-like folding, the extra seconds it took to prepare, and thought, "I'll never get that past the operators and the board." Once again, kudos to Greg for seeing through the technical challenges and recognizing a big idea when it was sizzling in front of his face. Fortunately, Greg had just heard of Tom Wagner's insight about missing the portability CUO, and this was clearly a shoe-in product. Now, remember how we said that even the greatest CMO can make the occasional mistake? Greg almost stuffed up Crunchwrap by insisting on calling it a Crunchwich. This was a moment when sandwiches were hot, and there was a certain logic to suggesting the new product would have the same portability and functionality as a sandwich. Luckily, his team at the time claimed to have held a focus group, where the name Crunchwich lost to Crunchwrap. With hindsight, Greg suspects that the focus group might have never happened, and this was simply his team easing him into a good decision he didn't want to make.

The Crunchwrap launched in 2005, and was a brilliant example of functional relevance in action. It answered both of our questions:

What category use occasions do we want to own?
In this case, tasty, unmessy, and portable.

and,

How do we do this distinctively?

By offering a riff on the taco that is completely unique, but also absolutely in line with Taco Bell's existing line of products.

In fact, the Crunchwrap ticked all the R.E.D. boxes. It was highly portable and thus functionally relevant. It was highly distinctive. And, when we marketed it, we came up with the "Good to Go" campaign, which featured our Crunchwrap guy showcasing how functionally relevant the Crunchwrap was, by highlighting how it fit right alongside other technical marvels, like a "smart" wristwatch (way ahead of its time), or a classic car tricked out with modern amenities.

Relevance, Ease, and Distinctiveness in Balance

All elements of R.E.D. coming together to work in concert with each other is critical, and it's crucial to keep it in mind as we move forward throughout the book. In this case we had a functional relevance problem. But solving a functional relevance problem in a way that then creates an ease problem or a distinctiveness problem is not a solution. As you work through this book, remember that no element of R.E.D. exists in isolation. For instance, we could have launched a sandwich, which would have been functional, but not distinctive. We could have made something that gave you endless options to customize, but that would have lost marks on ease. And so on. Instead we created a unique, functional hit. To date the Crunchwrap has sold over 1.4 billion units, worth about $4 billion, and it remains a perennial best seller.

A few years later, when both of us were working on the problem of Taco Bell Breakfast, putting together a variation of the Crunchwrap seemed like a logical idea. We formulated a version with eggs, bacon, and hash browns: nothing too spicy or overly flavored, since mornings are about "safe" food. Instead, it was a tasty, energizing, and distinctly Taco Bell take on breakfast. It was highly distinctive, highly Taco Bell, and another hit.

The second part of the equation was our marketing strategy: we had the insights gleaned from our ego psychologist to guide us. The original Taco Bell breakfast spots from a previous attempt at cracking breakfast several years prior had a heavy metal guitarist on a bus, thrashing the electric guitar and screaming "Flavor!" to wake up the sleepy and bored McMuffin eaters. With the benefit of our research, we now saw this was a somewhat misguided approach, neither comforting nor "pumped up," and at odds with a morning eater's unconscious anxiety at leaving the safety of their home.

We knew from our research that we needed to accomplish two things: make this new thing (the Breakfast Crunchwrap) comfortable by anchoring it to an old thing that feels familiar and safe (the McMuffin) and presenting our product as an incremental enhancement (cooler, more satisfying) on its competitor.

Habits are by definition things we do without thinking. Since our customers weren't making a fully conscious choice about their morning breakfast choice, we couldn't simply offer an alternative to the McMuffin. It wouldn't register as a viable option, since our morning customers weren't fully aware they were making a decision in the first place. So, we needed to make their old standby feel just a little uncomfortable, and on a subliminal level open the door to an alternative experience—one that wouldn't make them feel discomforted.

Our eventual campaign took both these insights to heart. We worked with Deutsch LA to produce a series of commercials with the objective of creating a two-horse race against McDonald's, or, as Greg likes to say, "poking the bear." For the first spot we found twenty men named Ronald McDonald—who generally bought their breakfast at McDs—and took them to Taco Bell to have them experience the Breakfast Crunchwrap (they loved it). By making the spot a joke on the name of our rival, we were able to anchor the Breakfast Crunchwrap to something that felt familiar and safe while simultaneously offering something more exciting than the George Costanza McMuffin.

For the second spot we presented a George Orwell version of McDonald's as Communist Russia, with a loudspeaker waking people up to the sounds of "Happy, happy, happy: same breakfast, same breakfast, same breakfast." Then you pan to a hexagonal graffiti and our luckless breakfast eaters break out of the gulag to join a younger, happier, hipper crowd at Taco Bell. It was fun, but it was also just uncomfortable enough to subliminally sprinkle the seeds of doubt in our customers' minds.

The one risk with this campaign was that, by using the name *Ronald McDonald*, we were highlighting another brand's distinctive asset and making McDonald's *more* mentally available in our customers' minds with *our* advertising. We placed a bet that the resulting buzz and conversation about what Taco Bell had done with McDonald's would outweigh those benefits, and luckily we were right. The launch of Taco Bell Breakfast became the only successful launch out of seven attempts and continues to grow and remain profitable today.

Just How Important Is Distinctiveness to Winning at CUOs?

Yum! does thousands of innovations around the world each year, from far afield stuff like the Doritos Locos Tacos in the US and the Chizza in the Philippines (a fried chicken breast filet with pizza sauce and cheese on it; trust us, don't scoff until you've tried it!) to closer-in dishes like the delicious San Francisco Sourdough Pizzas in the Middle East. Most of these are either moderately or wildly successful. But every once in a while, we have a failure. Catherine Tan-Gillespie was brave enough to share her biggest failure with us for the sake of education. As CMO of KFC in Australia, she launched the KFC Pulled Pork Sandwich. Yup. Let that one sink in for a second: Kentucky Fried *Chicken*'s Pulled *Pork* Sandwich. Kind of hurts to even think about it, doesn't it? Anyway, no surprise, it failed. In fact, it was the *only* month with negative same store sales growth in over three years!

The brand recovered, and so did Catherine—as evidenced by the fact that she's now the global CMO of the brand and in charge of all 150 countries.

Functional relevance should tap into what is *distinctive about you.*

Sometime in the 2000s, Greg had his own brush with failure. Word came down from Yum! to all three brands: develop lighter, dieting products. It was a well-intentioned ask. The diet category was booming and people were trying to get healthier. Greg was president of Taco Bell at the time, though, and he struggled to figure out a way into this CUO that made any sense for the brand whatsoever. Well, as fate would have it, at that very moment, a loyal Taco Bell customer named Christine wrote a letter to the company about how she had lost fifty-four pounds by eating Taco Bell tacos, "Fresco style" (served without sour cream or cheese).[7]

Christine is a great lady and her story was real, true, and genuine. Greg jumped on the opportunity. Perhaps this was a huge category use occasion Taco Bell could actually win in? The marketing team got the brief, and came back with a campaign they called "The Drive-Thru Diet." Okay, not bad. It's tongue in cheek, self-aware, and arguably could be somewhat distinctive. Until you look at the tagline: "Soft Taco. Hard Body." Oops. This campaign is a great example of a brand trying to own a category use occasion it has no obvious right to play in, as evidenced by the fact that the moment they made it distinctive (i.e., edgy and rebellious, in true Taco Bell form) it got really weird.

If we had done a CUO growth study, we would've found a big bubble in the extreme lower left quadrant: a lot of people wanted to diet, but few were using Taco Bell or even would consider using it for that purpose. By trying to fulfill Yum!'s request and be relevant so far out of our ballpark, the marketing materials we put together ended up being far off-brand.

The print campaign was in shades of turquoise and green, and featured Christine, in a bikini, or alternatively in khakis and a button-down, holding a taco. Our brand identity is built around a twenty-five-year-old, skateboarding male. So building a campaign around a sophisticated woman, with a color palette that didn't invoke Taco Bell in any way, made zero sense. We had created a campaign with some Taco Bell distinctive tonality to it, but executed it in a way we thought would be relevant to moms. Not good.

Even worse, Greg used his veto vote (for the one and only time in his career) to push this through the unwilling franchisees. Not only did the campaign flop, culturally influential websites slammed us for the whole concept. You don't need me to analyze the risk/reward ratio on that one.

Even really good marketers can make mistakes. Kudos to Greg for being willing to own his. The team he assigned to the project did the best they could given his insistence on pursuing the diet menu items. He's never downplayed this story, and he's learned the core lesson of functional relevance.[8]

So, lesson 1: Yum! rewards swinging for the fences and doesn't punish the failures—the true hallmark of an innovative company (remember Greg's guiding principle: smart, heart, and courage). But Lesson 2: Why did it fail? And how can we prevent more of those costly failures?

In a bid to figure out what the recipe was for success, Collider Lab crunched the data from over 1,500 product concepts we had tested around the world in our own Predictive Markets Concept Evaluator. Basically, this tool asks hundreds of survey respondents to invest their money (real or fictitious, depending on the country's gaming laws) in the concepts they think will be the most successful. If they select the concept most other respondents chose, they can double their incentive. The methodology is far more predictive of real behavior than a normal survey that asks about their own individual preferences. Turns out, we tend to lie to ourselves and say we'll probably buy that salad. But we're pretty accurate when it comes to knowing what *others* will do: skip the greens and go straight for the pizza.

Anyway, we tested all the products and found the hands-down, #1 factor that predicts success of a product. Can you guess? Greg Dzurik, who also leads our data science team, explains, "We were shocked when we saw the results. We thought metrics like, 'How much does the product break through the clutter?' or 'How modern is the product?' would be the strongest predictors of a product's success. But the distinctiveness metric was much more predictive than other metrics (it had nearly five times the impact in predicting success as visceral excitement, for example). So, if your product is highly distinctive, your chance of success increases dramatically." In other words, is it something that only your brand could do? Doritos Locos Taco at Taco Bell? Check. Pulled pork at KFC? Not so much. As a matter of fact, it's about the most opposite you could get from distinctiveness. And, unfortunately, the most opposite we could get from success.

At the other end of the win-fail spectrum was Taco Bell's launch of their fries in 2018. Clearly, there's nothing Mexican(ish) about fries. Fries, in other words, are not distinctive for Taco Bell. That's why they've always been considered a no-go at the company. If it's not distinctive, just don't launch it. But they did. Melissa Friebe, their VP of Marketing, explains, "When I brought up the idea to do fries—again!—people rolled their eyes in the office. How many times had we had this pointless conversation? But then I said, 'We're not launching fries. We're launching Nacho Fries,' and suddenly the eyes stopped rolling." The launch turned out to be the most successful product launch in Taco Bell's history, selling over fifty-three million orders in just a few months. Distinctiveness strikes again.

Exercise: Understand Needstates, and Experiment with Creating New CUOs That Are a Logical Extension of Your Distinctive Assets

How many needs have you had today? Let's tally up Ken's. He had to get out of bed this morning, which he did successfully, thanks to his Alexa alarm. He had to dress: the aforementioned AG khakis, Stance socks, and Stance underwear, Harbor surf shop T-shirt, and Nike Air Jordan 1s. Food and drink: Japanese Sencha in a VSCO-girl approved Hydro Flask mug. Bob's Red Mill overnight oats eaten on the road with To-Go Ware bamboo utensils. After that it's a blur of needs, and the products he chooses to meet those needs: iPhone Apple Watch, Audible, and a quick episode of *Pod Save America*. By the time he's made it to the office, he's used more than twenty-five products, which he's chosen for a variety of reasons that encompass all elements of R.E.D. Functional relevance is pretty straightforward:

> I have a need.
> Do you have a product to fulfill it?

Most of us have family of some kind: children, pets, "chosen family," parents. Our needs might involve taking care of those loved ones. We have interests and hobbies: so our needs include biking gear, craft supplies, a car that will get us to a remote creek for kayaking or fishing. We have belief systems: environmental, political, social. Our needs could be shaped by wanting products that align (or don't) with these beliefs.

As a quick exercise, write down every need you have had over the last twenty-four hours: anything that requires you to make a purchase, or use an existing purchase to satisfy it. Ask a friend from a different background to do the same. Now look at the lists. Every one of these needstates is a category use occasion—in other words, an opportunity for a brand to create or promote a product that will meet your specific need at that moment. Imagine you have a coffee shop in this example:[9]

- Why: I need something to wake me up, something to indulge, something to socialize.
- When: I need something midmorning, early evening.
- Where: I need something to eat in the car, as I walk, in the restaurant.
- Who: I need something for the office, for a group of friends, for my kids.
- What: I need a cup of coffee, a snack, a dessert.

Understanding which CUOs are most successful for your brand is key to developing a stepping-stones approach to expand and develop your CUOs. Let's take Starbucks as an example. They've done a phenomenal job of building upon their existing CUOs in a logical and methodical way. Early in their expansion phase, we imagine that they realized that savory lunches and snacks would be crucial to their long-term success. These are big CUOs and a second reason for a loyal Starbucks customer to visit the café over the course of a day (especially important for a coffee chain after the morning rush is over). However, Starbucks probably realized they couldn't go from coffee to offering lunches in the blink of an eye. Very few folks would buy it and they most likely would not have been profitable. There had to be a logical process of building up other offerings in order for the addition of savory food to make sense. Our outsider observations of the Starbucks CUO trajectory would be something like this: First they built up an offering of sweet, dessert-like drinks. Then, they doubled down on sweet pastries. Only then did they expand into savory breakfast sand-wiches, and from there—finally—to savory lunches and snacks. It took a few years, but it was logical, it made sense to their customers, and each addition was given time to "settle in" and become a familiar part of their consumers' routine before moving on to pushing the next CUO.

Functional Relevance Conclusion

Brands That Grow Are Brands That Grow Their CUOs

Think of Toyota vs. Mini Cooper. Toyota has a car for just about every use occasion, whether you need something rugged for outdoor adventures, something electric to be easy on the environment, something classy to show off your status, or something practical to get you from A to B with no fuss. Mini Cooper, until relatively recently, was limited to the child-free, or empty-nesters, who lived in urban areas, and didn't have to worry about carrying large items in their car. They have since expanded their line to include the larger Countryman, but they are still meeting relatively few CUOs. Mini is highly distinctive, but not likely to grow dramatically unless they meet more CUOs. If you want to grow, you need to meet as many CUOs as possible, something that Toyota has done far more effectively than Mini.

Be Open to CUO Growth
Outside of Your Usual Sales Environment

Taco Bell–branded tortilla chips were one of those "why didn't we think of it earlier" innovations that Collider Lab developed when challenged by Taco Bell to come up with a "one-hundred-million-dollar idea" over lunch. The three flavors, Classic, Mild, Fire (and Diablo as a limited-time offer), are sold in grocery and convenience stores rather than Taco Bell locations, and sell between $20–30 million a year. Sometimes the functional relevance innovation is getting your product in unexpected locations, and in front of people who might not normally consider your brand.

Stay True to Your Distinctiveness

Fulfill as many use occasions as you can, while still remaining true to your distinctiveness. Think of Arm & Hammer Baking Soda, which from the 1920s–1960s was a kitchen staple, relegated to the baking shelf, or a moldering corner of millions of refrigerators. By emphasizing the power of baking soda as an ingredient, and reframing the brand around the idea of its functional relevance as a deodorizer, and emphasizing its distinctive quality, Arm & Hammer was able to systematically expand the product line to encompass laundry detergent, household cleaners, first aid products, and toothpaste and mouthwash (among many others). Experiment with the Arm & Hammer approach and see if it will apply to your brand. But stretch too far and you'll encounter failure. Samsonite tried launching a line of clothing. Cracker Jack made cereal (actually, that sounds delicious, but probably too candylike for a breakfast cereal back then). Dr Pepper launched meat marinade. Zippo decided it was a good idea to sell a Zippo-branded perfume. It wasn't.

Primary Data Is Key

To discover the CUOs your brand could grow with, you'll need data. Specifically, you'll want to commission a study that sizes each possible CUO in the category, while at the same time measures just how difficult it would be for your brand to win in those usage occasions. It's not enough to buy an existing study off the shelf. Not only is the information rarely specific enough to your brand, you will also lose the invaluable experience of *doing the work.* One of the first things you'll need to do for this study is to catalog as many usage occasions as possible in the category. To give you an idea, we usually identify about 130 of them. Many are tiny (I ordered food online because I was stuck on the phone), and many are overlapping (I wanted something exciting and I wanted something innovative). But we deliberately try to cast a wide net to find the unexpected. If it's tiny or doesn't make sense in the results, there's nothing lost. This creative exercise alone is eye opening, as you'll have to go well beyond the basic occasions you already win in.

7

Social Relevance

"I'll Have What She's Having!"

FOUR YEARS AGO, when Greg and Collider Lab were developing the ideas you are reading in this book, we sat down to hash out the concept of social relevance (see Figure 7.1) and how exactly it would apply to our customers and the Yum! world in general. Ken explained that the two levers of social relevance are simple:

1. I trust a friend or influencer more than I trust a brand or expert.
2. The more I hear something repeated, the easier it is to recall, the more positive attributes I assign to it, and the more importance I give to it.

. . .

SOCIAL RELEVANCE:

THE ABILITY OF A BRAND TO CONSTANTLY BE A TOPIC OF CONVERSATION IN SOCIAL, CIRCLES, USUALLY BY CREATING UNEXPECTED STUNTS AND ACTIONS...

MISSION TO THE EDGE OF SPACE
Red Bull STRATOS
FELIX BAUMGARTNER

RED BULL

JUMP FROM SPACE

PALM SPRINGS
THE BELL
A TACO BELL
HOTEL & RESORT

TACO BELL

TACO BELL HOTEL

...BECAUSE THE MORE PEOPLE TALK ABOUT A BRAND, THE MORE EVERYONE FEELS IT'S THE BRAND TO BUY.

FIGURE 7.1

Social Proof

The first point is an example of something called Social Proof. Social Proof is our very human tendency to assume that if most of our peers are doing something, it must be the correct thing to do. Think of the last time you wandered down a street in a strange town, looking for a Sunday morning brunch spot. Did you pick the empty place, or the café with a line of people hovering at the door, jostling to get their names on a list? We believe this tendency to assume that other people have evaluated the existing options, and made the best choice among them, is partially a product of consumers shifting their trust from governments and institutions toward what their friends, employers, influencers, and celebrities say.[1] The Edelman Trust Barometer found that there was a 10 percent point decline in business trust between 2017 and 2018 (from 58 percent to 48 percent).[2] During the opening weeks of the coronavirus crisis, nobody listened to experts or brands telling them there was no need to stockpile, and instead rushed to the store to fill up on toilet paper and water bottles simply because their neighbors were doing it. Even more telling, Trust Working Group (a group within the UK Advertising Association) did a study that revealed that public favorability toward advertising was just 25 percent in December 2018, meaning distrust was at 75 percent![3]

Now, to be clear, we don't believe that for advertising to work it must be trusted. That's simply not the way advertising functions. Instead, advertising builds salience in consumers' minds by building and reinforcing memory structures. This salience leads to sales. But the fact that consumers *don't* trust advertising does raise an interesting point: Who do they trust? What opinions are they relying on when they need an opinion to make a decision? The answer, of course, is each other. That's why brands such as Glossier are turning to their superfans to help promote their products and spur growth.[4]

To understand just how influential an influencer can be, consider this: it took Tom Ford's beauty brand—launched in 2006—ten years of glossy ads, supermodels, and the backing of Estee Lauder to reach a half billion dollars in sales.[5] In Q3 2020, Kylie Jenner will close a deal with Coty for a 51 percent stake in her beauty business. The deal values her brand—five years old at the time of writing, which manufactures its product in a nondescript California town called Oxnard, and has had between eight and twelve employees for much of its existence—at $1.2 billion.[6] To date, Jenner has marketed her makeup line almost exclusively on her social media pages, which means she is leveraging her social relevance to reach a combined following of over 232 million followers with a bare bones marketing budget (obviously some of those followers are following her on multiple platforms, but still . . .). As of this writing, Kylie is embroiled in some drama over the actual value of her company; nonetheless, the fact that she was ever in a position to make such a deal demonstrates that she is a potent figure of the power of social relevance.[7]

The Availability Heuristic

The second way in which social relevance works is what is known as *the availability heuristic.*[8] We are all highly influenced by whatever information we have either heard or read in the recent past, and we give that information a lot of importance. This bias about past experiences can affect our thinking when making a decision in the present. A well-publicized shark attack will keep swimmers out of the water and cause a decline in drowning deaths, because the shark attack is so much more memorable—and widely discussed and written about—than the much more common drownings, which were never publicized enough to deter swimmers. State and national lotteries focus their advertising efforts on past winners, because by reminding us that people have won, we believe that winning is more likely than it actually is. When we create an ongoing social conversation, and keep peoples' attention on our brands, we're essentially making the brands feel more important, or "the thing to do." The availability heuristic is a mental shortcut, and, boy, do humans love shortcuts. Unconsciously defaulting to an available idea or belief saves us the time and energy that might be required to consider other, less available ideas.

One of the more impressive examples of a social relevance activation in the Yum! world comes from down under. For the last fifteen years, KFC has been sponsoring cricket, a sport most Aussies are absurdly passionate about. Every year, the brand encourages fans to wear the distinctive KFC bucket on their heads. That's right. The empty bucket of chicken. On their heads. And thousands have. Sally Spriggs, KFC Australia's marketing co-director, and co-creator of this bizarre moment in culture, explains, "The KFC Buckethead Army, as we call them, is now such an ingrained phenomenon that every year we produce specially designed buckets with the brand logo upside down, so when it's worn, you can read, 'KFC,' right-side up." Cricket has an incredibly high television viewership in Australia. So, you can imagine the value of this social relevance activation every time the camera pans over a sea of spectators wearing the product packaging on their heads.

The success of this, and hundreds of other activations around the globe, has boiled down to one simple social relevance mission: our brands must be present in the conversation. The more buzz there is about them, the more people will use them. This is obviously much easier said than done, so to help our marketing teams be more effective at it, we have a couple of simple rules.

Make a brand party-talk worthy.

and

Leverage a brand's distinctive assets.

Party-talk worthy means that a moment—be it an ad, a marketing stunt, or something completely bizarre, such as the Taco Bell Wedding Chapel in Vegas—is so unexpected, so of the moment, and so much fun that anyone who sees or hears it feels compelled to share about it with their friends and coworkers. Pizza Hut dropped the "Pie Top," a retro-ish 1980s sneaker equipped with a button that ordered you a pizza to be delivered to your house. For the thirtieth anniversary of *Back to the Future II*, the Hut debuted a mini-pizza designed to look like the pie Marty's mom pops in the rehydrator. Neither of these items were mainstream products; instead, they were designed to be talked about, shared, and discussed. In an interesting side note, the Pie Tops are now highly collectible, occasionally going for as much as a grand on StockX shoe exchange.

The reason why "party-talk worthy" is important is that for someone to share something with their friends, they have to feel it makes them look smart or cool or especially dialed-in to what's happening. Nobody is going to share something that makes them look dumb or corporate or outdated. So, our rule is simple: Is your idea something that someone would be proud to share at a party because it makes them look cool? Or is it something only a corporate dweeb would find cool?

When Pizza Hut in Taiwan launches unexpected "flash offers" of Bubble Tea pizza, Stinky Tofu pizza, or Durian pizza, people feel like insiders when they tell their friends about it. The combination of incredibly buzz-worthy ingredients and extremely short windows of availability make the news irresistible. Just across the strait, in mainland China, Pizza Hut has a collection of desserts they call the "dirty series," which capture the trend of messy, deconstructed desserts. Every single diner immediately posts their treat straight to their WeChat. It's not socially relevant if it's not party-talk worthy.[9] Most of us would rather look smart than stupid, rich than poor, and hip than geeky.

Leveraging a brand's distinctive assets is just that: whatever you do to create socially relevant content has to leverage the brand's core distinctive brand assets. Otherwise, your cool "party-talk worthy" event will be mis-attributed and end up helping your competitors. Pizza Hut Hong Kong launched an Ikea Swedish Meatball pizza, and at the same time Ikea launched a full-sized version of that little pizza protector we use at the center of our pizzas. The resulting buzz was clearly linked to the unique use of both distinctive assets (the Swedish meatballs for Ikea, the pizza protector for Pizza Hut).

More on this in a moment, but first, back to that conference room, in the spring of 2016.

PIZZA HUT × IKEA Pizza

Everyone wrapped up the conversation and Greg mulled over these ideas for a minute. Finally he said, "Well, then I guess the presidential election is as good as over." Since the campaign had just recently started in earnest, Ken was confused. Perhaps he'd misunderstood the point of social relevance? As if reading Ken's thoughts, Greg said, "No. I get it. But if social relevance is real, especially if it's distinctive, then the only way this ends is with Trump as president." Of course everyone present laughed, because there was no way that was going to happen! But it turns out that the Trump team leveraged Trump's undeniable, off-the-charts distinctiveness and social relevance to the hilt. Every shocking statement was instant party-worthy talk. Every rude, abrasive thing he said spoke right to his distinctive, brash character, and every mocking tweet refreshed those distinctive memory structures to earn him billions of free airtime from MSNBC to Fox to the outer limits of the internet. Think about the parades of experts countering his wild claims with heavily fact-checked data. Or Clinton, earnestly debating a man whose responses were boiler-plate trolling a la 4chan, or "rising above" his obnoxious behavior at their three televised bouts (exactly the opposite of what she should have done). None of them understood the problem: if you supported Trump, then he was your friend, your influencer, the scrappy upstart who would tell you the truth and who you trusted to offer you a fresh, party-talk-worthy take on a boring old product: politics. Clinton, or any of the well-intentioned talking heads, was the dull, lumbering Blue Chip Brand, insisting you believed what they wished you to believe and doling out information and ideas on their slow-enough-to-be-analog timeline. The same could be said of a whole host of distinctive character-type, socially relevant leaders around the world: Bolsonaro in Brazil, Duterte in the Philippines, Maduro in Venezuela, Orbán in Hungary, and Johnson in the UK.

Alexandria Ocasio-Cortez, the US congresswoman, has used social media, specifically Instagram Live, to hold AMA-style social media conversations to build a connection with her constituents, demystify the mechanics of how Congress works, showcase her favorite Instant Pot recipes, and create party-worthy talk that everyone from Laura Ingraham to AOC's millions of followers are compelled to share and discuss. Recently she started playing the red-hot game *Animal Crossing*, visiting supporters' islands to leave notes/doodles in their bulletin boards, and even gave a commencement speech.

On the GOP side, first-year congressman Dan Crenshaw stepped into *SNL*'s Weekend Update studio to get comedic revenge on Pete Davidson for the latter's jokes about Crenshaw's very distinctive eyepatch. His nimble and good-humored beatdown of the comic gave the newbie politician a massive boost in the public consciousness, and established him as a face to watch. Likewise, AOC's distinctive assets, be they Millennial tech savviness, a passionate defense of the workingman and -woman, or a bold red lip, have helped to make her a national figure as well—something most first-term members of Congress can only dream about.

I'm guessing our editor would prefer we don't discuss politics in this book, but I'm afraid we must. Because the 2016 election, and the 2018 midterms, are compelling examples of how social relevance can bounce a small, scrappy brand light-years ahead of its larger and more established competition. In fact, social relevance is one of the few places that being an upstart brand is a significant advantage, so, if that describes you and your product, listen closely. The key element here is this: if you have a distinctive voice, and can use it in a memorable way, you can pull that first, "I trust you" lever. Yes, you still have to get your cultural relevance, functional relevance, ease, and distinctiveness in place, but if you can initiate and nurture a meaningful social relevance presence, then you are much more likely to be able to develop an irresistibly watchable persona with millions of potential customers.

If you are part of a bigger brand, then you need to think differently and more creatively about how you are going to spend your PR dollars. Hint: Don't waste too much paper and time writing press releases, or traveling to conferences to make some grand pronouncement. Instead, work on developing a passionate, online group of people who are going to care enough to talk about what you are doing, and share it with their friends. That Taco Bell Hotel cultural moment? Almost all the influencers we invited wrote glowing (and funny) reviews and stories about "The Bell" hotel, and it led to 4.4 billion impressions. A massive return on a fairly modest investment. Plus, it was just plain fun to do.

Before we go further into the nuts and bolts of social relevance, let's elaborate on the origins of social relevance theory, and develop the ideas we've touched on above.

The Evolution of Social Relevance

Many of the strategies that we've developed at Collider Lab are based on evolutionary biology and the science of human behavior. As we already discussed, early humans found safety in numbers, and a common identity in shared stories. Another thread in this story is the way our ancestors began to learn from the experiences of the other sapiens in their community. If everyone in your immediate tribe uses a specific waterhole, and returns safe every evening, with no losses to lions, waterborne amoeba, or warring tribes, you are more likely to trust that waterhole. Your friends trust it, you trust your friends, and therefore it feels safe to trust their recommendations. Now, suppose you catch wind of a brand-new water-hole! None of your fellow early humans has gathered water there. You have no reports of its safety. It is closer, which is a big benefit when you spend much of your day in search of water. You are, however, naturally nervous about using the watering hole. Suppose there are lions? After all, lions have to drink water, too, and if they're not at the established watering hole, perhaps they are at this one. The potential benefits of a new, untapped resource pale compared to the possible dangers of using it. Instead, you continue to join the throng of your trusted friends, waiting for their turn at the familiar, safe water source.

Fast-forward ten thousand years, and many of our decisions are still being made by this simple metric: "Do the people I trust, trust this product?" This applies to impulse buying, too. The more you feel those around you trust the product, the more likely you are to buy it on impulse with less second-guessing or debating. It's as simple as "they have it so I should have it, too."

How to Create Social Relevance

This first lever—"I trust you more than I trust a corporation"—gives you and your brand an opportunity known as *earned media*. Earned media is the buzz and word-of-mouth that is created through social channels like Instagram and TikTok. Your brand's presence on social media and other popular platforms dictates its Share of Buzz (SOB). Brands have to go about creating this buzzy content—and supporting influencers who are doing it independently—in a deliberate way. You cannot predict what will go viral (and anyone trying to offer you a service that guarantees your content *will* go viral is a BS artist), but you *can* consistently make noise with your brand and get talked about in a seemingly organic fashion. This is incredibly valuable: whatever brand is most salient in a consumer's brain is more likely to be purchased. Note, paid advertising, and Share of

Buzz, work in concert together. As Les Binet and Peter Field say in their influential research paper, *Media in Focus*, "brands only tend to get significant levels of earned media online when they have both owned and paid media in place as well. In other words, to get people talking and sharing, you need to provide great online content and you need to promote it with some kind of paid advertising."

Now, I'm guessing your rebuttal to the idea that salience is king will be the obvious: suppose my brand is memorable for *bad* reasons. Well, we'd counter by pointing you back to our waterhole. So long as people that your customers trust, trust this product, your customer will be more likely to pick your brand and you will continue to come out ahead.

As you move forward, bear these core ideas in mind:

1. Creating moments in culture can have a big impact on brands.
2. As it becomes harder to "buy" attention, brands need to "earn" it, too.
3. Brands that increase their Share of Buzz are more likely to grow their market share.
4. In a world of mistrust, marketing actions speak louder than words.

The Five Paths to Social Relevance

Make Your Brand Part of the Entertainment Itself

One day, a creative at our ad agency was at a WWE event, and noticed that the audience booed the commercials shown between matches. From there, they came up with the idea for how Colonel Sanders could save WWE fans from the annoyance of seeing commercials during live events. This led to KFC bemusing fans of the 2016 WWE SummerSlam by running a two-minute commercial starring WWE Intercontinental Champion The Miz—

playing an anthropomorphic chicken, Pupper Cluckers—challenging Colonel Sanders, played by wrestler Dolph Ziggler, to a wrestling match. Kudos to the wrestlers for keeping straight faces as the characters insulted, belittled, and taunted each other, first in a "commercial" for the fictional Pupper Cluckers restaurants, and then, in a fog of dry ice, appearing in the ring in front of a live audience. It was absurd, but neither wrestler broke character. At one point, Pupper Cluckers pulled off his feather wing to slap the Colonel with it. Now, a few folks hated it. A lot loved it. But love it or hate it, they *all* talked about it. The ad had become part of the evening's entertainment, and, like the other matches that evening, the audience rooted for the heel (Pupper Cluckers) or the face (The Colonel), but the real winner was KFC. George Felix, the then head of advertising for KFC US (now the CMO of Pizza Hut US), explained how they landed on such a memorable sponsorship. "When we approached media integrations on KFC, we put a rule in place that we didn't want any 'logo slaps' or generic sponsorship opportunities. Our premise was that if we could bring a creative idea that was distinctive to KFC and also showed that we understood the WWE audience, we could add value to the fan experience." That mentality, adding value to the fan experience, is the critical component in making your brand part of the entertainment itself. Doing that in a distinctive way? Home run.

Part of social relevance is finding startling and unexpected ways to become the entertainment: Tinder created a bumper car ride to allow single-and-looking people to "bump into each other." In 2016, Airbnb, in conjunction with The Art Institute of Chicago, listed a rental room on the North Shore designed and decorated to look like van Gogh's bedroom in his beloved *Yellow House* in Arles, France. The designers meticulously re-created van Gogh's brushstrokes, crooked lines, and vivid colors to create the experience of being immersed in his painting.

All three of these examples are brands finding an unanticipated and impossible-to-predict way to become part of the entertainment. They aren't specifically about selling an end product, more about leveraging the brand's DNA to create a party-talk worthy moment that can contribute to a bigger cultural conversation—and the brand's place in culture. These are great examples of magnetic marketing: making distinctive work that attracts people to the brand.

So, make some noise. Sounds easy, but in practice it's much harder. Fortunately, we've got a fun little wheel of primers for you to kick-start your journey to social relevance. For each one of these sections, ask yourself, "How can my brand [blank]?" We'll use examples from other, brilliant brands that have produced excellent party-talk-worthy and distinctive moments in culture.

Be the Good Citizen

Lacoste replaced its iconic alligator with images of endangered species around the world in order to raise money and awareness for conservation. The camping supply retailer REI closed all its stores on the busiest shopping day of the year (Black Friday) to encourage people to go outside. The investment company State Street Global Advisors created an art installation on Wall Street of a "Fearless Girl" to champion women in business leadership positions. Burger King pulled off a stunt where their customers received damaged hamburgers as a way to raise awareness around bullying.

Be Useful

Offer an unexpected benefit to your customer. IKEA created an ad for cribs and other baby furniture that also functioned as a pregnancy test. Adidas developed a sneaker that doubled as a metro pass.

Be the Instigator

Sometimes your brand has an opportunity to provoke, or create a strong reaction, either in response to its own products, product delivery issues, or bigger cultural moments happening around them. In early 2018, a new delivery contract left many of our KFC UK branches without any chicken.

At the peak of the disruption, 646 branches were closed. As you can imagine, this was a problem.[10] Rather than offering some kind of banal, "sorry for the inconvenience" PR message, the KFC marketing team reworded their signature acronym, and ran a print campaign that showed a classic bucket with the letters "FCK" written where the KFC normally goes. Meg Farren, KFC UK's fearless CMO, explains, "Our customers were still angry as hell that they couldn't get their chicken, to the point where Tower Hamlets Police had to tweet, begging customers not to call the UK's version of 911 to complain. But, by acknowledging how FCKed up the situation was, we were able to get ahead of some of the bad publicity, create a socially relevant moment, and show solidarity with our frustrated customers." It worked. Total sales were back at pre-crisis levels four months after the disruption.

Don't be afraid to say out loud what your customer is already thinking. KFC UK did this again in 2018, when they laid the groundwork for their new, chunky skin-on fries by paying to promote tweets about how *bad* the original fries were (this prompted Burger King to reply, "*Weird flex but okay*"). Once they had established how much their customers hated the original fries, KFC UK launched the new, improved product to great amusement of all, including those original trollers.

Be the Pop Culture Creator

Finally, embrace your brand's power to create pop culture moments through smart and unexpected collaborations. Taco Bell has partnered with Forever 21 to create a ridiculously 'grammable clothing collection. Cheetos in turn worked with F21 to create Flaming Hot makeup palettes. MAC and *The Simpsons* likewise partnered to create a Marge Simpson–inspired makeup line that emulated the famous matriarch's suburban glam beauty looks. Adidas and Arizona Ice Tea collaborated on a brilliant sneaker line in 2019, selling both the cans of tea *and* the sneakers, printed with the instantly recognizable Arizona cherry blossom designs and the signature Arizona pinks and blues, for $0.99 in a pop-up shop in NYC. Ikea

UK and Ireland collaborated with designer Virgil Abloh on a curated collection of household goods that reflected his droll style—for instance, an AstroTurf green rug, printed with the words "wet grass." The brand even added quotation marks around their storefront logo in honor of Abloh's signature "logo" style. Don't be afraid to do something that seems ridiculous; however, make sure there is some kind of logic to it, it remains true to your distinctive brand assets, and you embrace it without hesitation.

Social Relevance Conclusion

In early 2020, we noticed something interesting about the late Millennials and Gen Z focus groups we were interviewing and working with. As they discussed their interests and temporary, short-term cultural obsessions, we realized that many of them hadn't actually watched the shows or movies they were recommending. Repeatedly, an interviewee would drop an opinion, like, "*The Boys* is brilliant, you should watch it." But, when pressed for more details about plot, tone, or character, the enthusiast would have to admit, "Well, I haven't actually watched it yet. But I heard it's good." Think about this for a minute. These pop culture moments are so socially relevant and impactful that these would-be viewers are vouching for them without even seeing them. The more we dug, the more we realized that there's no shame in being called out about not seeing the shows.[11] Instead, claiming to have seen or read something you actually hadn't is accepted as part of the ongoing swirl of cultural communication. (Interestingly, men are much more likely to falsely claim to have seen a show than women are, according to a 2016 study conducted by Hulu.) As we mulled over the implications of this, we realized it backed up all our theories about social relevance and pushed them even further than we'd considered. Our focus groups didn't even have to watch these shows in order for them to be salient, or at the top of their mind. Instead, these shows and movies had become so culturally relevant, memorable, and mentally available that our focus groups were willing to vouch for them without any personal experience of the content or quality of the product. If you're not sure social relevance is important to you and your brand, think about this paradox for a minute: it's worth the risk of being called out by your friends if it means you can claim to be socially relevant. In fact, it's so important that there is essentially no stigma to the false claim. Social relevance is a powerful currency (see Figure 7.2), so make sure you are using it to your best advantage.

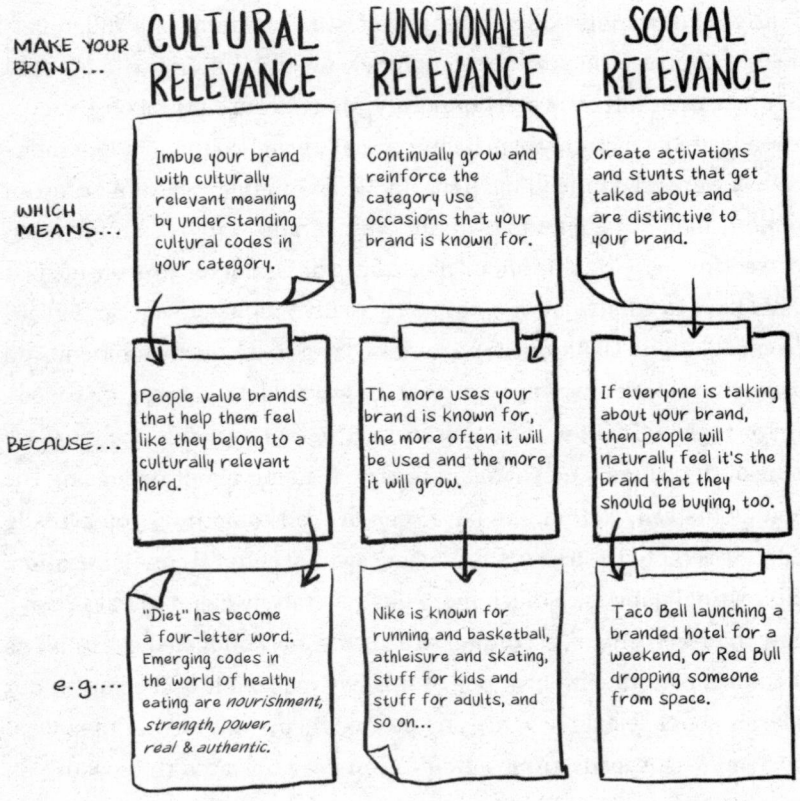

RELEVANCE OVERVIEW

MAKE YOUR BRAND...	CULTURAL RELEVANCE	FUNCTIONALLY RELEVANCE	SOCIAL RELEVANCE
WHICH MEANS...	Imbue your brand with culturally relevant meaning by understanding cultural codes in your category.	Continually grow and reinforce the category use occasions that your brand is known for.	Create activations and stunts that get talked about and are distinctive to your brand.
BECAUSE...	People value brands that help them feel like they belong to a culturally relevant herd.	The more uses your brand is known for, the more often it will be used and the more it will grow.	If everyone is talking about your brand, then people will naturally feel it's the brand that they should be buying, too.
e.g....	"Diet" has become a four-letter word. Emerging codes in the world of healthy eating are *nourishment, strength, power, real & authentic.*	Nike is known for running and basketball, athleisure and skating, stuff for kids and stuff for adults, and so on...	Taco Bell launching a branded hotel for a weekend, or Red Bull dropping someone from space.

FIGURE 7.2

8

Easy to Access

E ASE IS EVERYTHING. All the other facets of R.E.D., and of marketing in general, are important. They can be significant levers to get your customers engaged and interested in your product. Ease, however, is exponentially more important. We tend to think of ease as the biggest sail on the boat. Distinctiveness is the secondary sail, while relevance (or rather, the lack thereof) is an anchor that can kill all your speed.

Simple ease actions—removing the need for a password on an app, adding a default order to a user's profile, or opening a multi-lane KFC drive-thru-only location (as in Newcastle, Australia)—can lead to overnight growth for an individual brand or location. (Nikki Lawson, the current Global Chief Brand Officer of Taco Bell, co-created the multi-lane drive-thru as part of a challenge to enhance sales.) TikTok doesn't require a username or password to view its content. This ease, along with the app's addictive content, helped it become the seventh most downloaded app of the 2010s. That's a whole decade, folks, even though it was only available for the last three years of it![1]

Reducing ease can also lessen harm: blister packs reduce suicide rates because accessing the pills is no longer easy.[2] The lack of large bottles full of pills and the time it takes to pop out each individual pill in a blister pack may be enough to deter some of the potential suicides. Relevance and distinctiveness can make your brand more mentally available and appropriate for the times, but only ease can, with a few tweaks, pull your rivals' customers into your locations overnight. So, ease can be a powerful disruptive force—and the next two chapters will give you ideas about how to engage its full power.

One of the quirks of R.E.D. is that the most powerful component is also the simplest to explain and understand. Remember Ken's preference for Vosges chocolate, but his habit of eating Snickers? As we discussed then, Ken, like 99 percent of our fellow human beings, is deeply lazy. He will sublimate every other consideration—taste, texture, organic vs. conventional, price—to the very simple question of, "What product is easiest for me to get?" It doesn't matter that Ken is committed to eating well, or that he can run a mile in a pretty handy time. When he wants a blast of sugar, he'll reach for the instantly available, corn syrup–infused, partially hydrogenated treat every time.

Here's your insight from this: Ease is everything.

How to put it in practice? Make your product more physically and mentally available than your competitors.

So, that's the ease chapters.

Well . . . for the sake of our word count we should probably elaborate, and there are some interesting observations and intriguing opportunities for companies who are willing to reconsider the nuts and bolts of how they do things. At Collider Lab, we divide ease up into two core ideas.

The first idea is:

Easy to Access

This is simple. In marketing terminology we call impediments to purchase, *friction*. Ease of access means giving your customer more opportunities to buy from you, and limiting any obstacles, or friction, between the customer's purchasing decision and the actual purchase. These can be physical friction (like multiple clicks on an app to buy the product) or psychological friction (so many choices that it makes it hard to decide). We'll have a simple but effective exercise called "Ease Safari" for you to try at the end of this chapter. So, as we move through this chapter, look at your own consumers' journey, and hone in on areas where you have insufficient opportunities for purchase, or are creating friction, and preventing people from buying your product.

The second idea is:

Easy to Notice

We'll talk about this in the next chapter, but for now understand that easy to notice is how present your brand is in your consumer's life. Does your customer see or hear your message? Even more important, do they remember it when they are in the store, or the shopping environment? This chapter will be the one place where we will talk about sparking an emotional response in a consumer. But before you get all excited and warm up your computer to fire off an angry email at us, let me clarify: emotional response is not the same as emotional connection. We still dislike the idea of emotional connection as a branding tool, as we've stated multiple times. So hold that email. Or better yet, change the subject and send us a hello. We'd love to meet you and establish a real, human-to-human, emotional connection.

Easy to access (see Figure 8.1) is all about making your product easier to purchase. This should be a top priority for all modern marketers, because, out of all the facets of R.E.D., ease offers the greatest opportunity for disruptive innovation. All that is required is getting some clarity about the friction your customer is experiencing when they purchase your product. You don't need to reformulate your product, revise your marketing strategy, or lower the price below your competitors. You don't need to run expensive surveys to try and understand the psychological underpinnings of your core customer. All you need to do is find ways to increase the *physical and mental availability* of your product. Why is Amazon the vast, all-seeing monolith that controls almost 50 percent of all online retail transactions in the US?[3] Because it has made almost every product in the world physically available to almost every person in the world. At the height of the coronavirus crisis in April 2020, brick-and-mortar stores across the US were shuttering; publishers like Conde Nast were laying off seasoned writers; Airbnb, the wildly successful disrupter of the accommodations category, laid off 25 percent of its workforce; and the airlines were crisscrossing the skies with fewer passengers than crew. At the same time, Amazon's stock hit a record high of $3,200 on July 13, 2020.[4] Ease is everything: Amazon continues to remove physical frictions by eliminating checkout with its "Just Walk Out" technology at Amazon Go stores.[5] At the same time, their innovations that remove psychological frictions continue to drive sales. Every item you buy, for instance, will automatically bring up other related products that pair with it, instantly removing the friction of trying to figure out, say, what size bags go with that trash can you just bought. Same goes for their star rating system. A 4.5 star rating or above instantly removes the psychological friction that makes you pause, wondering if the product actually works. We don't commonly see massive disruptive possibilities in relevance or distinctiveness. However, an ingenious ease innovation can change your business's fortunes overnight.

Companies that make purchasing easier than their competitors will, in most cases, win, no matter what the circumstances. This is why Snickers beats Vosges chocolate. At the end of this chapter, we'll have a few

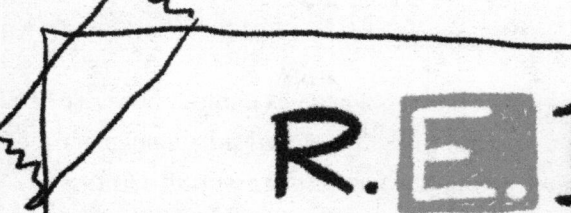

EASY TO ACCESS:

STRIPPING ALL FRICTION (BOTH PHYSICAL AND EMOTIONAL) OUT OF THE BUYING PROCESS, MAKING IT AS SMOOTH AND EASY AS POSSIBLE...

 **DOLLAR SHAVE CLUB**

DOLLAR SHAVE CLUB

DISRUPTED THE CATEGORY BY REMOVING ALL PHYSICAL & PSYCHOLOGICAL FRICTION; THEY MAIL IT TO YOUR HOUSE, AND YOU NEVER HAVE TO REMEMBER.

... BECAUSE HUMAN BEINGS WILL NEARLY ALWAYS CHOOSE THE EASIEST OPTION OVER TIME (AND THEN POST-RATIONALIZE THEIR DECISION).

FIGURE 8.1

exercises for you to do, to explore how you can make your product more physically available. But take a minute to think of some of the friction your customer experiences in buying your product. What are some opportunities to make what you sell more available to more people, with minimal friction between the initial moment of need and the end purchase?

The Power of Ease

The evolution of the at-home movie rental is a great example of how ease can be a disruptive force on a par with the San Andreas Fault. Remember when Friday night films involved getting in your car (often with all the other interested parties in your household), driving to your neighborhood Blockbuster, finding the new releases section, swearing under your breath when you realized that none of the cardboard placeholders had an actual tape behind it, and finally finding a compromise movie that no one *really* wanted to see? Then came the waiting in line, and the moment where the cashier wouldn't rent you a movie unless you paid $20 of late fees. If the clerk was a real jerk, he would add in some rewind fees to boot. Finally, a good hour or so later, you and your family would get home, your good mood having evaporated somewhere along the way. With the benefit of hindsight it's obvious just how ripe the movie rental business was to be radically remade by a disruptive company. Every step of the movie-renting process was full of friction, often in obviously ridiculous ways, such as memberships that didn't transfer between stores, and a convoluted process of coming into the store to reserve a copy of a major new release in advance.

You probably don't need me to tell you the second part of this story: in 1997, Netflix was born, offering a subscription model with no late fees, free shipping, zero driving or human interaction, and an ever-growing selection of movies and box sets.[6] The company even introduced the word "queue" to the US. In 2000, Netflix offered to sell itself to Blockbuster, but the deal was rebuffed by the incredulous brick-and-mortar behemoth.[7] We all know how that ended (though you may be surprised to know that Blockbuster itself survives with one final location in Bend, Oregon. Ideal for your much-needed hit of retro-friction!). Innovations in ease can change the world faster than innovations in any other area of R.E.D.

Interestingly, Netflix made one of its very few blunders when it attempted to separate its DVD and streaming rental services, rebranding the former as "Qwickster." Under this strategy, subscribers who wanted access to both DVDs and streamed content would have had to pay more, and maintain separate queues for both. Netflix, after years of removing friction from home entertainment, was suddenly adding friction back into the experience. Subscribers were furious, tech and entertainment blogs had a field day, and Qwickster quickly disappeared, proving that adding friction and subtracting ease is always a terrible idea.

One holdout to this model is RedBox, which was founded in 2002 by the McDonald's business development team as a convenience kiosk. After years of declining fortunes, RedBox has recently started to expand its kiosks, betting that the rock-bottom prices will remain compelling to users unwilling to pay higher streaming rental fees (and who are interested in trying new video games, something Netflix doesn't offer).[8]

It helps to get creative with how you think about friction and ease. In certain cases, things that feel like benefits can actually detract from the experience of purchasing your product. An example of this would be when the friction in a purchase is too much choice, as in the famous jam example in Barry Schwartz's *The Paradox of Choice*. (Customers offered a choice between six flavors of jam are far more likely to make a purchase than customers offered a choice between twenty-four flavors of jam. Note, this study has since been hotly debated, but we tend to see that simplifying menus leads to increased sales.)[9] Other potential sources of friction are purchases that have to be made frequently, or too many unanswered questions about a product. Direct to Consumer brands have experimented with different strategies to resolve these obstacles, such as memberships (for instance, Harry's Shave Club and Dollar Shave Club). Thrive Market offers delivery of food from top-selling, organic brands at wholesale prices. Warby Parker allows customers to try on five pairs of glasses at home before making a choice. Third Love uses a sophisticated questionnaire to help a customer pick the right bra size without the annoyance and hours out of your day to get a professional fitting (also a significant functional relevance benefit). It is yet to be seen how many of these innovative and disruptive brands will survive the pandemic (looking at you, mattress-in-a-box peeps). Some were great ideas that were unable to scale up in time. For the most part, DTC provides a fantastic opportunity for consumers to access better quality goods at affordable prices by cutting out friction like storefronts and virus exposure. But ultimately, the core reason that DTC will remain strong is for the same reason Ken will keep on eating his Snickers: physical availability and our inherent laziness.

DTC isn't the only game in town when it comes to ease though. Take a close look at your consumer's life and decision journey and you'll find endless opportunities to streamline and simplify. Pizza Hut in Taiwan, for instance, offers a "delivery to parks" service on their website with multiple designated meetup locations at popular national parks, so consumers can picnic with Pizza Hut in the outdoors. (Side note: the insanely beautiful Elephant Mountain trails in Taipei are on Ken's bucket list!) Pizza Hut Hong Kong lets you redeem some of your loyalty points to skip the line at their very popular dine-ins. Walk into a Pizza Hut in Singapore and you can order and pay from your own mobile device while sitting at the table. We'll give you some tips on coming up with your own ease innovations a little further on.

For an incredibly creative example of ease, check out KFC China's "Rainy Day Pop-up Menu." It's a brilliant solution for a major problem in China. When it rains, delivery orders shoot up from five hundred thousand a day to nine hundred thousand a day, slowing the whole system down. To meet demand, the team in China created a pop-up digital store that would automatically be activated on people's phones when it rained. The brilliance was that it curated a menu that made ordering take no longer than five seconds, and that menu was specifically chosen because it would make the cooking and order fulfilment faster at the restaurant. In the end, the consumer got an unbelievably seamless experience, the restaurants could deliver it faster, and sales went up an additional 4 percent.

Closer to home, The Habit Burger blew us away by opening pop-up drive-thrus within a few days of the coronavirus lockdown, and innovated a workaround on their ordering system, allowing more friction-free pickups for customers. It was quickly imitated by the other, exponentially larger, Yum! Brands.

Cognitive Dissonance

If you're a fan of science fiction, you've probably watched your fair share of *Westworld*-esque thrillers about humans and robots grappling with the idea of free will. We all like to believe that we are in charge of our own destinies, and that we shape those destinies with a lifelong string of choices, each of which reflects our truest nature and desires. This, like many of our beliefs about our behavior, is nonsense. Just as HBO's *Westworld*'s Dolores and Maeve fought to uncover their own inner voices, we are often unaware of what we really want, and why we want it. For the most part, we know what we *should* want (in Ken's chocolate example, something sophisticated, refined, organic, and fair trade, which he can eat with a warm glow of self-righteous congratulation, knowing he's made the world a slightly better place with his purchase). However, because our core directive puts ease above everything else, we rarely end up making the choice we think we want.

So, what happens when you make a choice that contradicts what you believe to be true about who you are, your values, and what you prioritize in life? As our brains struggle to reconcile two opposing beliefs, the uncomfortable feeling can slowly become unbearable, until we use rationalization or denial to force the two opposing ideas into alignment. That feeling is called cognitive dissonance, and it can be a powerful tool in the hands of a marketer who knows how to use it. In Ken's chocolate example, he might tell himself that, "I guess it really isn't that bad," or, "Well, I need to spend less money." He now has a reason for why he picked the Snickers bar. And here's the important part: How much money do you think you would've had to spend in advertising to convince Ken that Snickers actually tasted good? You would've had to pelt him with convincing ads and famous spokespeople for years before he would consider that just maybe Snickers wasn't that bad. Instead, by making it physically available, he did all the work of convincing himself! With one simple tweak, he has resolved the discomfort he felt and he can proceed with his day, having convinced himself Snickers aren't gross. As a marketer, you can use the power of ease to change your customer's beliefs. It's often far easier and cheaper than oodles of ads. And yet so many marketers gloss over ease. Don't forget: it's why the candy section is at the checkout. (One of our very favorite marketing minds is the great Paco Underhill, who continually shows in his books, including *Why We Buy,* how slight adjustments to the positions of racks results in radical increases or decreases in sales, just because of those incremental increases or decreases in ease. For instance, the checkout candy is actually positioned for the second or third person in line, not the first, who is too focused on checking out to think about the candy.)

The Benjamin Franklin Effect

One of our favorite books on the topic of cognitive dissonance is Adam Ferrier's *The Advertising Effect.* Ferrier, a clinical psychologist turned marketer, explains the phenomenon best with a parable called "The Benjamin Franklin Effect." The story goes that Franklin famously disarmed his fiercest political opponent by asking to borrow one of his books. Once he'd finished the book, he returned it to his critic, along with a letter complimenting the quality of the book, and the discerning taste of the man who had lent it to him. His critic, perhaps reading the warm and complimentary letter by the fire one evening, would have certainly experienced some intense cognitive dissonance. After all, he had dedicated years to insinuating Franklin was untrustworthy, corrupt, and so forth. These two things were irreconcilable in his mind: the action of engaging with Franklin on the topic of the book, and his feelings of Franklin as an unworthy rival. As a result, he was forced to adjust his opinion of Franklin to be able to accept the action of lending him the book, which he'd already undertaken. The critic never said a word against Franklin in public again.

What is the takeaway from this story? Simple: your actions have to be aligned with your emotions. It's incredibly hard to try and change a person's emotions, and then use that shift to influence their behavior. Marketers try this every single day. But it's much simpler to change people's actions. Benjamin Franklin knew he could make rational appeals to his rival until the sun went down, but it wouldn't change his adversary's deeply rooted beliefs about Franklin. He could, however, create a situation where his rival was cornered into behaving like an ally instead. You can't lend Benjamin Franklin a book and then believe that he's a terrible human being. Lending books and exchanging pleasant letters is what friends do, so surely . . . that means you are friends?

This dynamic, whether used by Franklin, or by a contemporary marketer, looks something like the right-hand column on this flowchart (again, hat tip to Ferrier who first crystallized this concept in the world of marketing).

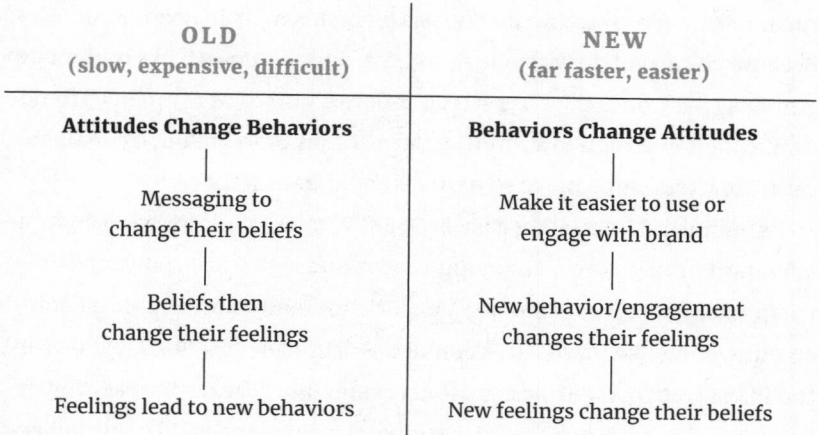

OLD (slow, expensive, difficult)	NEW (far faster, easier)
Attitudes Change Behaviors	**Behaviors Change Attitudes**
Messaging to change their beliefs	Make it easier to use or engage with brand
Beliefs then change their feelings	New behavior/engagement changes their feelings
Feelings lead to new behaviors	New feelings change their beliefs

It's a fascinating, mind-bending way to think about the role of your marketing. It flips everything most marketers think on its head. Curious about the genesis of this insight, we reached out to Adam recently. He's now running an award-winning ad agency in Australia called Thinkerbell. He explained that as a clinical psychologist he often worked with criminals and was always struck by how they had so convincingly and completely post-rationalized their actions—no matter how heinous. During those years, the lesson crystallized in his mind: if you can get people to act, they will justify those actions for themselves. It's a powerful thought. The more easy your brand is to use or engage with, the more likely it is consumers will convince themselves they like it.

Ease in QSR and How to Translate It to Your Business

Our actions rule the day, and our emotions bend to that, not the other way around. Let's bring this idea back to the marketplace. As your customer goes throughout the day, they are going to make choices based on quantities as simple as what side of the road they are driving on. Ken fills up his car at one Chevron station that he passes on his morning commute. Why? Because he can pull in with one right turn, and he knows there is a smooth entryway back onto the busy street. It doesn't matter how many promotions Mobil or Exxon offer him. A few pennies off a gallon, or a rewards card, are irrelevant compared to that simple transaction.

Refining and improving ease is QSRs' version of discovering cold fusion: potentially game-changing innovations with vast power to erase friction, enhance our customers' experience, and improve sales. Look at an innovation like Pizza Hut's contactless curbside pickup. David Graves, the Pizza Hut US Chief Brand Officer, explains, "We developed it in response to the pandemic (just drive up to the store and we'll come out and put the pizza in your trunk). Not only does it remove multiple layers of friction (going in the store, waiting in line, etc.) but, in a moment when fear was also adding to the friction, we were able to make the process of picking up dinner feel safe and predictable." Our Pizza Hut competitor Dominos developed a hit with their "Zero Click" app in Australia. Once you get past the hassle of downloading the app and setting up a profile, the app will order you a pizza anytime you open it. No worries if you butt-order it; you have a ninety-second window to cancel the pie.

With our own brands, we've focused on innovations such as the afore-mentioned multi-lane drive-thru in KFC Australia. Five lanes of full-speed chicken love! Just order ahead on your app and drive up to one of the toll-booths surrounded by the aroma of eleven herbs and spices coming from the nearby kitchen. We'll hand off your order faster than a pit-stop tire change at a Formula One race. And no burning rubber smell!

The amazing KFC marketing team in China is constantly at the leading edge of innovating on ease. Their loyalty program has an unbelievable 200 million members in it, who can order their favorite meals in just a few clicks. But in 2018, they took ease to a whole new level with a digital idea that effectively grew their store count from 5,800 to 580,000 overnight and to over two million in just a couple months. To do this, they gave ev-eryone in China the ability to create their own KFC store on WeChat, Chi-na's largest social media and messaging app. Consumers could design their own digital stores and sell actual products in them. As a reward, they would get additional KFC discounts and freebies for themselves. With just a couple of clicks, consumers could order their product and, thanks to geo-location, it would be ready for them at their nearest store. Suddenly, everyone's WeChat feed was filled with their friend's KFC storefront and ordering was that much easier.

Ease: Your Opportunity to React Quickly to Disruptive Events

One of the truly magical things about making your product easy to access is how the incremental changes in your customer's behavior—downloading an app, ordering an online delivery, placing an order at a kiosk rather than with a person—are irrevocable. During the coronavirus crisis we made an interesting discovery. Many of the small frictions that had prevented our customers from adopting new habits—for instance, creating a user account and choosing a memorable password—were smoothed out by necessity.

Even Ken's wife, who had refused to download the Taco Bell app for as long as he'd worked on the brand, finally caved when she realized it would remove multiple human interactions from her order. She now uses the app—or other apps like it, for our other brands—daily. And she's not alone. Grocery delivery apps experienced record downloads during the coronavirus crisis—to the point that new and existing customers often outpaced those apps' ability to deliver goods.[10] Here's the important detail: now that Ken's wife is over the hump, we are looking at a permanent habit shift. Humans are very habit-driven, and that habit will remain until there is some kind of disruptive event that forces you to learn new habits. So what habits remain after coronavirus? The answer is simple: whichever are easiest. Yes, everyone you knew may have spent the coronavirus crisis baking bread or pounding cabbage and salt into sauerkraut. These aren't permanent habit shifts. In fact, we believe the current boom in cooking at home is simply a temporary, coronavirus-specific fad.[11] Why? Because all these new pastimes involve *adding* friction to your life. And anything that adds friction will fade away before it becomes a habit. Just think of all the pickle-making and victory-gardening during World War II. Those vanished in a hurry after VE Day. Things that make life easier, on the other hand, will persist, and the use of digital tools to order and get a delivery is going to continue. And grow.

In spring of 2020, McKinsey China completed a study about digital deliveries of grocery items. During the lockdown in Wuhan—and indeed throughout much of China—residents began ordering groceries online and getting them delivered. McKinsey was curious: Would people be relieved to finally be able to return to markets and pick their food in person, or would the new app delivery system persist? Over 55 percent of respondents were adamant that they were going to keep this new system of buying groceries. Any ease innovation is going to stick as long as you can get people onboard with the initial decision. But if there is a learning curve, it's going to be an impediment.[12]

Greg and his wife, Carolyn, have experienced this firsthand. After years of shopping at their local markets, they switched to Shipt during coronavirus. They are now converts to ease, and will continue using Shipt rather than go to the store. This is a global phenomenon, even as apps like Insta-cart struggle to adjust to their new role as an essential delivery service rather than an indulgence.

The Delicate Balance

There is one caveat to the "ease over everything" model. Shortly before the coronavirus outbreak, Collider Lab did a study on what the customer service guidelines moving forward should be. We came back with the phrase "Helpful Humanity." This phrase symbolizes the tension between ease and the human desire to engage with other people in a way that adds warmth, intimacy, and connection to a retail encounter, but doesn't add friction at the same time. Your task as you move forward with implementing easy to access ideas will be to make sure you hold onto the right balance of human interaction. It's tempting to automate everything, and if you've read Yuval Harari's books, it may seem that automation is inevitable (with potentially terrifying side effects for humanity). Every piece of research we've ever done on customer experience, though, points to humans liking humans. That doesn't mean you can't repurpose those humans to more meaningful jobs, like helping customers vs. mechanically taking their orders. But it does mean you probably don't want to dehumanize every aspect of the customer interaction for the sake of ease. Removing humans from every customer interaction will always be a mistake.

Ease Safari

Now it's time to apply your learnings and evaluate your brand on how well it delivers on ease, relative to its competitors. For this exercise, you'll be going on an Ease Safari.

For this example, we'll have you walk through the purchase of your own product and your competitor's as well. The objective is twofold. First, to compare the friction of the purchase of your product vs. your competitor's. Next, find friction that exists in both cases. Is there an opportunity to create a disruptive innovation that eliminates the friction and becomes a competitive advantage for you? This exercise can be done for a product that is sold at a store or online. It can also be done for a retailer. You will be looking for both physical friction points, especially if you're a retailer (too many clicks, multiple decisions in the ordering process, etc.), and psychological friction (that feeling of confusion, fear, or doubt as you're going through the ordering process. Stuff like, "Is this the right size frozen meal for a family of four?" or "Which version is better, ultra, super, or extra?"). You'll fill out the Ease Safari rubric on the next page to help you size up your purchasing journey.

- First, decide on the main channel that you'd like to test for this exercise. This could be your own website, your brick-and-mortar store, a retailer or aggregator website that sells your product, convenience store, grocery, and so on.
- You will test the same channel for your product and your competitor's product. For example, if you decide to test delivery, you'll be testing your brand's delivery experience with your competitor's delivery experience.
- Next, choose the competitor brand you'll be comparing your brand to. Write both your brand and your competitor's brand in the boxes at the top of the scoring chart.
- Now comes the fun part. As a "real" consumer, go ahead and go through the entire shopping experience with your own brand, and then with your competitor's brand.
- As you go through each part of the consumer decision journey, keep track of how much friction or pain you experience as a consumer of that brand.

EASE SAFARI DIAGRAM

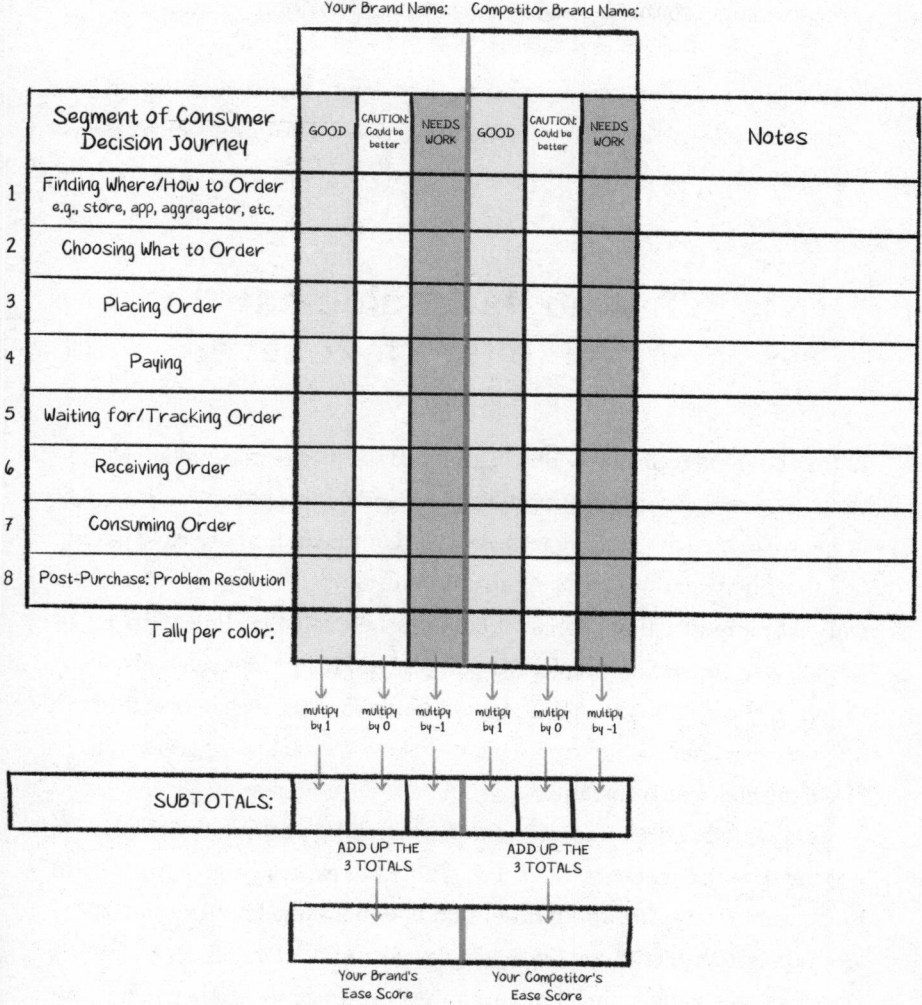

FIGURE 8.2

Fill out the Ease Safari rubric (Figure 8.2) to document your experience by placing a check (✓) to indicate which of the following best represents your experience:

Green Zone: none or almost no friction. The brand is doing well.

Yellow Zone: some friction. The brand could be doing a better job.

Red Zone: severe friction at one or more points that causes serious doubt or exasperation in the ordering process. The brand definitely needs more work on this.

Taking Psychological Friction to the Next Level

In the above exercise, we briefly introduced the idea of psychological frictions. They are the uncomfortable pauses and doubts you sometimes feel going through a purchasing journey. The confusion that arises at having to choose between similar-sounding options or the sense of anxiety that's caused by knowing that people are standing behind you in line. We reached out to Rory Sutherland, to get his perspective. He's the vice chairman of Ogilvy in the UK and the cofounder of a behavioral science unit within the agency. He walked us through what he believes to be Uber's greatest psychological friction innovation.

"Why is using Uber less stressful than catching a cab? Surprisingly, it's not the speed at which the Uber shows up! The reality is that if you were to look around for a cab, you'd often find one more quickly than you would an Uber. But as people, we find great comfort in predictability, and that's Uber's magic. Request one and not only do you know exactly when it will show up, you can actually see where they are on the map as they're heading toward you. They've eliminated the discomfort of unpredictability."

It is exactly these sorts of psychological friction innovations you should be looking for in your purchasing journey. A great place to start is Rory's book *Alchemy*, but we also recommend spending some time on a Wikipedia entry titled "List of Cognitive Biases." Believe it or not, it's one of the most readily accessible, yet comprehensive sources we've found that pulls together a lot of these quirks.

Find Your Disruptive Ease Opportunity

There are massive ease innovations waiting to be discovered in your product, guaranteed. Sometimes uncovering them requires coming at a problem sideways and finding opportunities in the seemingly smaller elements of your business. In the 1980s, Taco Bell—and every other QSR—was trying to both streamline costs *and* improve the customer experience. The team pondered packaging, recipes, and staffing. They chewed over tweaking the way orders were assembled. And then one guy pulled out his calculator, did some calculations, and said, "We're losing millions of labor hours filling soda orders. And for what? We're just slowing people's orders down. Let's just turn the machine around, let customers fill their own soda orders, and save ourselves millions [this has turned into billions over time now]." Stunned silence: This was one minute of sheer brilliance that translated into a radical and disruptive shift in the QSR category. Forever. Across nearly every country in the world. Customers loved it immediately, and they embraced creating their own custom blends, going back for refills, and enjoying the hygiene benefits of fewer hands handling their beverages.

So, how do you replicate this kind of "a-ha" moment in your own business or category?

The first is straightforward. Gather people from across your organization. If you're a small business and it's you and your spouse or partner, that's great! If you're part of a bigger organization, then bring in frontline employees, product developers, delivery managers, marketing and PR team members, and IT specialists. It's even better if members of these groups can mingle and share insights with each other (remember the Collider Lab theory that states that the biggest innovations come when disparate groups collide with each other). Go through the entire consumer decision journey, from the first moment your customer wonders, "What's for dinner?" to the completion of the purchase. On a whiteboard, or using Post-its, identify every small moment of friction. It could be something as simple as the difficulty of verifying that all parts of a large order are in the bag, or anticipating a smelly spill in your car if your order falls off the seat on the drive home. You can consider ways to help busy parents calculate the complete nutritional content of a custom meal. Once you've identified your sources of friction, try the same exercise with your competitors, and rank how you did vs. those competitors.

Then, come up with different ideas to skip around each of these steps.

Every moment of friction is a potential opportunity. Look back at our soda example. In retrospect it is a stunningly simple innovation to solve a nagging moment of friction in the order process. Interestingly, there was nothing problematic about the old-fashioned way of serving a soda behind the counter. Customers accepted it as the status quo, employees were used to doing it, and it wasn't a problem beyond the fact that it was adding seconds to the completion of an order. Part of ease is finding opportunities in the things that are "working fine." This is where talking with your frontline employees is essential. Another takeaway from ease is that ease innovations are often mutually beneficial, simplifying life for the person selling a product, and improving the product for the person making the purchase.

Are there moments in your customer purchasing decision where you could turn over part of your employees' responsibilities to the customer in a way that is mutually beneficial, and feels like a service enhancement to your customer? Think about how the process of using a credit card has evolved from handing over your card to a sales rep, to doing the entire swipe and sign process without any human contact with the employee.

Is This a Good Investment?

Say you discover an ease opportunity. The next question is determining whether this is something you should respond to or not. We have a very simple way to answer that question: if there is a disruption in your category that makes it fundamentally easier to get your product, you should invest immediately (see the Blockbuster and Netflix example). Aggregators such as PostMates, Just Eat, and FoodPanda are controversial in the restaurant business, but, applying the formula, we realize that, yes, food aggregators are making the customer journey fundamentally easier, which points to the idea of aggregated ordering and delivery being an innovation that likely has its place in the modern world (if they can figure out financials that make sense). If your ease innovation comes back with the observation that people are switching to curated menus, complex order personalization, and bespoke presentation, then no, don't invest in it. It needs to be fundamentally easier to deserve your investment.

Easy to Access Questions

- What friction is your customer experiencing when buying your product?
- How can you anticipate and reduce friction? Will a subscription model work, or predictive ordering?
- Can you simplify pricing and fees to remove anxiety or confusion about cost?
- Can you identify that specific friction that gives your customer an opportunity to end the purchasing decision? How can you fill that space with something engaging enough to continue the purchasing process?
- Can you align with other categories to "piggyback" on their ease? For instance, Taco Bell partnering with Lyft for a late-night, en-route snack opportunity.

- Can you deliver directly to the customer, even when they are out in public rather than at home or at their workplace?
- Can you create a default choice to speed up the ordering process?
- Can you preselect products for your customer, based on their preferences? For instance, Emirates partnering with Spotify to select the perfect travel destination for their passengers based on those individuals' playlists.
- Can you allow your customers to virtually experience what you are selling, with zero commitment? For instance, apps that simulate pieces of furniture within your home. Or makeup, "try before you buy," with Rimmel and other brands.
- Can you create specific sales media for your product, such as GM's built-in e-commerce marketplace on their dashboards?
- Can you eliminate wait times?

Easy to Access Conclusion

One final example of the power of ease. WhatsApp noticed something concerning during 2020. People were using the app's "message forwarding" feature to send conspiracy videos to their entire contacts list. These theories, often centered around demonizing the very people and entities who were trying to solve the crisis, were literally going viral. WhatsApp realized they had a problem—and that if they were credibly accused of censorship they would have another, albeit different, problem (their parent company, Facebook, chose this path, but resolved to flag similar content as conspiratorial or unverified news). Instead of censoring the forwarded information, WhatsApp tweaked their settings so that any link that WhatsApp categorized as "highly forwarded" could only be forwarded to individuals, rather than groups. By adding friction to messaging, WhatsApp was able to slow down the spread of conspiratorial theories, and give truth a chance to catch up with the falsehoods. It remains to be seen how much control citizens are willing to accept, but the lesson is clear: if you make the sharing more difficult, there will be less sharing.

So, friction can be used both ways. Cut it to speed things up, add to it to slow things down. Amazon took a very similar approach to WhatsApp during coronavirus. With too many homebound social isolators ordering everything from Toilet Golf to Bacon Floss (yes, the products are what their titles suggest), they had to slow things down to prioritize more essential items like thermometers and biohazard bags. So they literally slowed things down by adding weeks of delivery time to your "critical" Toilet Golf order, and even removed some brilliant friction-reducing up-selling tactics like "customers who ordered this item also ordered the following." Even if you're not experiencing a pandemic, ease is ripe for creative innovation to influence consumer behavior.

9

Easy to Notice

"I've learned that people will forget what you said, people will forget what you did, but people will never forget how you made them feel."

—MAYA ANGELOU

T HIS CHAPTER IS about a quality we call *easy to notice* (see Figure 9.1). Easy to notice is primarily about the efficacy of your media: Is the mix of radio, TV, online, out of home, and print ads working to get your brand noticed? And is the creative breaking through and memorable? More importantly, will your product be at the top of your consumer's mind the next time she has to make a purchasing decision? As we move through this chapter, we'll discuss ways to make your product mentally available.

Why is this important? Let's suppose that you make clothing. Specifically, let's say you focus on active wear for runners. Your average customer will only buy your product once or twice a year. So, how are you going to make sure that when your customer is in the market for some running shorts, she is thinking of you? If you listen to your social media

R.E.D.

EASY TO NOTICE:

1. USING MASS MEDIA TO REACH ALL CATEGORY USERS WITH A...
2. BREAKTHROUGH CREATIVE THAT CAUSES AN EMOTIONAL REACTION...

TikTok

ONE OF THE BIGGEST DIGITAL PLATFORMS IN THE WORLD IS ADVERTISING ON TV.

...BECAUSE

1. ADVERTISING WORKS BY BUILDING MEMORY STRUCTURES IN LOTS OF PEOPLE OVER TIME, WHICH ARE ACTIVATED WHEN THE NEED ARISES.
2. MESSAGES THAT CAUSE AN EMOTIONAL REACTION ARE BETTER REMEMBERED.

FIGURE 9.1

sales reps, they'll tell you that you need to focus on highly targeted advertising to people who are looking for shorts at that precise moment. They'll promise that they can deliver your message to a very narrow group of people, something like female runners in their forties with a special eye for style and currently in need of shorts.

Unfortunately, this strategy of highly targeted niche marketing is usually nonsense. We've done a deep-dive analysis of several of our businesses around the world with the help of an agnostic marketing attribution company.[1] These types of companies take all of your sales data and match it up very carefully with all of your media spend, using some pretty advanced modeling. In country after country, we've found the same thing: on average, we pay about a $5 CPM ($5 "Cost per Mille," or in normal talk, $5 to reach one thousand people with a message) using broad-reaching media, while our highly targeted media can regularly cost $25 to reach a supposedly more refined group of one thousand people. In one case, in Canada, we discovered we were paying $118 CPM! And here's the real catch: while we were paying an average of five times the cost, the media was only about two times as effective. We don't claim to be math geniuses (Ken's math is nearly as bad as Greg's spelling), but this does seem like an absurd bargain. If we're paying five times more to reach people, the campaign would have to be five times as effective for it to make sense.

In every analysis we did around the world, we never once saw an ROI that made any sense. It has become clear to us that the pressure we were putting on our media investment was ridiculous when we were doing precision targeting. There is no way we're getting enough in additional sales to make up for 500 percent more in media costs. And before you say that a $25 CPM sounds unnaturally high and you have a cheaper way to target with precision, do a true calculation of your actual cost. Factor in the price of all the martech and adtech junk you had to use and the additional labor hours it took to create these complicated campaigns. You'll quickly find $25 CPM is a lowball estimate.

Highly targeted media almost never pays out, mostly because it's incredibly expensive. Then why, oh why, is the ad and marketing world in love with this approach?

Two reasons:

1. FOMO. They see their competitors and other marketing brethren doing it, so it must be right and what will my CEO say

if I'm not doing it? That I'm old school? That I don't
understand the new world of marketing?

2.   Marketingland has fallen in love with the siren song of
     short-term sales and activations. We say siren song because if
     you chase that goal too hard and too single-mindedly, you're
     going to smash your brand on the proverbial rocks in the long
     term. Let us explain.

Advertising works by creating memory structures in people's minds so
that when the need arises for a product or service in your category, that
memory structure is activated and they think of your product or service
before your competitors'. You create these memory structures by targeting all your category users with consistent campaigns, delivered over the
long term. The more memorable and consistent the advertising, the
stronger the memory structure. The greater number of people that have
your brand's memory structures in their mind, the more sales.

What highly targeted media promises, however, is something else entirely. The purveyors of these products pitch the idea that, instead of
building memory structures in lots of people's minds, you simply have to
appear at the exact right moment with the exact right message for the
exact right individual, and they'll buy your product. The industry has absolutely loved this mirage of an idea! First, the folks that sell the extremely
expensive media make a killing, then the companies that sell the extremely expensive tools to create these highly refined targets make a killing, and finally, the CFOs at the brands can finally sleep at night knowing
that they have a clear measure of what their media dollars are actually
doing. The CMO, at least in the short term, can also feel like a winner because he's being a "modern marketer"! But then, of course, the whole
house of cards comes crumbling down a few months later when sales start
suffering. Why? Basically, you've chosen to stop building your brand, stop
reinforcing memory structures in lots of consumers' minds, and instead
placed all your bets on short-term activation with far fewer consumers.
Time to update that resume!

Why is highly targeted media so dangerous to long-term sales? Angela Richards, a brilliant media-minded director of marketing at KFC in Australia, is quick to point out that,

> At its core, what highly targeted media promises is zero wastage, or at least less wastage. In other words, targeting promises it will reach only the people that are in the market for your product and no one else (i.e., no media dollars are "wasted" on other, random people who aren't currently interested in your offer). Even if this were possible, it's incredibly important to understand that wastage is not actually waste!

What Angela means by this goes back to the previous paragraph: long-term sales and real brand growth comes from creating memory structures in lots and lots of people's minds. Precision targeting focuses only on the few that are supposedly in the market for your product at that very moment. So what the Highly Targeted People would consider waste (consumers not in the market right now) is not waste at all! They are the consumers who are going to buy your product in three months. (Or were, before you decided to stop messaging them and instead sink all your money into that cool targeting thing with Facebook.) This is where you have to be careful with your Marketing Mix Attribution analysis. Too much efficiency is a bad thing.

Now, let's say you're fine with paying five times the price to target your message for some reason. Would dumping everything into the highly targeted approach still be a mistake? Yes! Remember way back in chapter five where we talked about Douglas Holt's point about successful brands being imbued with meaning? That meaning is what makes Nike more than some random company that makes shoes. Nike means Michael Jordan and *Just Do It*. Nike means belonging to the herd of cool sneakerheads, and Nike means progressive-minded athletes who break conventions. That meaning is what makes Nike such an incredibly valuable brand. Well, that meaning is created in culture, in social moments, in broad, loud public spaces, and, of course, in advertising that uses broad-reaching media so that it can be seen by culture and the public. It's not created in Jim's Insta-feed with a message about how comfortable the shoe will fit his size 10½ foot with a flat arch.

So What Works?

If targeted niche marketing isn't the golden ticket to increased sales, what is? In nearly every single real analysis we've done around the world, our marketing attribution partners have come back with the same result: dump those narrowly targeted $25 CPMs whose ROIs don't make any sense, and instead invest in much lower-cost, widely targeted media that gives you, get this, real brand growth over the long term. So yes, we are believers in low-cost media that targets all or nearly all of the consumers in your category, even if that means "wastage."

KFC in Australia is an absurdly successful brand—one that both Greg and Catherine Tan-Gillespie used to run personally. The team there attributes a significant part of that success to their media strategy. Again, Angela:

> Over the years, we've deliberately changed our media and communications planning. We truly embrace media as a brand investment in who will buy in the next two years. To create shared cultural meaning and mental availability, we need people *outside* the immediate purchase opportunity to understand us so that when it comes time for them to indulge in some delicious fried chicken, we are the first brand they think of and the last brand they have seen.

So, is there *ever* a role for hyper-targeted media? We reached out to one of our favorite writers on the topic, Shann Biglione, who has led strategy at several large media agencies around the world. Shann does believe there is a role for highly targeted media, but cautions that you have to go into this with eyes wide open, a desire for experimentation and learning, and a laser-clear objective.

Generally, personalization is far from a sure bet for brands, especially if the purchase is serendipitous and low involvement—a reality for a majority of consumer brands. Where the act of buying is more planned with more layers to the decision process, then it can work to a degree. Likewise, categories with a high cost of acquisition might find it easier to justify the costs involved. In the case of cars, for instance, playing to the several rational factors consumers are researching can be profitable. Then the higher CPMs can make more sense. The key is to keep a very close eye on the real cost of the endeavor—the tech, the creative work, the corporate hours spent making it happen, etc. Always ask yourself, "Is the juice worth the squeeze?" If not, then don't do it.

Now, here's the next argument we hear from marketers. "Okay," they say, "I won't target thirty-eight-year-old suburban moms with golden retrievers at $45 CPMs, but if I look at my surveys, 20 percent of my consumers are responsible for 80 percent of my sales! Surely focusing my media on those heavy users is a no-brainer, right?" Well, Byron Sharp's work questions the validity and notion of acting upon the 80/20 rule (known as the Pareto Law). If you base your marketing strategy on this philosophy, it would seem to make sense to target your heavy users on Facebook. Why worry about the other 80 percent if they are only buying your product once or twice a year? Instead, focus all your energy on the 20 percent who make the bulk of your sales. It's a similar argument to the niche targeting one above: target a smaller segment that will supposedly be more profitable to you.

Unfortunately, although it seems logical, this thinking is also a trap, and one that can paint your brand into a corner. As Sharp's math readily points out, your light users are incredibly important for your brand's growth, often representing up to 50 percent of your sales if you measure it correctly. But we also believe there is another, more nuanced reason why targeting only your heavy users could lead to the long-term decay of your brand.

Recently we worked with a well-known name in the health and wellness category. They had coasted for years on selling the bulk of their products to a small fraction of the population. Let's call these buyers "extreme users." This was fine for years, but eventually health and wellness evolved. The category moved away from the hard-core, gym rat workout mentality, and toward a more Goop-y, plant medicine, and Moon Juice vision of wellness. Now, our client was stuck. They had tailored their brand and their message (their cultural relevance, if you will) to extreme users for decades. They had ignored every other group of potential customers, ignored all the emerging cultural codes in the category, and inadvertently made their brand feel unfriendly and unwelcoming toward the burgeoning holistic wellness community, despite having plenty of products this community wanted to buy in their stores. Our client had fallen into what we call the Pareto trap, and revealed a dangerous side effect of pursuing only your heavy users. One day trends will change, and your extreme users will die out, replaced by people who are actively repelled by your product mix, marketing, messaging, or branding. (We argue that this is why heritage automotive brands like Lincoln and Cadillac have also struggled.)

The biggest point, however, is what we mention above: the idea that you rely on 20 percent of potential customers, and ignore 80 percent (or 50/50, depending on the Pareto Law math you believe in), means you're actively avoiding light buyers, who will only purchase your category a fraction of the time heavier users do. These light buyers, though, are an incredibly important part of your business today, and may become an even more important one tomorrow as some of them become heavier users. Users can change from year to year, even though most marketers assume their behavior remains consistent.

The Law of Buyer Moderation explains that heavy users tend to become lighter users, while light users tend to become heavier users.[2] Why? Because life changes. One year you're single and having fun and a heavy user of airlines, rental cars, and tequila as you discover the world, and the next you have kids and don't board a plane once in the entire year. Not that we're bitter. So, rather than rely on your extreme users, it's savvier to target *all* your potential users, and keep your brand salient with them all. Once you understand this concept, the idea of spending five times normal rates to target likely buyers with niche marketing makes less sense. Instead, you need to reach all buyers, cost effectively, with a memorable and distinctive message, so those potential customers build up a set of memory structures related to your product that can trigger a sale when the need arises. You want to pay the lowest cost possible to reach the most users of your category possible.

The enemy is not social media, though, and in fact the CPMs can be lower for paid social than TV depending on the country you're in. The potential enemy *is* some folks trying to sell you hyper-targeted marketing. Most of the time, these individuals are connected to digital display media or one of those cool adtech or martech gizmos, and they vastly overpromise returns. Time and time over, though, mass audiences prove to have a higher ROI, especially over the long term. It's one of the reasons TV is still king in many situations. The Senior VP for Marketing at AMEX explained to *Ad Age* in 2016 that TV is still vital to their marketing, and that one day of broadcast is equivalent to two weeks of digital.[3] Even more telling, one of the hottest digital properties in the world in 2020, TikTok, is currently running sixty-second ads on . . . you guessed it, television.

The question, then, becomes when and how is it appropriate to use one-to-one marketing? We think of advertising and media as having at least two main roles. One is building those memory structures in lots and lots of people. The other is conversion, or triggering an immediate sale. One-to-one does a good job of the latter with a small group of consumers, and you could invest a small portion of your budget in doing that. Sasha Wolfe, Taco Bell's Director of Media, explains, using a potential dishwasher sale as an example,

> If you do a great job of making your product top of mind but when someone is actually in need of a dishwasher you are absent, you may miss out on a sale since specs and other functional info may be important at that time. If you only focus on the conversion piece, you miss out. But if you do both and in the right balance, you may be unlocking something interesting.

What is the right balance? That depends on your category and the role the rest of your media is playing. But we firmly believe that in nearly every case the *vast* majority of your media should be building those memory structures with all category buyers.

If you reject the niche marketing mirage, and use mass media as your centerpiece, you have a better chance of ensuring that your potential customers have been exposed to messages about your brand.

And that's only half the equation. It's not enough that she saw your TV spot, or online campaign. It needs to have made enough of an impression that she remembers it, and when the soles of her running shoes finally wear out, or her dishwasher finally shudders to a halt for the last time, your product is at the top of her mind.

Make It Memorable

We've mentioned salience repeatedly throughout this book. The root of the word salience is the Latin verb *salire*, meaning "to leap, jump, or dance." A salient idea, memory, or image will literally leap to the front of your mind, seemingly unprompted and out of nowhere. Of course, this isn't really true, and we will explore how and why the brain remembers some things and not others in the next few pages. The important thing to consider throughout this chapter is that when an idea or an image is very mentally available it raises the level of importance of that idea or image in your mind. Because this memory is easily accessible (or salient), you perceive it to be important. So, when your dishwasher breaks down, and an image of a kindly Maytag Man jumps into your mind, you trust yourself to have paid more attention to the most relevant product. You now give that brand priority over all the other dishwasher brands.[4]

Emotional Response as Marketing Magic

Once you understand salience, the next question is, "How do I create a salient campaign?" The answer to this question is in the science of what memory is, and why people remember certain moments more easily than others. As you read through, remember that R.E.D. views emotion differently from most marketing strategies. We are not concerned with creating an emotional connection. We are only concerned with creating an emotional *response*.

Our understanding of how our memory works is still evolving.[5] It is generally believed that our ability to experience distressing emotions like fear and anxiety gives us an evolutionary advantage, warning us of dangers and compelling us to behave more carefully than we might have otherwise. Warmer emotions, like love and joy, allow us to bond with each other, and tighten the social structures that have kept us safe in a dangerous world. One study suggests that even heartbreak has an evolutionary advantage, teaching us resilience and fortitude in the face of emotional devastation.[6] In the context of R.E.D., *which* emotions are affecting us are less important than the fact that we are being affected by them.

No matter the reasons and the methods, our lives are shaped by our emotions, and our emotional responses to external events. These emotions affect how we remember our lives as well, because a memory that is tied to an emotional response becomes more mentally accessible, and easier to recall.

Think of a memory in which you were deeply afraid. Perhaps you lost sight of your child for a few, agonizing, minutes. You can probably recall your surroundings, perhaps the sounds and smells of a summer day. Along with that, you might relive the physical sensation of your heart pounding, your palms sweating, and your brain's hyper-alert state. Psychologists call this phenomenon flashbulb memories: we clearly remember details such as what we were doing, eating, or wearing when those specifics are linked to emotionally significant (often shocking or surprising) events. I'm guessing you know exactly where you were when you heard the first news about a plane crash on 9/11/01; however, do you have any crystal-clear memories of what you were doing the morning of 9/10/01?[7] Probably not.

Some memories, perhaps the birth of a child, the fear of coronavirus, the death of a parent, a World Cup win, or a marriage proposal received with joy, are permanent. All those other moments—the long commutes, leftovers for dinner, and that same dumb fight with your spouse—fall away over the years. It's those moments that are linked to a defined emotional response (rather than a general sense of happiness or sadness) that stick. As marketers, we can use this psychological phenomenon to create a lasting memory in a customer's mind. If you are able to link your ad with an emotional response, then the memory of that marketing impression stays salient. When your customer is prompted, perhaps by that first ominous rattle coming from her aging Kitchenaid, the emotional link to your ad makes her memory of it easier to access. She remembers, seemingly out of nowhere, laughing at the tagline, or perhaps feeling a tug of sadness at a poignant or bittersweet story line. *What* she feels doesn't matter. It could even be disgust, perhaps at a joke she considered in poor taste. Maybe your lead actor reminded her of her ex-husband and she felt a flash of anger. That's okay. All that matters is that she remembers your spot, and, right as her dishwasher goes dark for good, she is typing the name of your brand into her search bar.

How to Trigger
That Emotional Response

Easy to notice is understanding that humans are deeply lazy, and that we will buy the product that is physically most accessible *and* most salient in our mind.

Now that you've built the right media plan and are creating break-through work by ensuring your creative causes an emotional reaction, we can talk about the next, trickiest bit: making it distinctive. Distinctiveness is the second ingredient to salience. It's so important, in fact, that we've broken it out into a separate letter (D) and series of chapters. Several modern marketing theorists will break ease into two ideas, mental and physical availability, and call it a day. But we find that problematic. When you do this, marketers tend to discount the importance of distinctiveness. They assume that by simply having a great media plan and creating a breakthrough message that causes an emotional response, they're doing everything they need to do to create an effective message. This is the kind of stuff that wins in advertising festivals around the world: the one, brilliant, quirky, and hilarious TV spot. Unfortunately, in many cases, these tend to be commercial failures because they're missing the most important ingredient: distinctiveness.

We define distinctiveness as the unique, ownable, and, most importantly, consistent use of distinctive brand assets. Without this bit, all your smart media and breakthrough creative just won't do much. People will see your ad and laugh, sure, but they'll fail to remember who the advertiser was. As a matter of fact, most ads globally are attributed to the wrong brand. That's the effect of not having distinctive work, and why we break out D as a separate section of its own. It's that important.

— 10 —

Distinctiveness Mythbusting

O NCE UPON A time, products were simply options that sat on a shelf. A consumer's choice was minimal, often with only a small range of options between various cereals or other goods. Some categories were not so much marketed as they were enhanced with an additional functional benefit. From the 1800s to the 1940s, grain, food staples, and other perishable items were often sold to farm wives in printed cotton sacks that the women could repurpose as fabric for clothing or quilts. Eventually, product manufacturers and marketers realized they could differentiate their products by promoting some advantage to their brand over all their competitors and thereby encourage consumers to buy their box of cereal or other goods. This would seem to make sense, but as we've learned—and hopefully you have, too—consumers don't buy products for rational reasons.

Byron Sharp is probably the most famous marketing guru to criticize this concept of differentiation. He stated that when brands seek to differentiate themselves, they miss the fact that consumers are more swayed by distinctiveness than differentiation. As you probably realize by now, we love Byron Sharp. Sharp's message is beginning to take, and marketers increasingly accept that trying to make rational appeals to consumers about the various attributes of their products doesn't move the needle on sales. Here's where we've developed Sharp's work, and added our own Collider Lab spin, to make it more practical. We think marketers are still focusing their energies on the wrong problem when it comes to trying to create salience for their brand and getting it to stand out in the marketplace. Their mistake is focusing on the *what* rather than the *how*.

> The *what* is your message, and the case you are making for your product, be it emotionally, culturally, or rationally.

> The *how* is your distinctiveness. Are you sharing your message in a way that will build salience?

In the upcoming chapters we will break down the elements of distinctive: *unique*, *ownable*, and *consistent*. For now, though, let's focus on brands that have succeeded by creating what we call distinctive brand worlds, and conversely, why some marketers are still relying on refining, focus grouping, and tweaking their messages but neglecting the element of their message that actually matters, *how* you say it. We can't overstate how fundamental this mistake is. We've worked with dozens of major brands over our combined sixty years in marketing, and in the vast majority of cases, marketers obsess endlessly over the precise messaging and then simply hand off the *how* to an agency, cross their fingers, and hope for the best.

As we've mentioned before, we work closely with Wieden+Kennedy in Portland. They are one of the most awarded and celebrated advertising agencies in the world. They have created some of the most famous campaigns in history: Old Spice, the KFC Colonel campaign, Nike, and Bud Light's "Dilly Dilly." The list goes on and on. They've also been named "*Ad Age*'s #1 A-List Agency of the Year" in 2018, 2019, and 2020. We believe a big reason for this is their insistent focus on distinctiveness. While trying to decode why they are so successful, Britton Taylor, one of their brilliant directors of strategy, explained to us,

> When it comes to making advertising, there are a few different places you can start. You can begin with a consumer insight. Or you can start with a category insight. But what makes W+K special is that we almost always start with the brand. What's the truth of this brand? What makes it special? When was it at its best? When we have a new piece of business, we typically dive into the archives long before we do anything else. We're looking for the truth and the magic. When you find it, the trick is to figure out how to bring it to life in a new, interesting, and provocative way. This is our secret sauce for distinctiveness.

Frankly, it's such a fundamental lever in advertising, it boggles our minds how few ad agencies get it. We can't begin to tell you the number of meetings either of us has been in when the agency has presented "a whole new, exciting direction for the brand" that has nothing to do with what made the brand successful to begin with. As Kristi Woolrych, the CMO of KFC in Australia, points out, "Consistency is harder—we get bored of ourselves faster than consumers do—but it pays off in the long run." Still, it's a small minority of advertising pros that understand the importance of this approach. Even more depressing is when we see a new CMO start at a brand and immediately dump their distinctiveness. It's usually the self-serving, short-term mindset of the CMO that drives this sort of decision, and it rarely serves the brand well in the long run.

Remember back to the beginning of the book where we talked about how we wanted to do things differently at Collider Lab. One of our new beliefs was that it is better to be distinctively off than blandly okay. If you are noodling around for weeks or months, trying to refine the perfect message, trying to uncover the deepest, most obscure consumer insight imaginable, you are never going to be distinctive. We see brands all the time who have spent months refining the messaging, passed it along to their agency, received options, and, by the time the whole process is finished, have work so bland it's utterly worthless. It is better to commit to a concept that is distinctive, even if slightly flawed, than to settle on a compromise so insipid it does nothing at all.

It goes back to that Y in the road we talked about earlier. If you think consumers are rational, then sure, spending months refining your message makes sense. If you realize consumers are irrational and are driven by a series of biases and heuristics (subconscious mental shortcuts like "what brand stands out most in my mind"), then those months of noodling were wasted energy. In nearly every case, devoting more energy and effort to distinctiveness is what pays off.

One way to do that is to focus on your brand world, and make sure that it is distinctive and compelling. Look at Away Bags. Yes, they've had some Slack-related CEO drama, but they took a product that was essentially the same as their competitors (i.e., Samsonite) and created a brand world that was pretty distinctive: an alluring, global-minded, young, hip, and fashion-forward brand world. Now, bear in mind that when they describe their actual product features they are touting much the same benefits as the legacy luggage brands. However, they worry less about describing how the product works and more about exploring the relatively distinctive #globaltraveler lifestyle that makes them feel unique.

Taco Bell has a very defined brand world: rebel, explorer, and entertainer. It also helps that the product, Mexican-inspired fast food, is distinctive in itself. Disney World's brand, the Magic Kingdom, is more important than any of the individual products they sell. You simply have to mention the name to a consumer for them to access a memory structure about what Disney is, what kind of experience it offers, and whether they want to go there.

Distinctiveness is critical because 80 percent of marketers spend most of their time trying to nail that differentiation message of why you would choose a legacy luggage brand over Away, or another theme park over Disney. Instead, they should be focusing on doing what those two brands do so well, creating that distinctive brand world identity, which makes the product so instantly memorable for the consumer. Back to the Y in the road: this is another opportunity for you to understand and respond to the arm of the Y that will allow you to create an emotional reaction and build salience.

Like all elements of R.E.D., distinctiveness is not enough on its own. Your distinctiveness must also have relevance, and ease. Years ago, Greg and Taco Bell had a ton of success with a promotion called the Volcano Taco, a bright orange taco with extra hot sauce. They decided to push the idea of colored food, and launch the Black Jack Taco, complete with pepper jack cheese to ramp up the spiciness. They filmed a sophisticated spot, with a glamorous palette of black and white, and launched. The taco sold pretty well, but there was no incrementality. Meaning, the promotion succeeded with existing Taco Bell consumers, but didn't bring in *new* consumers, or persuade the existing ones to ramp up the frequency of their visits to Taco Bell.

Here's the problem with the Black Jack Taco: it was very distinctive, but there was no cultural relevance. A casual Taco Bell user was happy to try it, but it didn't align him with any specific herd. The concept wasn't exciting enough to be socially relevant, and our franchisees actively disliked it because it required extra steps for their employees to assemble the order. However, it was still a valuable learning experience. Taco Bell does nine or ten promotions a year, and part of the process is to religiously review the promotions once they are completed in order to understand what succeeded or failed. That discipline paid off. We were able to understand that the Black Jack Taco didn't work because, while it was highly distinctive, it wasn't relevant. In the end, we took the core idea of colored and flavored taco shells and partnered with Doritos to make the Doritos Locos Taco, a huge hit. (If you're confused about whether to prioritize your R, your D, or your E, we'll give you a simple strategy in the final chapter to figure this out.)

So, make sure you are distinctive, but make sure you're also relevant, and that you're adding, rather than subtracting, ease at every turn.

— 11 —

Distinctiveness

A S WE'VE MOVED through the book, we've explored how the different facets of R.E.D. work: Relevance is about making sure your product is relevant to your customers' needs, and to their lives, and allows them to align with the herds that best represent them. Ease is about making sure your product is both easy to find and use, and stays at the forefront of your customer's mind. The final piece of the puzzle is distinctiveness (see Figure 11.1). Being distinctive is about making sure that your product stands out, won't be mistaken for a competing brand in your category, and maintains a consistent voice that is visually and emotionally unmistakable.

The three elements of distinctive are:

1. Unique (especially in your category)
2. Ownable (you can realistically own it for the long term)

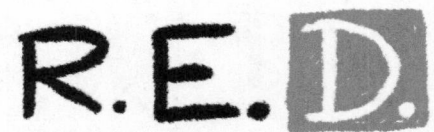

DISTINCTIVENESS:

BRANDS THAT USE UNIQUE OWNABLE AND CONSISTENT ASSETS AT EVERY TOUCHPOINT BECOME DISTINCTIVE AND STAND OUT CLEARLY IN CONSUMERS' MINDS.

KFC US

KFC US'S CONSISTENT USE OF COLONEL SANDERS HAS LED TO INCREASED SALIENCE AND SALES.

... BECAUSE PEOPLE TEND TO BUY THE BRANDS THAT THEY MOST EASILY RECALL. SIMPLE AS THAT.

FIGURE 11.1

3. Consistent (visually and emotionally, across touchpoints and across time)

These elements add up to create a distinctive world that is salient, easy to remember, and aligned with an emotional reaction. Your distinctive assets are what help build memory structures, something that is critical to successful marketing, but woefully underappreciated.

A memory structure within marketing is a consumer's long-term awareness and familiarity with a brand that has been built up over the years and decades and that is triggered by specific distinctive assets. This can be the physical appearance of a product: a vintage Coke bottle, a Barbie doll, or the silhouette of any number of cars, from a Mini Cooper to a Porsche. It could be a jingle, or a tagline, or a character who remains consistent, even if the casting changes over the years. It can be a sound (the Snapple "pop" when you open a bottle) or even the way a product feels. For instance, think of the appealingly rough "peel" texture of a glass Orangina bottle in your hand (the unique shape of the bottle is itself highly distinctive).[1]

Academics have thrown huge amounts of money at understanding what they call *sensory marketing*, debating the wisdom of doubling down on a noisy product like potato chips by putting it in equally noisy packaging, or determining whether it is possible to tell a can of Coke from a can of Pepsi, simply by listening to the hiss of the escaping gas when you pull the tab. Investigating whether icy-cold beer sounds more appealing when poured than merely cold beer is a legitimate thing to study. However, the R.E.D. approach is simpler: the only thing that matters is whether these assets are unique, ownable, and consistent—and, in turn, that these elements are used to build memory structure in consumers' minds. Iconic brands and products that have built lasting memory structure by nailing unique, ownable, and consistent include:

Virgin Atlantic. This is one of our favorite examples, and we'll examine it in more detail in the next chapter. In their early years they relied on the buffoonish charm of Richard Branson to market their brand (which led to many photo ops of him manhandling flight attendants on the aircraft stairs in exotic new destinations). More relevantly, they upended every idea of how an airline brands itself by ditching the conventional signifiers of safety and security: soft gray and navy blue color schemes, and a discreet sense of sophistication and luxury. Instead, they created a world full of glamor with scarlet uniforms (designed by punk provocateur Vivienne Westwood), and a purple and red color scheme that gives even the economy class cabin a Studio 54–like decadence. Interestingly, Virgin Atlantic is still a relatively small airline, albeit with outsized salience in flyers' minds. Many of their customers are leisure travelers who fly once or twice a year, max, which makes being distinctive and salient even more crucial, since those flyers aren't going to be focused on earning frequent flyer perks like mileage or status.[2]

KFC. We'll talk more about the Colonel, and how he was rejuvenated as a brand asset in a few pages, but for now, let us just share a quick example. KFC in India was running advertising that had a misattribution rate of about 40 percent. Only 60 percent of people who watched those ads, in other words, correctly identi-fied they were for KFC! That's nearly half of the media going down the drain, or worse, help-ing competitors. Moksh Chopra, the brilliant CMO of KFC India, explains, "The brand advertis-ing in India was not distinct and pretty much mirrored the QSR category code—four friends, a joke, and the food." Once R.E.D. was implemented, they quickly spotted their distinctiveness problem and radically changed their approach. They launched an Indian version of the Colo-nel, doubled down on the iconic  KFC bucket, focused on the brand's colors, and saw their attribution scores soar to 88 percent. The result was instant: KFC India's top of mind recall scores hit their highest level in the brand's history.[3]

Memory Structure

As brand consultants, we are there from the beginning of the marketing process through to the completion of the final campaign. We work with in-house teams to refine what it is they are selling, help as ad agencies get involved, and as the final work is generated. We review creative with the client, advising on subtle tweaks and nuances that might go unnoticed otherwise. Despite our best efforts, the amount of time that is *still* wasted on worrying about emotional connection (not a thing) is obscene. Equally galling: how little time is spent worrying about distinctiveness. We get it. Distinctiveness is not something that is taught to young marketers. They think it's something for the creatives to worry about. The creatives in turn are more focused on generating something new that will differentiate this year's campaign from last, perhaps by changing up a color scheme, retiring a character, or coming up with a new tagline. In 2010, Gap tried to change its logo from the classic blue box and Helvetica font combo into something more "contemporary." Instant, outraged backlash. The new look lasted a week before Gap folded and announced they were returning to their most distinctive asset. Ditto Coke and New Coke.

The marketing world is not built to incorporate or understand the importance of distinctiveness. Research methodologies often miss distinctiveness altogether, even though it is often the most important element in marketing. Tropicana discovered this when they redesigned their logo in 2009, stripping away the distinctive "straw-in-an-orange" design. The rebrand was greeted with anger and derision, and lasted a few months before Tropicana hastily returned to their iconic look. Afterward, the then-president of Tropicana acknowledged that the brand had underestimated how important the straw and orange were to their ultra-loyal users, and that this passion for the iconography had not "come across in research."[4] Mess with your distinctiveness at your peril!

These kinds of changes are usually done for the sake of change itself and will dilute your brand's distinctiveness. Marketers will argue that the changes make the brand more relevant, but we say BS. Though they are both needed to work in concert, distinctiveness beats relevance, so be careful what you change. Many creatives find that their goal of making the client happy, and serving a brand's needs most effectively, is also swayed by the hope of creating something that will look good in their portfolio, and maybe get them that glorious summer trip to Cannes, and an elusive Golden Lion. Let's just say this now: if your ad campaign wins a Golden Lion, you have most likely done a disservice to your brand by severing connections to the past, and coming up with something both new and unnecessary. Now, if you can win at Cannes while sticking to your distinctive brand assets, then you actually deserved that trip to Cannes. You've made something both distinctive and breakthrough (Cannes is only rewarding you for the breakthrough, but the increase in sales is rewarding you for the distinctiveness!). Clients—meaning brands—rarely prioritize consistency in tone and content, but consistency builds salience.

Ignoring your customers' existing memory structures in favor of creating a radically different brand identity in the hope of fostering emotional connection is absurd. Clear your mind for a second, then think, "My family wants fried chicken for dinner tonight." What came into your head? I'm willing to bet that for most of you it was a flash of the Colonel, white suit and all, or some other distinctive asset: maybe the bucket, the color scheme, or the number eleven. It doesn't matter whether KFC is your favorite chicken brand. It's irrelevant if you have a favorite local hole-in-the-wall that makes amazing jerk chicken. When it's up to your brain, your brain goes to the most accessible memory, and the one with a strong emotional reaction. Think of the emotional reaction like a chain, which allows you to pull the memory up from the depths of your subconscious: up comes the Colonel, no matter what your personal preferences or beliefs about food.

Distinctiveness = Correct Attribution

Let's look at another core benefit of distinctiveness that we've only touched on so far: creating a truly distinctive campaign is your best way to ensure that consumers correctly attribute your work to your brand. Misattribution is a huge problem in our industry. A Nielson survey from 2016 found that 75 percent of consumers *cannot* correctly identify the ad and brand the day after watching the ad. At the same time, a proprietary Collider Lab study from 2019 showed us that a highly distinctive campaign will be correctly attributed up to 95 percent of the time (don't ask me who the 5 percent of survey takers that attribute the Colonel to McDonald's are, although we're betting some illicit substances were at play during the survey taking).[5]

This is a key reason why building those long-term memory structures is so important. It's fabulous if your potential customer saw your spot the day before she made a purchase in your category—but if she misattributed your work, then there's a good chance a more salient brand will pop up in her head when she's picking between you and your rival. Suppose you are the CMO of Delta, or American Airlines, and your customer saw your new ad last night, highlighting the joys of visiting London on a clean, sanitized, and efficient 777. Maybe you emphasized the Wi-Fi connectivity, your antiviral cleaning products, or your new leg room options. Right after that, she saw a Virgin Atlantic spot, shot to look like the James Bond opening credits, complete with passengers reclining in a giant martini glass, and being tucked into beds of literal clouds. Do you really think that your sincere attempt to pitch the benefits of an on-time departure, robust disinfectant, and in-air Facebook availability is going to make a dent against that? In fact, a 2017 survey in Australia found that the most remembered TV ad was, "no brand / no ad," meaning that 57 percent of those surveyed couldn't remember an ad they liked. Even worse, 66 percent surveyed were unable to remember an ad they *disliked*—suggesting that viewers were for the most part completely unengaged with the ads they saw.[6] So, if new campaigns aren't connecting, what about revisiting what you've done in the past?

Existing memory structures that stem from distinctive brand assets are amazingly powerful: Fairy dish soap in the UK brought back their vintage packaging for their fiftieth anniversary in 2010. The old-style opaque white bottles with red cap were regularly used on a children's TV show, *Blue Peter*, as materials for building rockets, cars, and other projects. A survey found that 40 percent of adults were reminded of their childhood by the retro bottle. Even more impressively, the adults remembered *what* they had made with the Fairy bottle: 53 percent made a toy rocket, 40 percent made a pencil holder, and 22 percent made a flowerpot. That's a memory structure that has lasted for decades, and it's invaluable.[7] Why would you discount those distinctive memories of childhood, imagination, and adventure (all within the safety of the kitchen, and your mum's loving presence) for "something new"?

We'll discuss these ideas more throughout the chapter, but for now, hold onto the thought that building distinctive brand assets is incredibly valuable. Remember our Y in the road. Once again, you have a choice to make. You can build a strategy around the outdated idea that people are buying your product for a carefully thought-out reason. Or, you can take the other path, and work around the reality that people are choosing your product because of physical and mental availability.

The Problem

There's no way to say this delicately, so let's just jump in: sometimes the problem with sacrificing distinctiveness and ignoring distinctive brand assets comes from the top—usually because a brand-new CMO has been brought in to revive or refresh an ailing brand, and feels huge amounts of pressure to deliver something new and breakthrough, quickly. Greg points out that CMOs feel as much pressure to comply with the rules of their herds as any other groups do. CEOs feel the same pressure. So, when a CEO sees her competitors marketing their purpose, she feels a ton of pressure to do the same. When she instructs her CMO to deliver that purpose, he is going to feel compelled to do just that. It can be incredibly hard to break free of that groupthink that pervades even the highest levels within an organization.

When we are brought on to advise a new CMO, our #1 piece of advice is to dig into the archives, and look for existing distinctive assets. (Stay tuned till the end of this chapter, where we'll guide you through an exercise for determining which distinctive assets are worth working with.) Most brands that have been around for multiple decades have incredible resources to review: old campaigns, old logos, and discarded color schemes or fonts. Dig deeper and you might find brand myths and legends. If you're truly lucky, you'll find characters that are worth exploring. Perhaps the founder was an ornery old fellow with a quirky backstory that can be retold entertainingly for a contemporary audience. As you'll see in the exercise, there are various markers to consider when isolating which asset will help you strengthen or revive memory structures about your brand. For now, though, the main thing to consider is whether they are unique, ownable, and consistent.

Reviving existing assets can be controversial. Perhaps they are burdened by baggage about other aspects of the business that were struggling at the time. They may feel too culturally and socially irrelevant to be worth reviving. However, if you have the vision and fortitude to do the work of sifting through the archives, you may find a new approach for old ideas.

In January of 2014, Kevin Hochman had his own experience of digging deep in the archives when he took over as CMO of KFC. Kevin had a storied career as a marketer. He, along with George Felix and Wieden+Kennedy, was responsible for the resurrection of Old Spice, another brand that leveraged its distinctive assets—manliness, a nautical theme, and the eternal stylishness of tying a sweater around your shoulders—to reboot an ailing brand. When he arrived at KFC, he found the brand languishing behind Chick-fil-A, and adrift on a sea of indistinct marketing that emphasized everything *except* the brand's distinctive assets.

Previous CMOs, beholden to the prevailing wisdom about emotional connection, and feeling compelled to find a new approach to the KFC problem, had gotten seriously off track. The result was advertising so indistinct, so unmemorable, and so un-salient that it made no impact on sales. One campaign, "I Ate the Bones!" built around a new boneless chicken product, was wrong in the worst kind of way, being too creepy and weird to be distinctively off. The then-marketing chief admitted to *USA Today* that the brand was "taking our hero product and drastically changing it."[8] As well as deemphasizing family meals, and downgrading the significance of the iconic bucket (even tweaking the colors to modernize the graphic design), KFC was also looking to expand into multiple new product lines that moved further away from the core product. The then-CMO confidently predicted that boneless chicken was the way of the future, and that in the near future nearly all KFC's products would have shed their bones for good.

One question: Why? Clearly the brand was struggling, but every move the team took was moving KFC *further away* from its distinctive assets and anything existing and former customers knew and liked about the brand. It's strange to look at advertising that is less than ten years old, and see no focus on the distinctive assets, be it the Colonel, "11 herbs and spices," the bucket, the red and white color scheme, the "Finger Lickin' Good" tagline, or the classic drumstick. Customers who were interviewed about their experience said they liked not having to eat around the bones, and were willing to pay a little more for the boneless experience. However, that's not the kind of response that builds salience, or will keep the brand on the top of potential customers' minds.

Instead of being unique, ownable, and consistent, the brand was betting everything on a single relevance upgrade that was okay, but had nothing to do with the actual brand, and was actively pulling away KFC from *everything its distinctive assets embodied.* (Remember, relevance is important, but the brand still has to be distinct if you want people to remember which brand is offering the relevant enhancement.) Now that we've implemented R.E.D. globally, there are several things about this KFC reboot that wouldn't happen today. Every one of those changes that were made back then were well intentioned, and done by smart folks. But knowing what we know today about marketing, we know why they didn't work.

Kevin and George pretended they didn't know at the time, but Yum! had specifically decreed that the Colonel could no longer be part of any advertising. Some folks in leadership felt that it wouldn't show the respect that the Colonel deserved, while others felt that showing the Colonel would make the brand feel old. Either way, Kevin was curious to know more about the brand, and its history. So, his very first action as CMO was to ask to see the brand archives. His second action was to shake his head in astonishment when he was led to a *cave* where the Colonel's archives were stored. For the next few weeks, Kevin and the creatives from Wieden+Kennedy opened up boxes and rifled through the Colonel's old marketing materials. They found boxes of old mandolin albums, drumstick paraphernalia, and evidence of the Colonel's many strange hobbies, obsessions, and former jobs. It turned out the Colonel was a quixotic fellow, who sold insurance and ribs, worked at a gas station, and tried his hand at multiple careers until he invented Kentucky Fried Chicken at the age of sixty. In other words, the Colonel was a colorful character, but one who many customers assumed was fictitious.

Kevin realized he had a treasure trove of distinctive assets in the Colonel alone. He was quirky, mercurial, eccentric, and utterly unique. Most interestingly, the Colonel was a natural marketer himself: he understood the importance of standing out, be it with his white suit, or the hair and moustache he bleached to match it. He hired a band to record a Christmas album. Why? Who knows! As they rifled through the boxes, Kevin and his team realized that the Colonel was multifaceted in a way that could work beautifully in a marketing campaign. Since he encompassed so many distinctive brand assets, they could use different aspects of his iconography to represent different products within the KFC family.

In KFC's heyday, when the brand was growing the fastest, every item in the restaurant had the Colonel's face on it. Why had anyone pivoted away from this? Can *you* think of another brand that does this? Likewise, the classic red and white stripes reminded people of happy childhood memories, but somewhere along the way the color had been modernized to a burgundy, which sucked all the fun and liveliness out of the design. Again, why? Finally, prior marketers had walked away from the bucket because it was seen as the old way of eating chicken. Kevin realized they had everything they needed to reboot KFC in front of them. It was simply a case of reframing these distinctive assets for a new audience.

The Return of the Colonel

Kevin, George, and the brilliant minds at Wieden+Kennedy devised an ad campaign built around a modern interpretation of the Colonel as a dandy raconteur, and all-around eccentric. Initially they cast Norm McDonald as the Colonel. Eventually Wieden+Kennedy suggested recasting the Colonel on a regular basis, both to keep customers guessing about who would step into the distinctive role, and to allow specific actors to reflect specific products, marketing strategies, and product developments. (George Hamilton for instance, was cast for an ad about "extra crispy" chicken. Later, Jason Alexander would be cast in a spot that riffed off of nineties sitcoms.) Note: Even as the casting changed, the character remained the same, meaning that the campaign and the brand's core distinctiveness remained.

Everything seemed poised for success: there was only one problem. Kevin had broken the one sacrosanct rule at Yum!: don't use the Colonel. Like the kid in the horror movie who offers to check out what's happening in the basement, Kevin had put himself in the way of a multimillion-dollar, career-ruining world of trouble. Within Yum!, the new approach was divisive, and there was pushback against Kevin for doing something so clearly against Yum! standards. A good chunk of the higher-ups thought, "This can't go out; it will ruin the brand forever." Before the first spot aired, Greg asked us for our thoughts. At the time, we thought we were simply being asked for an opinion, which was overwhelmingly positive. We didn't realize that our answer would determine whether the campaign made it to air. We thought, "This is amazing!" The spots were good— weird, incredibly distinctive, and radically breakthrough in a flat out bizarre sort of way. They were culturally and socially relevant, too. Over the life of the campaign, the Colonel was recast with recognizable stars and a constant stream of new characters that reflected the mood of the moment. And of course the spots were extremely easy to notice. At that moment, though, we fully supported it for the very simple reason that it was highly distinctive, and could only be KFC. The Colonel is so iconic that it's clear what he's advertising from the first moments of the spot. In addition, Kevin and Wieden+Kennedy had brought back the tagline "It's Finger Lickin' Good," and used other visual and audio queues to establish the Colonel as a modern reinterpretation of a classic American character.

Despite all the trepidation, the campaign launched, thanks to Yum!'s creative courage. Almost immediately we heard from a very vocal minority of the population who thought we were messing with the character of the Colonel—a frail old man in their eyes—and *hated it.* The people who liked the ads weren't brand ambassadors because there were so few customers connected deeply to KFC anymore. And that's when Greg doubled down on the strategy. He very famously stood up at the annual convention and said, "I would rather be hated and loved than ignored." Good call, because shortly thereafter, sales shot through the roof. After ten years of declining sales, KFC numbers started to tick upward. Yum! threw their support behind the new campaign, and encouraged Kevin to commit, making the spots funnier, whackier, and even more distinctive as they delved further into the Colonel's eccentric background.

Greg's key takeaway has since been related to every corner of the globe: it's okay to strive for some level of hate. If a certain subsection of your audience just loathes what you are doing then it means you are doing something daring and you are getting noticed. If your work is the equivalent of digital wallpaper, you're just wasting your time and your dollars. If you stick to your distinctive assets, leverage them in a culturally relevant way, make them easy to notice, and ensure the product is easy to access, you are well on your way to success.

— 12 —

How to Be Distinctive

THERE ARE SOME elements of this story that are hard to replicate, and out of your control. Yum! is incredibly supportive of their creative and marketing teams. Kevin is an incredibly brave marketer, who operates with great instincts, and has the conviction to go in 100 percent on big, bold ideas. It's a harder job to pull off a radical rethink of your marketing strategy without that level of personal confidence or corporate support. But it can be done. First, it's key to make sure your brand assets are:

Unique, ownable, and consistent

Unique, ownable, and consistent

and

Unique, ownable, and consistent

Did we need to repeat it three times? Well, yes, it's that important.

Let's break down how to tell if your strategy is unique, ownable, and consistent using the Virgin Atlantic strategy we touched on in the last chapter. Let's compare Virgin's branding to that of its bigger and older rivals, in this case, American, Delta, and British Airways.

This image is actually a compilation of existing print advertising from all three of American Airlines, Delta, and British Airways: not that you'd ever be able to distinguish one from another! They all use the same silver/gray, blue, and red themes. They have similar styles: snow-white mountains below silver wings, or idealized images of their destinations at golden hour. All of them make reference to the same things: where they fly, the joy of travel, reliability, safety, or service. None of these are negative attributes; they're simply too generic and not distinctive enough to mean anything.

Now compare that image to this collage of Virgin Atlantic spots. Yes, we get that these images are in black and white in the book! But trust us, the overwhelming impression is heady, intense, and saturated: each ad has a full-page purple and scarlet color scheme, overlaid with their hallmark skinny font, splashes of bold red uniforms, and not an inch of space wasted on touting generic attributes like reliability or safety—at least not without adding a heavy spin of "très chic-ness."

The ads are unique: purple where everything else is primarily blue. Sexy, when the other airlines' ads are corporate. Witty, when everything else is earnest. They are ownable: the world they've created could only belong to Virgin. And they are visually and emotionally consistent. Every ad uses the same assets: colors, tonality, and emotions.

No wonder they are easy to notice, and highly salient.

Of course, all things evolve, and the scourge of coronavirus is continuing to drastically reshape the aviation industry. As we write, Richard Branson is trying to sell Virgin Australia, and putting up his private retreat, Necker Island, as collateral for a loan from the British government to save Virgin Airways.

Mirror vs. Magnet

We touched on Mirror vs. Magnet marketing earlier in the book, but this concept really comes into play when we are discussing distinctiveness. Virgin is magnet marketing. Look at these other examples. On one side is a random assortment of beer commercials, promising a generic pleasant night out with your mates: mirror. On the other is Dos Equis's Most

Interesting Man in the World, promising who knows what kind of adventures: magnet. Imagine an assortment of blue, green, and yellow print ads for various butters and margarines: mirror. And the extreme close-ups and dark backgrounds of the Lurpak butter campaign: magnet.

Mirror advertising reflects back what consumers expect to see. It focuses primarily on the consumer and their lives, echoes their own everyday experiences back to them. A marketer might try to sell you on this strategy in the name of creating an emotional connection with your customer. After all, who doesn't love sitting around and enjoying a beer with your close friends? That's great, but if you can't remember the name of the beer, how on earth are you going to buy it?

Magnet advertising focuses on the brand. It creates a unique, ownable, and consistent world that attracts consumers in a magnetic fashion. Look at the Dos Equis ads: they've created an environment that can only exist in the Dos Equis universe. One where a dashing raconteur is feted by, and charms in return, various beautiful women, all while being effortlessly charismatic, devil-may-care handsome, and the best-dressed man in the room. We don't know about you, but our nights out on the town look more like the beer ads in the mirror composite. But why would anyone want to go there? Realistically we know we're not going to turn into the Most Interesting People in the Room, no matter how many Dos Equis we drink. The point is, we remember the campaign long enough to order the beer. (And if a little of that savoir faire rubs off on us, well then it was worth a shot.)

When Being Breakthrough Isn't Enough

One caveat, and something you should watch out for as you move forward. When you don't have a great idea, it's tempting to double down on unique, and hope that it sticks. As we mentioned in the very beginning of the book, at Collider Lab we believe in the value of committing to a distinctively off idea, especially if it's in contrast to something "correct" but bland. However, there is a world of difference between something that is distinctively off, and something that is just plain off. Mountain Dew's Kickstart *Puppy Monkey Baby* spot was certainly breakthrough, but it didn't actually do anything helpful for the brand. The spot was unique (it featured a character that was a hybrid of, well, a puppy, a monkey, and a baby) but it didn't feel particularly true to Mountain Dew, and it was wildly inconsistent with everything the brand had done prior. It seemed to come out of nowhere, had no logical connection to other existing marketing, and was just plain off.

Likewise, Kia's *Walken Closet* was a funny idea, and certainly break-through, but it was unconnected to the brand. Both spots nailed unique, but struggled with the more nuanced ownership and consistency. Break-through is important, and it's that first layer to get someone's attention—*but*—distinctiveness is what connects the breakthrough stuff to your brand. The nuances of this idea can be hard to understand and execute; we get that. But, if your team is encouraging you to go in a direction that feels *too* weird, then you need to look at the work through the same distinctive metric of unique, ownable, and consistent. Only move ahead if the work clearly checks all those boxes.

Greg and his team used the Aaker Model (sometimes known as the Brand Identity Model) to help identify areas of distinctiveness at Taco Bell. This idea was developed by David Aaker in his book *Brand Leadership*, and we found it invaluable. It's too complex to describe within the scope of this book, but we'd recommend reading it and working through the exercises if you are struggling to develop the right kind of distinctiveness.

At Taco Bell we were able to use the Aaker Model to identify a core set of key attributes that any Taco Bell product had to embody. These include things like:

1. Mexican-inspired
2. Left of center
3. Innovate and elevate
4. Engaging food

By testing every new product idea against this list, and rejecting any that didn't meet all of the items in it, we were able to sift through and reject ideas that *almost* seemed like a good idea for Taco Bell. The Aaker Model has also been instrumental in developing okay ideas to be great ideas. At one point, when every fast-food brand was offering ranch dress-ing, Greg was pushed to offer ranch dressing at Taco Bell. He pointed to the first attribute on the Aaker Model, and said, "It's not Mexican-inspired." The marketing intern (yes, intern) who had pitched the idea went away, thought about it, and came back with avocado ranch dressing instead. The avocado ranch was the perfect Taco Bell twist on a cultural favorite, and is now permanently on the menu.

Find Your Distinctive Assets

All of the magnet campaigns listed above leveraged distinctive assets to create a unique, ownable, and consistent strategy. Other magnet campaigns include Budweiser's "Dilly Dilly" spots, Arby's *We Have the Meats* strategy, and Mucinex's virulent green mucus character. All of these brands are also smart enough to ensure that their LTOs (Limited Time Offers) stay true to their distinctive branding, and don't try to make an impact by introducing them as an entirely different brand, with their own look, feel, and ideas. Arby's has been especially good at this. Have a look at this collection of their print ads, and notice how even the LTOs are firmly within the brand house.

The point is, all of these teams were able to isolate elements of their brand's essential character to make a magnetic appeal to their customers. So how do you do it?

In the last chapter we saw how KFC was able to sift through a physical archive to find physical objects that helped spark new ways to look at an existing asset: the Colonel. Of course, telling you to go "search your archives" isn't specific enough. So, let's break down what exactly you are looking for.

Building Your Distinctive Brand Assets: Old vs. New

There are two ways to create distinctive brand assets: the first is to do what Kevin and his team did. Roll your sleeves up, unpack those dusty boxes that were shelved in a warehouse sometime in the mid-eighties, and examine your brand's history with an eye to discovering something that might spark those long-dormant memory structures about your brand.

There are multiple reasons why this might not be applicable to your brand. Perhaps your brand or product is relatively young and you have limited assets to examine. Maybe your brand has been around a while, but previous teams never created or consistently used any assets to begin with. Or perhaps your assets were created deliberately to represent something that is no longer relevant to your category or society. The weight loss brand Weight Watchers, for instance, has been battling with their biggest distinctive brand asset for years: their brand name. As we mentioned back in the relevance chapter, dieting is no longer in vogue, so having a brand name and set of assets that consistently cue calorie restriction hasn't helped them much. As a result, they changed their brand name to WW and ditched their logo and nearly every other asset in their arsenal.

The other option is to create your brand's unique, ownable, and consistent distinctive assets; and there are multiple ways of doing this. A charismatic origin story is one way. Tesla has, like Kylie Jenner, a $0 traditional marketing budget (though who knows how much it cost to put that car in space). Their most distinctive asset is their founder, Elon Musk, and the word-of-mouth he generates.

If you don't have a charismatic brand founder, you'll need to do the work of creating your own distinctive asset. Beverley D'Cruz did amazing work at Pizza Hut UK, which had been flat to negative for five years when she came on board. She worked with Collider Lab and quickly discovered that one of the main issues was distinctiveness. The generic-feeling value ads weren't doing much for the brand or sales. She quickly put together a campaign called "Now That's Delivering" and turned the brand around. Beverley explains, "The key was consistency. We decided on our distinctive brand assets—the character, the playful, provocative tone, a bold sense of confidence, and the 'Now That's Delivering' tagline. Our attribution scores went way up, followed closely by our sales. We went from a −1 percent sales growth, to an amazing +15 percent before COVID hit (and then it went even higher)."

In this chapter, we'll break down these two approaches: reviving existing distinctive assets and creating new ones (see Figure 12.1).

Rejuvenating Existing Distinctive Assets

Part of retooling existing assets is the physical labor of shifting through all the existing materials and memorabilia you have available. We're not kidding about this part. Remember how we said that incoming CMOs feel an urge to start fresh and reinvent the wheel? This is an instinct as old as advertising itself. If you have a fifty-year-old brand, there will be campaigns and marketing materials in the archive that no current employee has seen and that no one has any recollection of. The vast majority of those will be trash, of course: an ephemeral CMO's bid for personal fame without any regard for the brand. But among the refuse you'll find some gems. Some of the original work, perhaps, will be inspiring and still ring true. That was certainly the case with Colonel Sanders's original work.

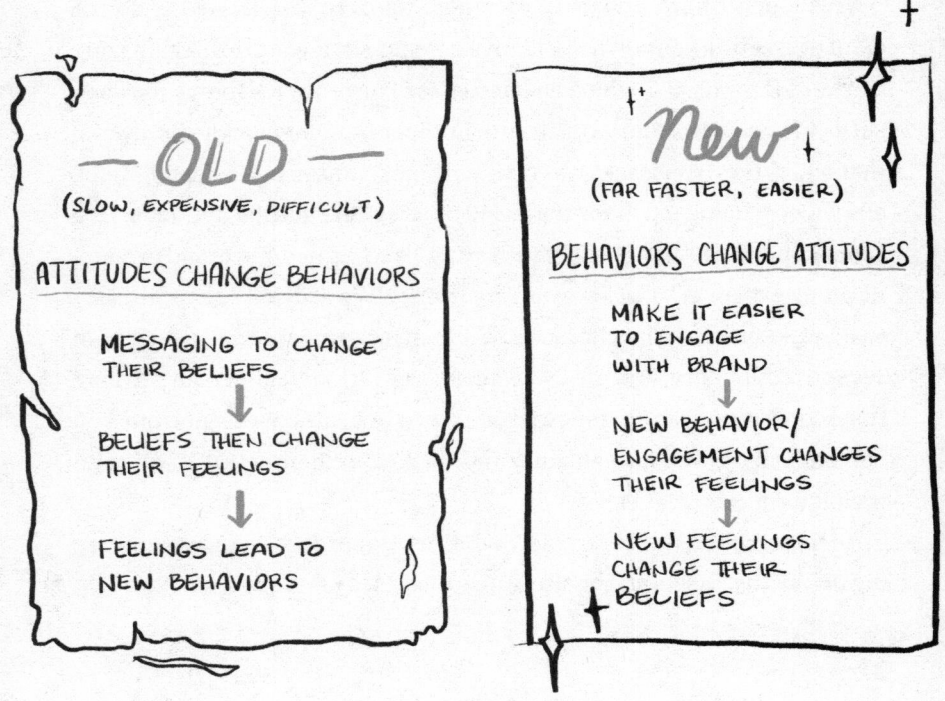

OLD
(SLOW, EXPENSIVE, DIFFICULT)

ATTITUDES CHANGE BEHAVIORS

MESSAGING TO CHANGE
THEIR BELIEFS
↓
BELIEFS THEN CHANGE
THEIR FEELINGS
↓
FEELINGS LEAD TO
NEW BEHAVIORS

new
(FAR FASTER, EASIER)

BEHAVIORS CHANGE ATTITUDES

MAKE IT EASIER
TO ENGAGE
WITH BRAND
↓
NEW BEHAVIOR/
ENGAGEMENT CHANGES
THEIR FEELINGS
↓
NEW FEELINGS
CHANGE THEIR
BELIEFS

FIGURE 12.1

Another great example is Barbie. The iconic doll was born in 1959, and she had a storied career as *the* doll that every little girl wanted to own. However, by 2014, the brand was shrinking and sales were down 16 percent. Even worse, Barbie lost her crown as the #1 toy for girls that Christmas (losing out to *Frozen*'s Elsa). This had never happened before. It wasn't that girls themselves no longer wanted Barbies; it was that their mothers no longer felt comfortable buying a doll that embodied such an absurdly slender figure. It doesn't matter if your target consumer loves your product; if your distinctive assets are disturbing to the person actually buying the product, you're not going to make that sale.

Barbie was ultimately able to turn around some of the decline when the brand team apparently rediscovered a quote from Ruth Handler, the original creator of Barbie. She said that Barbie represented "the fact that women had choices." This quote helped reframe the campaign around a more progressive and appealing vision of the doll.

The agency embraced Barbie's brand history, and showcased all that the doll had achieved over the years in her varied careers. Diverse Barbies, and tall, curvy, and petite Barbies, were added to the lineup. A #TBT Instagram campaign highlighted her empowering professional life over the decades. TV spots aimed at Millennial moms suggested that the dolls allowed their daughters to try out future roles, careers, and creative aspirations. By the end of 2015, Barbie sales were improving and have continued to grow since. Note that Mattel didn't tie the doll to a #girlpower-style "Purpose." Rather the campaign reimagined her cultural relevance, to allow her distinctive features to once more be appealing to little girls—and the adults who buy toys for them.

So, as you unearth assets, look for anything the brand hasn't fully used, or fully used lately. These could include characters, such as the M&M talking candy characters that were originally used in the 1950s and rebooted in the mid-nineties by BBDO.[1] The agency was tasked with resurrecting M&M's, which had slipped into candy-aisle obscurity.[2] Their answer was to give each color a personality, including outfitting the seductive "Green" in white go-go boots to hide her lack of ankles. BBDO nixed animation, and brought the characters to life in CGI, introducing the sextet of candies at the Super Bowl. The spots and the characters were instant hits. When Mars sporadically attempted to pull them out of the TV ads, so that they "wouldn't be taken for granted," they got immediate pushback from customers, who wanted to know where the characters had gone. It's been two decades, and the M&M candies are still the face and heart of M&M—and evidence that being unique, ownable, and consistent pays off every time.

Dig deep as you consider potential assets. In Australia, Tiger Beer leveraged its Singaporean heritage as a street beer by sponsoring a street food festival and doubling down on its image as the perfect beer for Singaporean street food. More recently, they sponsored a major initiative to help double the global tiger population, something that helps cement another unique asset, tigers, in consumers' minds.[3]

Nearly every airline in the world has attempted to rejuvenate the excitement of travel by bringing back distinctive assets from the glory days of aviation. For most it's limited to repainting an aircraft in retro colors. (Most recently, British Airways repainted three 747s in iconic designs from the fifties to the eighties.) Interestingly, JetBlue is a minority owner in the TWA Hotel at JFK, which was created during a $265 million *Mad Men*–esque renovation of the iconic Saarinen Terminal. JetBlue passengers now have the option to spend their preflight time in the heavily TWA-branded lobby, full of distinctive assets including a TWA Constellation Starliner remade as a cocktail bar. Perhaps suggesting that if your own archives don't go very deep, it's possible to benefit by co-opting the glamorous history of your spiritual predecessors.[4]

Evaluating Your Existing Assets

Once you've gathered your assets, you need to evaluate which are worth considering, and which should be discarded. A useful first step is to do a distinctive brand asset study. In this study, we show consumers brand assets—logos, color schemes, characters, or even jingles or taglines. This type of study removes the brand's names, so the survey takers are relying solely on the stimuli of the asset itself. Imagine the Pizza Hut roof without the words "Pizza Hut" written beneath it. Or Wendy's freckle-faced moppet without "Wendy's." Then you score your answers on three dimensions—the three As (see Figure 12.2). The first A measures the asset's *awareness strength* (as represented by the size of the bubble), meaning how many people are aware of the asset. The second A measures its *attribution strength*, meaning people correctly attribute it to the brand and don't confuse it with another brand. The third and final A is the *attention strength*, which measures how disruptive and attention grabbing the asset is. Any asset that lands in the top right quadrant is both highly attention grabbing and highly ownable. If the bubble is large, then it's a widely known asset that is immediately usable to the brand's benefit. If the bubble is small, then few people know of it, despite it being breakthrough and unique. These assets can be invested in to become even more valuable as time goes on.

MEASURE YOUR DISTINCTIVE ASSETS

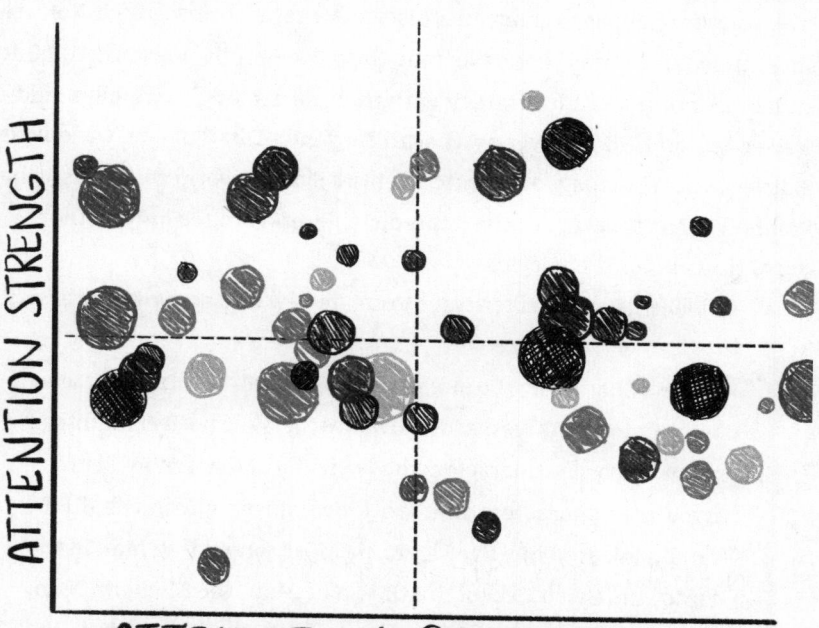

FIGURE 12.2

Creating Distinctive Assets

Let's assume that you didn't strike gold looking through your archives. We've encountered a few of those situations. Perhaps it's simply a new brand. Or maybe the historical search reveals that the brand has never really had a soul, story, or anything much that could be considered distinctive. Your next step is to create new distinctive assets from scratch. You are surrounded by brands that have done this successfully. Mastercard built an iconic, multi-decade strategy with their "Priceless" campaign. Budweiser has created a newer asset with its "Dilly Dilly" spots. Or look at Skittles, who've managed to create an entire Skittles world with "Taste the Rainbow." The spots are crazy, unpredictable, and limited only by the colors of the candies themselves.

We've identified at least ten ways to create new distinctive brand assets.

1. **Create a Character.** You already know who our favorite character is: the Colonel. As we discussed above, he's the perfect manifestation of a brand character who is vividly and indelibly distinctive. Other characters that work brilliantly within the R.E.D. framework are Tony the Tiger, the Most Interesting Man in the World, the Geico Gecko, the Old Spice Man, the Michelin Man, Poo-Pourri's Bethany, or another one of our old favorites, the Panda Cheese panda. You must stop everything now and look him up on YouTube.

2. **Build a Distinctive Brand World.** Building a distinctive brand world brings the brand to life and allows it to embody a particular look, feel, and aesthetic. Like the brand, the world needs to embody all the elements of distinctiveness: unique, ownable, and consistent. Glossier and Apple are two brands that have created a brand world that is highly appealing to their customers. The Skittles world does this with spots that are emotionally consistent throughout (i.e., the spots all have the

same straight-faced execution of wildly improbable situations, be they an exasperated witch losing patience with her Skittles-loving victim, or teenagers infecting each other with Skittles pox).

3. **Create a Consistent Ad Framework.** We'd argue that the most impactful way to build a distinctive asset is to create a standardized framework or story structure for commercials. These frameworks have distinctive beats that the audience can anticipate even when they haven't seen a specific spot before. Mastercard mastered this with the four-part "Priceless" framework that first lists and prices the necessary items for a particular activity, event, or moment; then shows characters enjoying the moment; then depicts the emotional moment that cannot be measured by a price tag; and finally closes with the classic "Priceless" tag. Snickers has a similar formula, showing an elderly person gamely trying to keep up during an intense physical activity. A friend has a nonsensical confrontation with them about their performance, throws them a Snickers, which they eat, and are thus magically transformed into their younger selves, able to fully join in the action once again while the voice-over intones, "You're not you when you're hungry." Take a look at Betty White's Snickers spot on YouTube. Or even better, the Brady Bunch Snickers commercial. A consistent ad framework *must* have an identical structure every time (our brains find comfort in repetition, and it's consistency that really builds distinctiveness). It must leverage the same story, same tension, and same idea every time, using different elements to differentiate it from the other spots in the campaign. And finally the structure has to be used every time in an overt and obvious manner. Don't try to hide your framework or you will lose distinctiveness. Creative ad agencies will bore of this approach after a few years, but discarding it is the same as throwing out one of your product lines because you're tired of working on it.

4. **Create Sticky Jingles, Catchphrases, and Taglines.** Geico's "Fifteen Minutes Could Save You 15 Percent or More on Car Insurance," KFC's "Finger Lickin' Good," and Frosted Flakes' "They're Great!" are classic examples of super distinctive taglines. Jingles can also be unique, ownable, and consistent through the years. State Farm's *Like a good neighbor...* has been used consistently throughout the years, resisting any impulse to try and update the tune to sound more contemporary. All of these jingles, catchphrases, and taglines are so memorable that they refresh our memory structures every time we hear them. But don't just think of your tagline. KFC in Australia has an incredibly successful value campaign that they've been running for several years now. Annabel Fribence, the then-marketing director, explains,

Every TV commercial has the same story arc to wire memory structure through repetition. This is the construct of every commercial: The protagonist is having a bad day, he sees a KFC value offer which he can't resist, and this gives him the confidence to flip the bird to social expectations and he exclaims, "Shut up and take my money," and their day turns around. Okay. Maybe you have to be Australian to get it. But it's so sticky, it's become a common saying. And it's made our value work so much more memorable.

5. **Own Key Sounds.** Think of the Taco Bell "bong," the Intel synth sound, or the 20th Century Fox orchestral flourish that plays over their logo before a movie. Harley-Davidson spent years trying to protect the V-twin engine's sound. All of these sounds are ownable by the brands in question and trigger instant associations with the products in question. Sounds can be incredibly evocative and create deep memory structures that last for years. The *Law & Order* "dun dun dun" is so recognizable that it has even been parodied on *Saturday Night Live*. Consider theme tunes and musical riffs, but don't forget to look at the actual sounds

your product makes, perhaps a specific sizzle, snap, or other distinctive audio cue.

6. **Own a Product or Service.** This one's trickier, but if you can "own" a particular place in your category it's incredibly distinctive. For instance, Taco Bell owns Mexican(ish) food in the US: so, anytime we advertise a chalupa, taco, or quesalupa, it is highly distinctive for us. The KFC bucket is highly distinctive, and although other brands might offer buckets, the concept of a bucket of chicken is indelibly linked with our brand. This only works if your product or service is nearly 100 percent attributable to you and only you, and it's generally rare to have a product that is so distinctive. If your market has multiple chicken chains or pizza brands, then perhaps your distinctiveness comes through in your packaging, your secret recipe, or your restaurant look and design. Other brands own their respective spaces so thoroughly that their product name has become the generic name for their category: Kleenex, Clorox, Q-Tips, and, in the UK, Hoover. If none of these apply, this one isn't for you, and you'll have to create distinctiveness through one of the other approaches discussed here.

7. **Do Stunts in a Distinctive Tone.** What do you think of when you consider Red Bull? They have pretty much claimed the extreme stunt space, whether it is flying small planes through inflatable obstacle courses or sponsoring parachutists jumping from the outer edge of space. Brands can find distinctiveness assets when they do stunts or other physical or digital activations that, when tied to culture, can create buzz, relevance, and topspin. Once again, consistency and ownability is key. The stunts will only work if they have a consistent tone and can be tied directly to you. Red Bull has nailed this with a consistent language and focus on extreme flying and flight-related adventures (after all, "It gives you wings!"). Other brands make it work with concepts

like the *Deadpool* movie posters that mock older films, or Tesla sending a car into space.

8. **Own a Cause.** You know how we don't love Purpose? Well, this is one area that's an exception. If your brand can own and build a specific cause into its business in a distinctive way, and which helps garner public attention and builds a connection with target audiences, then this can become a distinctive asset. This only works if the cause is unique enough to be ownable, and it is used in every (or nearly every) ad and touchpoint, not just CSR (corporate social responsibility). The brands doing this well include Patagonia, Tom's One for All (while it lasted), Dove's Real Beauty, and REI for their policy of closing on Black Friday. It's critical not to align yourself with a generic cause, but to find something that makes sense for your brand in a distinctive way.

9. **Own Certain Shapes.** Look at the shapes in your brand and product. For instance, the iconic Coca-Cola bottle, the VW Bug, or the 747. The Converse All-Star sneaker is unique, consistent, and ownable. Likewise Kikkoman soy sauce bottles and the Golden Arches. Consider ownable patterns and prints: Burberry's signature Burberry Check instantly identifies a product as belonging to the Burberry family (or a counterfeiter's version of it). Within the Yum! world we identify the Crunchwrap as a powerful "shape" asset. Ever seen a taco-like hexagon before? We also include unique fonts, color schemes, and other identifiers within this category.

10. **Own the Ritual.** Think of the Oreo cookie "Twist, Lick, and Dunk," or the Tim Tam Slam. These little rituals that are unique to specific brands, and passed down by generations, become an instinctive action for the person eating the product.

The Starburst Pink Freeze Drink

Here's one last thing to consider: sometimes the way to a distinctive idea is through asking yourself a seemingly silly question. One of Greg's approaches to breakthrough ideas is to ask his team an obtuse question that seems likely to only generate nonsense answers. Why? Because it gets people—especially people who are stuck after long days or weeks of trying to come up with a new idea—thinking about a challenge in a fresh way.

In 2014, Greg and his team were talking, when he asked them, "What is it that we like to eat, that we'd also like to drink?" One of the answers was, "We love to eat candy. What about drinking it?" Well, that's both an interesting idea, and an idea that doesn't necessarily seem to have a practical application. How exactly would you make a drink that tastes like candy anyway? The next week Greg happened to be at a conference where he met the Mars confectionary people. He introduced himself, they chatted briefly, and he asked, "Hey, would you guys be interested in doing a Starburst drink?" They responded, very logically and reasonably, "We don't make drinks, we make candy. And we've never really thought about it." Yet, very quickly, it dawned on everyone that this was actually a pretty brilliant idea for something breakthrough and distinctive that would be mutually beneficial to both brands.

A short time later, Mars approved the concept and asked Greg which flavor of Starburst he wanted to use. Here's where it pays to understand how different aspects of your product can make you distinctive. Mars of course could tell us which were the favorite colors in order of consumer popularity in the Starburst lineup. Among them was a deep cherry red and a pink strawberry. Mars encouraged Yum! to go to cherry red, as it is perennially the most popular flavor. Because Mars didn't make drinks, we reached out to our friends at PepsiCo to help us match the candy flavor and color to a drink flavor and color. They did a fantastic job and the flavors and colors were identical to the actual candies. They were duly photographed in the studio, and the team took a look at the shots to try and evaluate the best flavor to go with. The thing is, this was going to be the very first product that Taco Bell ever launched without using TV: our actual customers were going to be learning about this drink on social media. So how the colors looked on Instagram or Snap was critically important. It was less important which flavor looked good in the studio than it was which flavor photographed well out in the wild, where customers were going to be experiencing it themselves.

Greg and his team grabbed the drinks, drove to Laguna Beach, stuck the drinks in the sand, and experimented with taking shots of the various beverages backlit against the California sun and surf. The cherry red looked good, but the strawberry pink looked amazing. It was a unique color, could become distinctive with consistent use, and with the marketing support of both Mars and Taco Bell, was a winner. When the Starburst Pink Freeze was launched in 2014, sales were 300 percent higher than predicted. Following on from that success, Taco Bell then launched a Skittles (also owned by Mars confectionary) Strawberry Freeze drink. Both products are quite distinctive since they're not just another frozen drink. They're co-branded and that makes them stand out as unique, ownable, and consistent. Taco Bell got two great ideas out of asking the question "what do you eat that you would like to drink?" Collaborating with Starburst and Skittles made the drinks both more relevant (as you had a known expectation of the flavor) and also more distinctive because the candy was now in a drinkable format.

13

Distinctive Campaigns

DISCOVERING YOUR BRAND'S distinctiveness is a uniquely complex challenge, for the simple reason that being distinct requires standing out, sometimes in distinctively off ways. This can be tricky enough on an individual level, but within an organization with multiple levels of hierarchy and approvals? Almost impossible. However, it must be done. Without distinctiveness your brand is doomed; all the other R.E.D. innovations, no matter how well conceived, will struggle to gain traction if your end users can't recall exactly which brand or product it was that promised to be easy or accessible, or made them sit up and notice its social, cultural, and functional relevance.

How do you create a structure and a culture that will support distinctiveness? We've got our own strategies here at Collider Lab, which we'll share below. And, to bolster our ideas, we interviewed some key players at several large organizations. We wanted to figure out what strategies support distinctiveness, and what tried-and-true methods can stifle creativity and nudge you toward indistinct, anodyne work. Together, we've drawn up a culture guide to help you create an environment that is conducive to developing distinctive ideas. One of Greg's strongest beliefs is that CMOs need to occasionally (or often, as in Greg's case) go to research groups themselves. Yes, your people will tell you, "Why not just read the report?" However, you miss vital clues when you don't physically witness a research group discussing a product yourself. Facial cues, body language, a quiet sigh of exasperation or boredom while a focus group subject attempts to project enthusiasm. Eventually we built an in-house research facility at Taco Bell, so we could feed subjects directly out of our test kitchens, and make it easier for other members of the marketing team to pop in and observe ad hoc.

Some of these require buy-in from top management, and all of them demand confidence in the team executing the work, so—first step: make sure you've pulled together the brightest, most diverse minds your organization has to offer. This isn't a simple task, but remember the Collider Lab PhD dropout rule. Don't be limited by demanding specific credentials, especially academic. The world is full of brilliant minds who didn't have the time, money, connections, or interest to pursue an MBA.

- Keep a seat at your table for people who've taken different routes, and don't discount ideas because they came from an unexpected source.
- Mull over the word *collider*. All the biggest, craziest, and most innovative ideas come when multiple different worlds and backgrounds collide (as in MIT's famed building twenty, where the randomness of the office assignments, and the temporary nature of the building, led to individuals from disparate disciplines inadvertently meeting and tearing down and reconfiguring the internal spaces to suit their evolving collaborations and shared projects). This is especially crucial when you're looking for distinctive, and you're open to being distinctively off.

- Having voices in the room who can give you diverse perspectives and share their cultural references and life experiences is key. So, if you don't have coworkers or employees who sometimes surprise you, or bring observations that no one else on the team would have made, then ask yourself why you're limiting your team's potential with stultifying homogeneity.

- A traditional education at a "good" school is a great thing, but for the majority of people on this planet, it's also an almost impossible thing to achieve. Those thwarted learners have the same (or more) brains, drive, and ambition as the legacy admissions sailing through the Ivies. Don't discount them, and make sure your HR department knows you are actively looking for new hires who have unconventional backgrounds. (If you must stick them in the intern program, for the love of God, give them a livable stipend.)

- This may sound like Ken's and Greg's bleeding hearts breaking through, and it partly is, but this is also pragmatic, creative advice. You don't know what you're not seeing, until someone who *is* seeing it can point it out to you. This is crucial when you are brainstorming a breakthrough distinctive innovation. Give that person a chance.

Distinctive Organizations: The Culture and Structure of Distinctiveness

Depending on your position within your organization, you will have different levels of control over the culture in your workplace and the amount of creativity your coworkers feel confident sharing with their superiors. These are the telltale attributes of a company that prioritizes creating distinctiveness, and the more you can activate within your creative and executive ranks, the better. As always, do what you can. Even if you are only able to shift one small aspect of how business gets done, it's better than nothing at all.

What follows is our formula for building organizations that support and nurture distinctiveness. We created it by interviewing several of our marketing departments around the world that were creating consistently distinctive campaigns as well as marketing teams that haven't been as successful.

Align on Objectives and an Understanding of the Brand

"Everyone has a different idea of what we're trying to accomplish."

"If you really look at the objective, it's not about relevance, it's about a unique look, feel, tone, world, image. Not everyone understood that. Many still thought it was about the emotional connection or message."

"We need a common language and understanding of what distinctiveness is."

These three quotes came from three different and unsuccessful marketing departments. Consistently, across the board, the number one issue was that every team member was on a different page. Ultimately, at the heart of your work, you need to create an atmosphere that prioritizes and encourages the pursuit of distinctiveness. From the CEO on down, every person should know the value of distinctiveness. If they don't, educate them.

Avoid Overly Complicated and Prescriptive Briefs

"We set out to create a campaign **first**. Then later we worried about the individual products to be advertised."

This is key: If you brief every single product or offer as if it were its own product or brand, you'll never create a distinctive campaign. It's such a fundamental part of distinctiveness that it's easy to overlook. Every product, offer, TV ad, or whatever would look and feel different because it has its own idea. Instead, if you set out to find a long-term campaign first, and then worry about the individual activations later, it'll be easier to find success. Brief for the campaign, not the product.

Have No More Than Two Chefs in the Kitchen

"Our CMO did a mind-meld with the creative director at the agency."

Creative meetings in the marketing and advertising industries are notorious for having way too many people and way too many "devil's advocates." This is well meaning, but exemplifies a huge problem we see in marketing: the very human instinct to make sure everyone gets to have an opinion and input into the matter at hand. We think this is admirable in most facets of life, but deadly in creative matters. We want everyone to have an opinion, but frankly that doesn't help distinctiveness. Remember the Collider Lab rule that it's better to commit to something that's flawed but interesting, and give it 100 percent? That won't happen in this kind of creative democracy.

So, this one is a bit controversial, but it's been proven true over the years. Great marketing campaigns are not created by a committee. If you have a group of people, all with their different agendas, trying to create something they can all agree to support, you will end up with an indistinctive mess. Truly distinctive campaigns are created when the CMO (or marketing director, or head of advertising) and the creative director at the agency handling the account are aligned on a single vision.

Crown your two chefs: a marketing leader on the brand side, and the creative director on the agency side, and accept you aren't living in a democracy on this particular project.

Have a Clear Creative Vision

"Without a clear creative campaign, none of the midlevel or junior people know what to execute."

"We have tons and tons of ideas—but we don't have prioritization. What's the goal? We need focus. We cannot parallel path all the ideas—the agency will give us twelve ideas and we'll tell them to do it all."

Once your two chefs have honed in on a direction, they need to convey it effectively to the rest of the organization. Then, they need to empower everyone to confidently move forward with their assigned task. This is where everyone else in the organization gets to get their hands dirty with creative. Not every piece is birthed by the CMO and CD. Once the CD and CMO have mind-melded on the idea and main distinctive assets, they can loosen the bat a bit and let the other teams run with it. Set some clear guidelines, a sharp definition of the brand idea, and a clear list of "is/is nots" so you're not shocked by the outcome.

Don't Be Too Intellectual

"Sometimes there are so many graphs, charts, frameworks, strategies, layers of complicated emotional connection. Forget coming up with an idea, the challenge is just figuring out what it all means."

"Look at these graphs and charts! WTF are any of them actually about? I mean, why?"

Remember, while you make your earnest and PowerPoint-y presentation that half the people in the room are hard-core right-brainers. Even though they intellectually understand these visuals, odds are they aren't translating it in an urgent or compelling way. Instead of inundating your teams with data, try sharing information in a more narrative form. Share ideas, insights, and stories. Remember that distinctiveness is never about data, so starting with a data dump doesn't make sense. Tell stories, share experiences. Hope for a bit of intuition, emotion, and serendipity along the way.

Reduce Layers of Approval

"We had a great campaign, but we have so many layers of internal approval that eventually it got so watered down and vanilla that it was terrible."

"It's a decision by committee . . . it's not uncommon to have meetings where the agency is getting feedback from fifteen clients. It's viscerally painful."

"My wish overall for everything is fewer people in meetings. I get that we need to give junior people a chance to speak up in a meeting and get some experience. But when we have to go round the room and everyone gets to share an opinion . . . then the opinion of one random person throws everything off."

Limit the number of people who have decision-making power. Trust your CMO or marketing leader and reduce the layers of approval. If the CEO is signing off on every piece of creative, something is broken in your organization, and moving quickly, boldly, and creatively is out of the question.

Remember the Oatly example we used above. We asked John (their Chief Creative Officer) how they were able to create such bold work within an organization.

We don't have a marketing department. We have a creative department that we call the Oatly Department of Mind Control. We brief ourselves, do the work, and then approve it when we think it is good enough. No one in the company except Toni [the CEO] can stop anything we do, and we have a deal with Toni that as long as what we do is world-class he can't stop anything either, even if he doesn't like it. That responsibility and opportunity allows us to create something unique and ownable. Killing the politics of a marketing department can result in some interesting work.

Use the Correct KPI to Measure Success

"We use the wrong KPIs that are not correct to measure what we're asking—like brand reputation. It says that consumers still see us as leaders in the category, but that's not distinctiveness, is it?"

What key performance indicators are you using to measure your success? It's very easy to throw yourself wildly off target by listening to the *wrong* metrics. More traditional copy testing methodologies require consumers to engage their rational sides of the brain. These will be counterproductive to creating a breakthrough and distinctive campaign. This is the big flaw in most copy testing—you're asking your consumer to judge the campaign in an unnatural way. Your respondents are looking at the campaign with a logical, rational eye. They want to please you, so they are trying hard to analyze it thoughtfully. And this isn't how they're going to look at, process, and respond to your campaign, store design, or product innovation when they see it out in the wild.

Use the correct KPIs to measure distinctiveness. The ultimate KPI, of course, is increasing sales. But unaided top-of-mind awareness is hugely valuable. We also believe in testing ads AFTER they've run (with all the logos and brand names removed), and asking respondents three sets of questions: 1) Have you seen this? (breakthrough), 2) What brand is it for? (attribution/distinctiveness), and 3) Was the message compelling and why? (relevance). Some of our marketing teams will pull the ad off if the score is low and sales aren't going up. Painful, but important learning lessons.

Take Smart Chances

I do believe big organizations can suffer from status quo disease, and getting marketing leaders to take risks and lead the organization in a new direction is hard because it will always be safer to just let the brand blend in and not offend anyone or risk failure. This is particularly true when you have brands that are already well regarded. The temptation to leave things as they are and not take risks is always there. To be a great marketer you can't be afraid of failure, more so than just about any function.

—DAVID GIBBS, YUM! CEO

Fear will kill distinctiveness like nothing else. No one wants to be the person who signed off on a multimillion-dollar fiasco, or worse, okayed something so non-breakthrough that it didn't even make a ripple of "that sucks." The boldest, most distinctive campaigns in our industry were controversial when they were first revealed. Consider the Old Spice Man. He wasn't subtle: instead, he was absurd, over the top, and unique. Now look at an image from the campaign he replaced: a generically buff guy, carrying his mountain bike through a roaring stream. Take away the tagline and the product image, and it could have been an ad for anything from low-carb beer to life insurance. Now, look at the Old Spice guy. Now back at me. Now back at him. Oh, wait . . . Seriously. Look at Isaiah Mustafa on his horse. This was controversial. It wasn't a slam dunk getting Procter & Gamble to sign off on the concept. There were probably a lot of very concerned people, who thought it would kill what little market share Old Spice still had. Yet Old Spice is now a long-term campaign structure that has lasted over a decade. Today it even includes Old Spice Man's relationship with his Gen Z son, and the predictably quirky father and son miscommunications that occur between the two of them.

Don't let fear keep your work indistinct. Push through it, and have faith in your creative. If it's unique, ownable, and consistent, it's the right choice.

Avoid "Dissecting the Frog"

> "Once it goes through the machine, any interesting tension or creativity gets removed. And then somehow it's expected to still be bold and do miracles."

> "Historically on our end it's been a lot of people, a lot of opinions, a lot of research, a lot of insights—and when it gets to the end it's milquetoast and it falls flat."

There's an old "dissecting the frog" parable in advertising that many agency creatives will identify with. The brand buys a great campaign that's creative, distinctive, and breakthrough, but then they start overthinking it, picking it apart, tweaking it, cutting it, moving things around, and by the end of all that it's a weird Frankenstein. It's like taking a frog, dissecting it, stitching it back together, and then expecting it to still hop.

So, to achieve distinctiveness, just don't dissect the frog. Find the core of the idea, polish it, reinforce it, and double down on it, but don't dissect the frog.

— 14 —

Distinctiveness Exercises

Asset Mapping

Now that you've gotten a good rundown on distinctiveness and how it works, let's evaluate how good your brand is at being distinctive. Eventually, the idea is to do this using real consumer data through a high-quality consultancy, but this exercise can be a quick diagnostic for you to do in the meantime.

Let's get started!

1. First, think of all the distinctive brand assets for your brand, and fill out the first column with these assets. These assets can be things like a character, a brand world, an ad framework, jingles/taglines/catchphrases, a sound, a product, stunts, a

cause, or shapes/color schemes/typefaces. You don't need to fill up all fifteen slots.

2. Next, you're going to rate each distinctive brand asset (1–10) on three key factors (the three As):

   ■ Attribution Strength (how much people could correctly attribute this to your brand)

   ■ Attention Strength (how breakthrough is it, how much attention does it command)

   ■ Awareness Strength (how many people are aware of this asset?)

3. Finally, use the scores you gave on the table to map out your assets on the quadrants.

Let's look at an example before diving in. Think about Hello Kitty as a brand. Even though Hello Kitty is one of Sanrio's many character lines, Hello Kitty has become so distinct and well known that she is essentially her own brand. Taking a look at some of these Hello Kitty brand images below, what assets would you say are Hello Kitty's distinctive brand assets? How would we do this exercise for the Hello Kitty brand?

We'd start by listing their distinctive brand assets: Hello Kitty herself, her overalls, the iconic Hello Kitty font, her yellow nose, the iconic bow, Teddy Chum (the teddy bear Hello Kitty carries around), and so on.

Next, we'd rate each asset on the three As. Let's have a look at Hello Kitty herself. There's no doubt that she's very high (10) on awareness (most people that are engaged in the category have seen her, we'd bet). She's also very high (10) on attribution—in a sea of cartoon characters, she stands out and cannot be mistaken for another character. And we'd argue she's quite attention-grabbing as well (10). Faces, characters, and places tend to be more attention-grabbing than something like a simple color.

Let's try another asset in the Hello Kitty brand: Hello Kitty's bow. The bow has become somewhat of an icon and is an asset that's often used in place of Hello Kitty herself.

We'd therefore rank the bow as very high (9) in awareness—people know this iconic bow almost as much as Hello Kitty herself. How is its attribution? While other brands and characters have iconic bows, like Minnie Mouse and Betsey Johnson, each of those bows is unique in its own way. For this reason, we'd rank the bow pretty high in attribution (8). Attention, we'd argue, is somewhere in the middle (6): not quite a character, but not just a simple color.

Let's try one more Hello Kitty brand asset: Joey Mouse. He's Hello Kitty's friend, and he's the blue mouse that's sometimes pictured with her. You're probably thinking, "Huh? What mouse?" And if we showed you his picture (which we won't, because we don't want to prime you!), probably half of you would think, "Oh! I've seen him before. I think." The thing is, he's *low* (3) on awareness because he's not very well known at all (perhaps unless you're a true Hello Kitty fan), especially when he's not pictured next to Hello Kitty. What about his attribution? Could he be mistaken for other characters or attributed to other brands? We think so—at least currently—so we'd rank attribution on the lower end, too (3). Attention ranks on the higher side (6) though.

We'd do that for each of the assets we listed. Our final chart would look something like Figure 14.1, and we'd translate that to the mapping chart. Attribution is the horizontal axis, attention is the vertical axis, and awareness is the size of the bubble itself.

ASSET	ATTRIBUTION (0-10)	ATTENTION (0-10)	AWARENESS (0-10)
HELLO KITTY	10	10	10
RED BOW	8	6	9
JOEY MOUSE	3	6	2
OVERALLS	4	4	5
HELLO KITTY FONT	2	3	3
WHITE CAT SHAPE WITH WHISKERS & YELLOW NOSE	10	8	10
RED	2	2	2
PINK, RED & WHITE COMBO	6	3	5

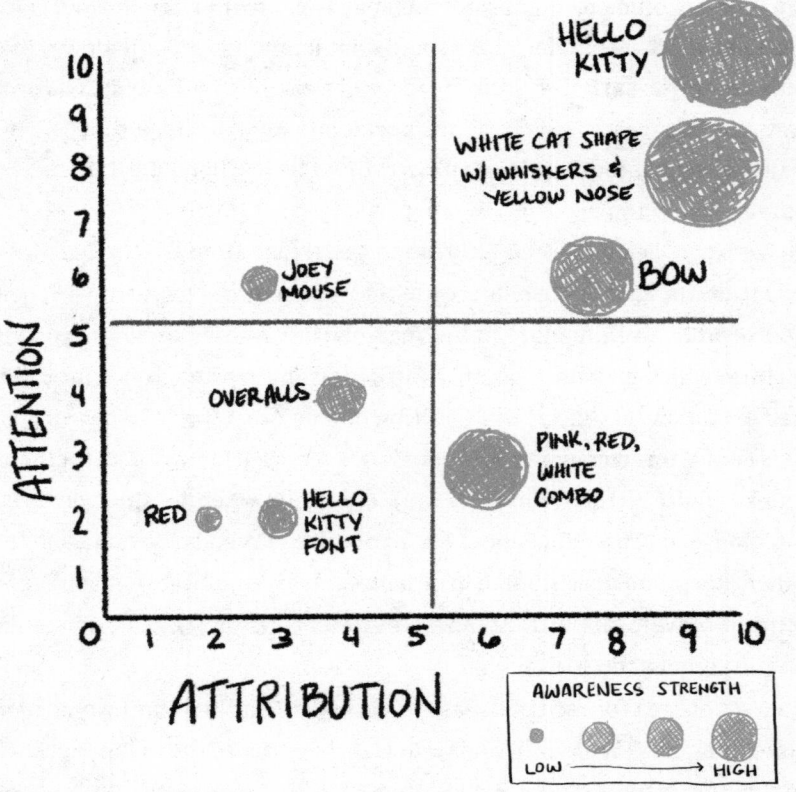

FIGURE 14.1

By plotting your assets on the distinctive assets mapping chart, you've created a visual diagnostic that should help you determine which assets are strong, which are opportunities, and which you should proceed with caution. In the case of Hello Kitty, we learn the following from this exercise:

Upper Right Quadrant: These are your major assets. Using them at every touchpoint will increase effectiveness of your communications.

- Hello Kitty herself
- White cat shape with whiskers and yellow dot nose
- Bow

Upper Left Quadrant: These are assets that capture a lot of attention, but aren't easily linked to your brand. Beware of using them outside of a brand-specific context. Otherwise, you may be unwittingly reinforcing your competitors' memory structures.

- Joey Mouse

Bottom Right Quadrant: These are clearly distinctive assets: they are easily attributed to your brand. The problem is that they don't capture a lot of attention. Use them as support and in combination with other, more attention-grabbing assets.

- Pink, red, and white color combo

Bottom Left Quadrant: These are problematic assets, as they are neither attention-grabbing nor easily attributed to your brand. Consider discarding them or using them only in combination with more attributable assets.

- Red
- Overalls
- Hello Kitty font

Note: *Little Bubbles in the Upper Right Quadrant* are potential gold mines. They command attention and are unique. Invest in them to make people aware of them and they should pay out for years to come.

This exercise is a huge opportunity for you and your brand to unearth treasures from your archives. It's also an equally important opportunity to help you decide which of your assets are worth investing in and which are best left aside. A brand can have too many assets to effectively build and defend, just as easily as it can have too few. Selecting the ones you really want to invest in over the longer term is an important part of success. And make sure to mix it up. You don't want all visual assets. Think of sounds and text lines, distinctive smells, or even signature customer service behaviors.

15

Making This Work

WELL, THAT'S ABOUT it! As we've shared, Collider Lab and Yum! have experienced exponential growth by using R.E.D. to shape our marketing strategies. We hope you do, too, and we hope this program gives you the fortitude to weather what is sure to be a challenging few years in business. Who knows what twists and turns the global economy will take between now and our publication date. What we *do* know is that with R.E.D. in your pocket, you will have a better chance than most of surviving the storms. So, where do you start?

Greg Creed has a classic quote that he shares when a brand is in turmoil and no one knows how to start fixing things. He simply says, "Don't try to boil the ocean." What this means is that when you are in crisis, and *everything*—your product, your marketing, and your in-store experience, for instance—seems to be part of the problem, you need to do the *opposite* of what your instincts say. Rather than sending off teams here and there to try and tackle all the problems at once, take a minute, and figure out what author Charles Duhigg calls your *keystone problem*. A keystone is the stone right at the top of an arch. Once you have a keystone in place, the mason can relax for a bit: she knows the arch is now structurally sound and will remain upright, and she can start tending to the other building tasks, or the landscaping, or her lunch.

Duhigg's classic example is once-ailing aluminum giant Alcoa, where then CEO Paul O'Neill identified workplace safety as the most important problem to solve. You can read a full account in *The Power of Habit*, but for now it's enough to know that O'Neill, very controversially, focused all his efforts on improving worker safety at Alcoa. This caused shareholders to initially worry, as they assumed sales would continue sliding and the value of their stocks would decline. There were many, many problems at Alcoa, and worker safety was not at the top of anyone's list. Instead, by fixing what Paul identified as Alcoa's keystone problem, he was able to turn the company around. That keystone acted a bit like a set of dominoes falling, to mix metaphors. His emphasis on worker safety led to managers connecting more with their employees, which led to more ideas about how to be more efficient, which led to better innovations, and on and on.

We take a similar approach when we use R.E.D. First, we take a step back and figure out what is the one core issue, and what kind of change is going to have the most immediate ROI. We do this because once you start having a little success, and you get some momentum going, you'll have the freedom to explore more solutions. Your CEO will breathe a sigh of relief, your team will start feeling more confident. Success begets success. And you have a much better chance of being successful if you focus on your one keystone problem.

This can be easier said than done. Most obviously, it's not easy to muster the internal fortitude that is required to focus boldly on one solution. But if you can muster it, then the big question becomes: What's the one keystone solution? It's a big question, so we don't take this step lightly. We dedicate several weeks of intense focus and research, and we use an approach we call the "The Four Cs." Don't worry, this isn't another complicated framework you have to lay on top of R.E.D. It's quite simply a way to ensure that you're looking at all aspects of your business while you're hunting for the keystone problem and solution.

The Four Cs (Okay, Three Cs and a B)

The three Cs is a classic business analysis framework developed by famed Japanese management guru Kenichi Ohmae. The *Economist* called him "one of the world's top five management gurus," and he wrote a book about his approach in the early nineties. His "Strategic Triangle" was made up of three Cs: *company, customer,* and *competition,* the three elements Ohmae-san felt had to be the basis for "all strategic thinking and planning." Being Collider Lab, we've mixed it up and added a fourth, *culture*—which, we hope you've gathered from the last few hundred pages, we think is absolutely critical to success. Also, we don't really think we're talking about the whole company—just the brand, so we made that a "B." So yeah, our "three Cs and a B" isn't quite as catchy as the original (sorry Ohmae-san!), but we find it more useful for our purposes. Still, we call it "the four Cs." Just because. The purpose of the four Cs is to help you ask all the questions that need to be answered before you can fully understand what is happening with your brand.

So, if we're doing the four Cs exercise right now, we might ask:

1. **Consumer.** What's happening in consumers' lives right now? How is the coronavirus shaping their confidence about their world? Are they experiencing fear, anxiety, or are they hopeful for a quick return to normal? What are the other factors shaping their lives? How is a potential economic downturn likely to affect their behavior? We then seek to answer softer, attitudinal questions about consumers' mindsets. Look at the TV shows

that are blowing up, or the widely shared memes or themes on social media. What can you learn that might help you understand where your customer's heart and mind are at?

2. **Category.** What brands in our category are on fire? Which are declining? What are those brands promising and why are they growing or shrinking? Anything we can learn from that? What CUOs are growing? Declining? Why?

3. **Culture Code.** What are the big cultural codes in my category? Am I in tune with them or not? In the 2011 Taco Bell example from chapter five, for instance, this would be where we started discovering how foodie-ism was impacting fast food. If you're in the news industry today, this is likely where you'd start unraveling culture's complicated search for, and rejection of, truth and fact.

4. **Brand.** Finally, what's going on with your brand? Start in the distant past. What did the brand once represent to consumers? What does it represent now? Why the change? How does it stack up to your competitors? Does it win with the right CUOs? Does it fulfill the cultural code? Or is it missing the mark? Why?

The Challenge

The four Cs analysis can take us as long as twelve weeks, if we have the luxury of time and we're unraveling a complicated mess of factors, like in the case of KFC South Africa, where every single one of the Cs was in a state of radical flux. But it can also be done much quicker, in a matter of a week or two, if necessary. In these cases, we divide and conquer a bit, and send individual team members off on their own C journey. Someone will dive deep into demographic and psychographic shifts to answer the Consumer C, while someone else goes through the Competition's C, watching old commercials, looking at their pricing structure, doing an in-depth social media analysis, finding industry-wide publications that break down each brand's strength and weakness. We all do gather for the culture code, though, and schedule group chats with relevant academics and cultural experts in the topic. This gives us all the important cultural context we need to decode what's happening in our individual C.

Finally, after a week or so, we all get together for a long internal brain-storm. Each person presents their findings, and after each presentation, we have a mini-brainstorm, where we discuss how what we just saw could be impacting the brand. It gets progressively more insightful as we hear each presentation and discuss each C, and by the end of it, we have a pretty decent grasp on the main factors affecting the category and brand. It's a messy process, and intentionally so. We're called Collider Lab for a reason. We come at the problem from multiple angles at once, with multiple hy-potheses at once. We analyze new data as it comes in, assess its relevance to the situation, and either incorporate it or park it off to the side. The trick is that we do all this within the confines of a framework we trust: Ohmae's plussed-up three Cs model. We're not just casting about wildly in the wind, hoping to strike insight gold randomly.

As a matter of fact, as we brainstorm, we have four giant sticky notes on the wall: Consumer, Category, Culture Code, and Brand, and as we dis-cuss each C, we throw up smaller sticky notes beneath that column. By the end of the brainstorm, each column has at least twenty potential answers. Then we circle, mark, or set aside the insights we think are most important to our situation. Many times, we're not 100 percent sure we've nailed it, so we build multiple four C "stories" and go off and do a little more research to figure out which is right. But at some point, we're pretty confident we've cracked the four C puzzle and we ask ourselves the big question: "What's the Keystone Challenge?" This is a tough moment. There are lots of factors floating around, and the instinct is to address them all, but in all of our years of doing this, we've never seen a marketing department suc-ceed by going after ten things at once. So we push ourselves, argue, and pressure test our hypotheses until we're sure we've landed on the one thing that needs to be addressed first. Everything else is collected, organized, prioritized, and set aside as next steps.

The key to this whole thing is the lens with which you're doing the analysis. And our lens, of course, is R.E.D. While we're looking at every C, we're asking ourselves, "Is this a cultural relevance problem or perhaps a functional relevance situation where we haven't expanded our CUOs enough?" Or maybe it's an ease of access situation, where our competitor's distribution is better than ours. Maybe as we look at the brand C we realize our advertising isn't very breakthrough and we are, therefore, failing with easy to notice. Or perhaps we discover, while doing the category C, that the competitors have developed far more distinctive brand assets and distinctiveness may be our core problem.

We know what you're thinking. Wouldn't it just be easier and do a R.E.D. analysis, step by step, and dispense with the four Cs? We'd love to say yes. But no. They both do very different things. The four Cs tells you *which way to look*, and R.E.D. tells you *what to look for*. The good thing is that the four Cs is just a simple map. It just helps point you to the big four quadrants and nothing more. There is no additional science in the way we use it. It simply ensures we are taking a deep look at the competitors in our category, the life of our consumers, the emerging cultural codes, and the brand itself. R.E.D. is the meat of the matter, and what is going to provide the answers you're looking for.

Once you've identified the keystone problem, prioritize solving it over everything else. Don't dilute your energy by trying to solve multiple issues at once. Instead, inspire a company-wide push to turn around this one aspect of your business—if indeed, it's a cross-departmental issue. Let's say our keystone problem is that customers find ordering from us too complex and slow (ease of access). We might define our solution as, "streamline an overly complex menu and ordering process." Now our whole team has one shared goal, from operations, to marketing and IT, and so on. We unite around this one goal, and encourage people to feel like this transformation will work. Then, when everyone involved in the brand sees that first success (in our example, conversion rates ticking up and sales increasing), we celebrate it and acknowledge that change is happening.

Remember how we believe it's more important to act with conviction than to dither and delay figuring out the perfect action to take? This holds true for a keystone problem as well. What you're looking for is the domino effect that follows bold action. Pick a problem, and solve it with conviction, and you'll start a domino effect. Once your teams see that forward momentum and feel progress, they'll be reinvigorated, and more hopeful in turn. Before you know it, you'll see a happier team, improved communication, increased efficiency, and better work.

In our classic Taco Bell example from the Cultural Relevance chapter, we realized that we were hopelessly out of tune with culture. Let's look at another example from the Yum! universe: KFC España.

The Fifty-Year-Old Bird

KFC has operated in Spain for over fifty years, but by 2018 the brand was in serious trouble. Sales were sliding, and the new marketing leaders, Jesus Cubero and Pablo Calavia, were under intense pressure from everyone to turn it around quickly. They engaged Collider Lab for an accelerated project, and after a couple of weeks of digging we started to get a clear picture of the situation. Our consumer analysis didn't detect anything unexpected. Sure, Spaniards were having a tough time financially, but our prices were in line with competitors. Our category analysis was, likewise, pretty uneventful: lots of low-cost brands were booming, but nothing shocking. The cultural code was about "access to socialization," as Spaniards love eating together and were in the midst of a financial crisis. But when we looked closely at the brand C, we saw the problem: the advertising from previous years wasn't unique, ownable, and consistent, and as a result, consumers were barely even acknowledging KFC's presence in the country. KFC's invisibility was so pronounced that several consumers we spoke to had to ask us, "KFC? That's the restaurant that sells . . . chicken, right?" Remember, we'd been in Spain for fifty years at this point.

If we solved the lack of distinctiveness, we'd also solve a corollary problem, that consumers who were aware of KFC had the impression that the brand was low-quality. (Remember, salience means that if people are talking about your brand, it will be more memorable, and consumers will assume that it must be good to be so widely discussed.) Jesus and Pablo are classic Yum! marketers: intuitive, bold, and quick to act. So when we sat down with them after a week and said, "We think your problem isn't quality or cultural relevance, it's distinctiveness," they both immediately agreed to pivot their efforts and address it. They instinctively understood the keystone problem. Instead of noodling, or testing, or talking it through with endless teams, or doing any more positioning work, they invited three very young, very creative agencies in Spain to help them land the distinctive idea.

A few weeks later, all three presented creative solutions that were light on positioning and heavy on distinctiveness. All we really wanted to say was that KFC sells good chicken, but make a lot of noise doing so. The agencies were allowed to use the Colonel, or any one of our distinctive assets. Eventually we selected a pitch that featured people dancing, and singing this absurd song, "chicken chicken." It was wonderful, ridiculous, quickly became highly distinctive, and led to double-digit growth for the next three years.

Here's the point though: by giving KFC España a big win, everyone backed off of the marketing team. The franchisees were delighted. They were busy again! The GM and regional leaders could breathe. They were no longer calling Jesus and Pablo and pressuring them to try something new. "Suddenly, we had all the credit in the world to try even more daring things," explains Pablo. "That initial success removed the immediate, defensive pressure and instead put us on the offense in the marketplace, which is far more exciting."

So, this is the key takeaway: *Momentum is everything.*

Once you have that first small success, everyone, from the CMO who knows she is one more bad quarterly report away from being fired, to the frontline employees exhausted by unhappy customers, can relax and take a breath. They see that change is possible, and more important, there are people in charge capable of pushing that change through. The old farmer saying that it is easier to turn a moving tractor is very true. Once you get a little momentum going, all sorts of opportunities open up.

Of course, we are making it sound easier than it is. It takes guts to pick a keystone problem and prioritize it, especially when the brand is flailing and management, shareholders, and franchisees are breathing fire and demanding results. But if our experience is any indication, you'll be rewarded if you can take a minute, do a four Cs analysis, find your conviction, and put the bulk of your resources behind that one thing.

At the same time, you have to be honest with yourself about the organization in which you work. Your keystone solution has to be something you can rally people around. John Kenny, from the Michelob Ultra example way back in the Cultural Relevance chapter, has this excellent piece of advice:

> Different organizations need to think about what strategy they are best able to pursue. Relevance requires a team that is not afraid to alienate cultural conservatives. Ease requires an organization that will be ruthless in its use of data and technology to improve the customer experience. Distinctiveness requires a commitment to switch from being a process-driven organization to a creatively driven organization, where storytelling, emotion, and originality are more prized than order, process, and predictability. Excellence in any of these is hard. Success is not for the faint of heart.

So, where do we all go from here?

Who knows what happens now. By the time you read this, no doubt there will be some kind of clarity about how business moves forward. At Collider Lab we are doubling down on collaboration. It's always been key to our success, but in the last few months since COVID hit, we've reached out to double the number of professors, experts, and cultural thinkers that we would normally expect to collaborate with. Why? Because sharing ideas, learning from our peers, and collaborating with like minds (and, more importantly, unlike minds) makes us feel less alone and better equipped to handle the strangeness of current times.

This kind of collaboration can be both external, with our wide range of experts, and internal. In the last few months, Yum! has created the R.E.D. LT, which Catherine Tan-Gillespie leads. All the global brand managers convene every two weeks to discuss what they're doing, what works, and what doesn't. This shared sense of struggle and occasional triumph has been invaluable.

Business isn't going anywhere. The challenges and joys of the jobs that most of us love so much will still be here, albeit in different forms than we have experienced in the past. With R.E.D. in your pocket, we believe you will have the confidence and skills to adapt to what is sure to be a fast-changing environment. We hope we see you out there, and more relevantly, we hope we see your breakthrough work, in all its relevant, ease-ful, and distinctive glory.

Good luck!

Greg and Ken

THE PURPOSE OF EACH RED COMPONENT

RED COMPONENT		WHAT IT IS	WHAT IT AFFECTS
R.	CULTURAL RELEVANCE	The deeper, culturally relevant meaning of a brand. Gives people identity and a sense of belonging to a herd.	The brand's overall DNA, reflected to some degree at every touchpoint.
	FUNCTIONAL RELEVANCE	The brand's ability to be known for fulfilling people's functional needs in the category: category use occasions.	The product or service itself, as well as the comms that connect those CUOs to the brand.
	SOCIAL RELEVANCE	The ability of a brand to be buzzworthy and talked about.	Stunts, buzzworthy activations in culture.
E.	EASY TO NOTICE	Creating salience with all category users through mass media and memorable creative.	The media plan and the advertising creative.
	EASY TO ACCESS	Becoming as readily acessible and friction-free as possible in the buying journey.	The distribution, retail strategy, e-commerce, and buying process.
D.	DISTINCTIVENESS	The brand's consistent use of unique and ownable brand assets to create an unmistakable brand that stands out.	The look, feel, and construct of all advertising, product, packaging, and so on.

Further Reading

AS WE'VE MENTIONED, at Collider Lab we like to read. A lot. Now, we recognize most busy marketers, ad agency execs and creatives, or brand builders don't have time to sit down and read on a regular basis. So . . . our suggestion would be assigning books to anyone within your organization who expresses an interest in reading a hot book, digesting its contents, and sharing what they discover at a regular book club within your organization. Ideas and inspiration are everywhere. New ways to understand how your customers think may pop up in unexpected places. Make sure you are tuning into big thinkers outside your category, whether it's TED Talk podcasts; smaller, niche pods on pop culture; social trends or current events; or academic articles digging into new discoveries in psychology, anthropology, sociology, and behavioral economics. We love to uncover new ideas—but we get that most people don't have the luxury to spend hours noodling out on their favorite podcast app. So, farm it out, then come together and share your insights and observations. And, if you hear or read or see something that you think is brilliant? Please share it with the rest of us!

Reading List from the Introduction

After finishing this book, you may want to read *How Brands Grow: What Marketers Don't Know*, by Byron Sharp, to understand the marketing revolution he's started. But then read a little Douglas Holt to understand the other side of the argument entirely. His book *How Brands Become Icons: The Principles of Cultural Branding* is a good place to start. Check out Paul Feldwick's *The Anatomy of Humbug: How to Think Differently About Advertising*, as it does a great job of going through all the old theories of marketing in much more detail than we do here. For a particularly rousing read, check out Phil Barden's essay in the excellent anthology *Eat Your Greens*. For an illuminating read on how cultural capital is a foundational marker of social class, check out Elizabeth Currid-Halkett's excellent book, *The Sum of Small Things: A Theory of the Aspirational Class*. We are indebted to professor Currid-Halkett for the endless hours she's spent on the phone with us over the years. Stephen Johnson's excellent book, *Where Good Ideas Come From: The Natural History of Innovation,* is an essential Collider Lab read (and where we got the name "Collider" from; he explains that the most eclectic, densely packed, and highly interactive places on earth are the ones that create the most new life).

Reading List from the Relevance Overview Chapter

For further insight into how humans make choices, read the classic *Thinking Fast and Slow,* by Daniel Kahneman. *Predictably Irrational* by Dan Ariely is a great deep dive into behavioral economics. Robert Cialdini's *Influence: The Psychology of Persuasion* is one of Ken's favorites because it's a pretty inspiring predecessor to behavioral economics. For an in-depth, excellent read on the herd dynamic, check out Mark Earls's *Herd: How to Change Mass Behavior by Harnessing our True Nature.* It's been a mainstay at Collider Lab for many years. If you're curious about differentiation between herds around the world, check out Geert Hofstede's 6 Dimensions Model online.

Reading List from the Cultural Relevance Chapter

The best book we've stumbled across that explains in detail the dynamics involved in cultural relevance is Holt's *How Brands Become Icons.* Clotaire

Rapaille's *Culture Code: An Ingenious Way to Understand Why People Around the World Live and Buy as They Do* is a captivating read, detailing how different categories mean different things around the world (although we don't agree with all his conclusions). Brené Brown's *Braving the Wilderness: The Quest for True Belonging and the Courage to Stand Alone* is an insightful exploration of what it means to "belong."

Reading List from the Functional Relevance Chapter

For further insight into the idea of how innovation in design and marketing has to remain within the limits of what your customer will find acceptable, read up on the MAYA Principle as originally conceived by Raymond Loewy.[1] It stands for *Most Advanced, Yet Acceptable*, and although it was originally intended for design, it works very nicely for expanding your CUOs as it pushes you to try new things, but not stray too far. David Taylor's *Brand Stretch: Why 1 in 2 Extensions Fail, and How to Beat the Odds* is a solid look at why so many forays into new CUOs fail. There's also lots to be learned from Anthony Ulwick's *Jobs to Be Done: Theory to Practice*.

Reading List from the Social Relevance Chapter

We enjoyed *Connected: The Surprising Power of Our Social Networks and How They Shape Our Lives* by two acclaimed social scientists, Nicholas Christakis from Yale and James Fowler from UC San Diego. Check out *The Wisdom of the Crowds* by James Surowiecki for more about the concept of social proof. Have a look at some of the most socially relevant media, stars, and influencers around. At the time of this writing, we'd suggest James Charles's show, *Instant Influencer*, on YouTube. Also, David Dobrik and Shane Dawson on the same platform, especially the latter interviewing controversial influencers like Jake Paul and Jeffree Star. Bon Appetit YouTube is a brilliant example of how you can move your brand to a new platform and dominate in it. Look at other niche influencers like bullet-journalist Amanda Lee (AmandaRachLee), dance instigator Charli D'Amelio on TikTok, beauty guru Jackie Aina, body positive beauty guru Tess Holliday on Instagram, motivational speaker Prince Ea, and Emma Chamberlain on YouTube, among many, many others. The idea isn't to emulate, copy, or follow them. Instead, look at these people as examples of how to understand exactly how social relevance is evolving in front of your own eyes. Times change fast, so ask your kids, new hires, or baristas for their tips of who to stream today.

Reading List from the Easy to Access Chapter

Rory Sutherland's 2019 book, *Alchemy: The Dark Art and Curious Science of Creating Magic in Brand, Business, and Life*, is a wonderful journey through the illogical-seeming mind of humans and our surprising approach to making decisions. Adam Ferrier's *The Advertising Effect: How to Change Behavior* is a Collider Lab favorite. Check out *Inside the Nudge Unit: How Small Changes Can Make a Big Difference* by David Halperin. It's a fascinating look at how the British government changed people's behavior with small nudges. Barry Schwartz's *The Paradox of Choice: Why More Is Less* is a classic full of surprising insights into how less really can be more (even allowing for the controversy over the jam study). Paco Underhill's *Why We Buy: The Science of Shopping* is full of insights into how to increase sales by adjusting how you position products and other store furniture. It's a really fun read, too, trust us!

Reading List from the Easy to Notice Chapter

This is a tricky subject, hotly debated, and with lots of money on the table for media companies and the martech/adtech crowd. So be very picky about your reading here. Search for neutrality above all else. The two fundamental reads come from the IPA in London: *The Long and the Short of It: Balancing Short and Long-Term Marketing Strategies* and *Media in Focus: Marketing Effectiveness in the Digital Era*. Both are easy, short-form PDFs

and are written by Les Binet and Peter Field. Keep a close eye out for whatever these two authors publish next.

Reading List from the Distinctive Chapters

Shockingly, there hasn't been a lot written about distinctiveness. Because
the marketing world has been so enamored with emotional connection,
brand love, and brand purpose, this incredibly important topic (far more
important than all those three philosophies put together) has been largely
ignored. The few exceptions to that are Jenni Romaniuk's *Building Distinctive Brand Assets*, which should be your first and most important selection. Afterward, check out *Iconic Advantage: Don't Chase the New,
Innovate the Old* by Soon Yu (even *if* the book talks about emotional connection and meaning).

Once again, we encourage you to do your own investigations and
research—there's a ton of fascinating information out there.

Acknowledgments

Greg Creed

To my parents, Albert and Moya Creed, who raised me to believe anything was possible.

To my amazing wife, Carolyn, and our now-adult children, Tim and Lauren. I am incredibly grateful and proud of you for putting up with the multiple relocations around the world as I pursued my career. I hope you feel that it was ultimately worth it!

To Su Mon Wong, my marketing lecturer (1976 and 1977) at the Queensland University of Technology (QUT), where I discovered my passion for marketing.

To Peter England, my first marketing boss at Lever & Kitchen (Unilever) in Sydney (1980–1982), who nurtured my love of marketing and taught me the skill of "less is more."

To P. D. H. (Dyrk) Riddell, my boss when I worked in Detergents Coordination at Unilever House in London (1987–1988), who taught me so much about the importance of cultural relevance in a global business.

To David Novak, a world-class marketer in his own right, who plucked me from Australia to be the CMO of Taco Bell in 2001 and who ultimately asked me to succeed him as the CEO of Yum! in January 2015.

To all of the marketing teams I have had the privilege to lead as CMO at KFC in Australia and New Zealand and at Taco Bell. In particular I'd like to recognize Atul Sharma and Chris Mort (Ogilvy), Jeff Fox, Bob Fulmer, Tom

Wagner, Debbie Myers, Martin Hennessy, Laurie Schalow, Lynn Hemans, Tracee Larocca, and Melissa Friebe.

To the wonderful executive admins I had the privilege to work with, including Judy Ecob, Rosa Dias, Karen Walters, Diane Savage, Donna Hughes, and Jennifer Henry.

To my co-conspirator, and the real "most interesting man in the world" (sorry Dos Equis, but it's true), Ken Muench. Ken: Thanks for suggesting we write this book together! It has been a little strange to cowrite during COVID, but I can't think of anyone else who I would want to write about brand-building with. Your vision, insight, and endless good humor has helped build Yum! into a marketing superstar. Nobody could have done it better than you!

And a final thank-you to everyone involved in making Taco Bell, KFC, and Pizza Hut a success over the years: everyone in the RSCs, but especially our associates in the restaurants. Your dedication, grit, and commitment has always inspired me to try harder. And finally, to our guests—the people who ultimately decide if our work is a success or failure: thank you! My career has been the adventure of a lifetime, and I am profoundly grateful to each and every one of you I met along the way.

Ken Muench

This book could've been written by Greg Dzurik, Catherine Tan-Gillespie, Jessika Gomez-Duarte, or any number of Collider Lab or Yum! marketers. It's a system that has been methodically built over the course of the last eight years and refined as new data rolls in and we find what works and what doesn't. So many people have had a direct hand in its creation and refinement that it's impossible to thank everyone who had a role, but here is my attempt. First off, to Caroline Greeven, who was with us daily throughout the writing process, pushing, prodding, reinterpreting, and politely making our nerdy marketing thoughts palatable to humans, thank you. Your patience, hard work, brilliant skills, and constant guidance were essential to this endeavor. Thank you to Jeff Fox, cofounder of Collider

Lab. I am clearly indebted to you for pushing us all to take the plunge and open our own shop. Your constant guidance and practical marketing (and life) advice these last ten years has been a touchstone for me. John Kenny and Michael Faschnacht, the years we worked together at FCB stand out as some of the most intellectually stimulating ones in my career. Thank you for pushing me to write the book and helping to mature the initial ingredients of the R.E.D. system. To the folks at Collider Lab who had a direct hand in creating several of the training exercises that later made their way into the book, thank you. And, of course, thank you for the endless hours over the years helping create the system and/or reading the manuscript over and over and over, always finding something smart to add or silly to remove: Shirley Mak, Jack Lettenmair, Abby Barnes, Emily Leung, Lila Faz, Nick Gomez, Dominick King, Taylor Leigh, Alex Tennis, Xitlaly Ruelas, Jessica Wong, Jamie Keen, David Medina, Aarika Hernandez, Angel Huang, Caleb Guan, Naomi LeDoux, Queenie Zhu, Sam Renzi, and, of course, the aforementioned Jessika and Greg. And to my cowriter, Greg Creed, I just have to say that I've never met a kinder, wiser, more empathetic human being who also happens to be a preternaturally skilled marketer and incredible leader (anyone that knows him also knows that this is still underselling him).

Notes

Chapter Three

1. Martin Pengelly, "Nike Sales Surge 31% in Days after Colin Kaepernick Ad Unveiled, Analyst Says," *Guardian*, September 8, 2018. Accessed at https://www.theguardian.com/sport/2018/sep/08/colin-kaepernick-nike-ad-sales-up.
2. Vanessa Romo, "NFL on Kneeling Players' Protests: 'We Were Wrong,' Commissioner Says," NPR, June 5, 2020. Accessed at https://www.npr.org/sections/live-updates-protests-for-racial-justice/2020/06/05/871290906/nfl-on-kneeling-players-protests-we-were-wrong-commissioner-says.
3. Byron Sharp termed this concept "Mental and Physical Availability" in *How Brands Grow*. He also credits some of these levers as being the vast majority of what drives a purchase.

Chapter Four

1. As Sharp says in chapter eight of *How Brands Grow*, "Scientific laws, theory and direct empirical evidence challenge the importance placed on meaningful perceived differentiation. Differentiation does exist, but the degree of differentiation is weak and varies little between rival brands, and it is far less important than is portrayed."
2. *LoveMarks: The Future Beyond Brands*, by Kevin Roberts, former CEO of Saatchi and Saatchi, is the definitive book about this theory.
3. Richard Shotton, "Fast and Slow Lessons for Marketers," *Guardian*, April 7, 2014. Accessed at https://www.theguardian.com/media-network/media-network-blog/2014/apr/07/thinking-fast-slow-marketers-consumers.
4. Jeff Bercovici, "Small Businesses Say Amazon Has a Huge Counterfeiting Problem. This 'Shark Tank' Company Is Fighting Back," *Inc.*, March/April, 2019. Accessed at https://www.inc.com/magazine/201904/jeff-bercovici/amazon-fake-copycat-knockoff-products-small-business.html; Stephen McBride, "Is This the Beginning of Amazon's Meltdown?" *Forbes*, January 2, 2020. Accessed at https://www.forbes.com/sites/stephenmcbride1/2020/01/02/is-this-the-beginning-of-amazons-apocalypse/#1509982d726c.

5. In his classic book, *Thinking Fast and Slow* (Farrar, Straus, and Giroux, 2011).
6. Yuval Noah Harari, *Sapiens* (Harper, 2015).

Chapter Five

1. D. B. Holt, *How Brands Become Icons* (Harvard Business Review Press, Kindle Edition), p. 2.
2. Now, poor distribution or a lack of product will never amount to big sales (it's the opposite of "Easy to Access!") but it does provide an opportunity to show just how passionate your users are about your brand. In the case of Oatly, very.
3. Holt, *How Brands Become Icons*, p. 4.
4. Now, you may argue, "Who cares about the aspirational class? That's not my target." But what the aspirational class loves today, the rest of the world loves tomorrow . . . out of sheer imitation and wanting to be "like the cool kids." This explains why people can simultaneously own fossil fuel stocks and Teslas. The cars have passed the cool kid test, and now everyone wants to drive them—no matter what their belief systems about climate change or Peak Oil.
5. Zoe Wood, "Oprah Winfrey and Jay-Z Tap into Rising Alt-Milk Star Oatly," *Guardian*, July 14, 2020. Accessed at https://www.theguardian.com/food/2020/jul/14/oprah-winfrey-and-jay-z-tap-into-rising-alt-milk-star-oatly.
6. "Guinness Targets Africans with Bold 'Made of Black' Campaign," *Ad Age*, August 28, 2014. Accessed at https://adage.com/creativity/work/made-black/36936; "Guinness: Made of Black," WARC. Accessed at https://warc.com/content/article/apg/guinness-made-of-black/105191.
7. Aimee Grove, "MEDIA: Taco Bell: Yo Quiero Profits, Not Just a Cute Little Dog," *PR Week*, July 31, 2000. Accessed at https://www.prweek.com/article/1240070/media-taco-bell-yo-quiero-profits-not-just-cute-little-dog.
8. Aimee Grove, "MEDIA: Taco Bell: Yo Quiero Profits, Not Just a Cute Little Dog."
9. "Most Innovative Companies, 2016," *Fast Company*. Accessed at https://www.fastcompany.com/most-innovative-companies/2016.
10. Daniel Kahneman, *Thinking Fast and Slow*, 2011.

Chapter Six

1. Jonathan Stempel, "CEO of Buffett-owned Brooks Running Moves Production Out of China, Cites Tariff Threat," Reuters, May 3, 2019. Accessed at https://www.reuters.com/article/us-berkshire-buffett-brooks/ceo-of-buffett-owned-brooks-running-moves-production-out-of-china-cites-tariff-threat-idUSKCN1S91DU.
2. Laylan Connelly, "Nike Surf Products Folded into Hurley Brand," *Orange County Register*, November 28, 2012. Accessed at https://www.ocregister.com/2012/11/28/nike-surf-products-folded-into-hurley-brand/.
3. "Cautionary Comments regarding the Myers-Brigg Type Inventory," *Consulting Psychology Journal: Practice and Research*, Summer 2005.

4. "These Are the Biggest Fast Food Franchises in South Africa," Businesstech, July 25, 2019. Accessed at https://businesstech.co.za/news/business/331387/these-are -the-biggest-fast-food-franchises-in-south-africa-2/.

5. Old Spice owns several other CUOs with their other scents and variants, including antiperspirants, face cleansers, beard care, and so on.

6. "Legacy's Truth Campaign Named One of the Top Campaigns of the 21st Century," *Tobacco Unfiltered* blog, January 14, 2015. Accessed at https://www.tobaccofreekids .org/blog/2015_01_14_legacy.

7. "Taco Bell's® Drive-Thru Diet® Menu Fuels Christine Dougherty's 26.2-Mile Run in the Marathon in New York City," BusinessWire, November 7, 2010. Accessed at https://www.businesswire.com/news/home/20101107005102/en/Taco-Bell%E2 %80%99s%C2%AE-Drive-Thru-Diet%C2%AE-Menu-Fuels-Christine.

8. Emily Bryson York, "Taco Bell Takes Heat over 'Drive-Thru Diet' Menu," *Ad Age*, January 4, 2010. Accessed at https://adage.com/article/news/advertising-taco-bell -takes-heat-diet-menu/141285.

9. To help you think of all the different dimensions of use occasions, we recommend using Byron Sharp's what, when, who, where, why, etc. as primers.

Chapter Seven

1. "Edelman Trust Barometer Archive," Edelman, January 1, 2019. Accessed at https:// www.edelman.com/research/edelman-trust-barometer-archive.

2. This number is for the "General Population." The drop in trust is even sharper for the "Informed Public": from 74 percent to 54 percent. (https://www.edelman.com /sites/g/files/aatuss191/files/2018-10/2018_Edelman_Trust_Barometer_Global _Report_FEB.pdf p.11).

3. "New Credos Report Highlights How Consumers Want Advertising to Change," Advertising Association, January 30, 2019. Accessed at https://www.adassoc.org.uk /policy-areas/new-credos-report-highlights-how-consumers-want-advertising -to-change/.

4. Cheryl Wischhover, "Glossier Is Going After New Customers with an Army of Reps," Racked, July 12, 2017. Accessed at https://www.racked.com/2017/7/12/15949530 /glossier-international-shipping-canada-uk.

5. Georgina Caldwell, "Tom Ford Beauty Poised to Become Billion-Dollar Brand by 2020," Global Cosmetics News, June 20, 2016. Accessed at https://www.globalcosmetics news.com/tom-ford-beauty-poised-to-become-billion-dollar-brand-by-2020/.

6. Tonya Garcia, "Coty's $600 Million Deal with Kylie Jenner Is Designed to Hang on to Her Social Media Star Power," Market Watch, November 23, 2019. Accessed at https://www.marketwatch.com/story/cotys-600-million-deal-with-kylie -jenner-is-designed-to-hang-on-to-her-social-media-star-power-2019-11-18.

7. "Kyle Jenner Sells $600 Million Stake in Beauty Line to Coty," *Ad Age*, November 18, 2019. Accessed at https://adage.com/article/cmo-strategy/kylie-jenner-sells -600-million-stake-beauty-line-coty/2216571; Tiffani Bova, "How Kylie Jenner

Built One of the Fastest Growing Beauty Brands Ever," *Entrepreneur*, July 20, 2018. Accessed at https://www.entrepreneur.com/article/317001.

8. Jason Collins, "Please, Not Another Bias! An Evolutionary Take on Behavioral Economics," *Jason Collins Blog*, July 30, 2015. Accessed at https://jasoncollins.blog /2015/07/30/please-not-another-bias-an-evolutionary-take-on-behavioural -economics/.

9. Jonah Berger, a professor at the Wharton School, talks about it in Chip and Dan Heath's *Made to Stick*: "How does it make people look to talk about a product or idea?"

10. Matthew Weaver, "Most KFCs in UK Remain Closed Because of Chicken Shortage," *Guardian*, February 19, 2018. Accessed at https://www.theguardian.com/business /2018/feb/19/kfc-uk-closed-chicken-shortage-fash-food-contract-delivery -dhl; Erik Oster, "KFC Responds to U.K. Chicken Shortage with a Timely 'FCK We're Sorry,'" *Ad Week*, February 23, 2018. Accessed at https://www.adweek.com/creativity /kfc-responds-to-u-k-chicken-shortage-scandal-with-a-timely-fck-were -sorry/; Alexandra Topping, "'People Have Gone Chicken Crazy': What the KFC Crisis Means for the Brand," *Guardian*, February 24, 2018. Accessed at https://www. theguardian.com/business/2018/feb/24/people-have-gone-chicken-crazy -what-the-kfc-crisis-means-for-the-brand; "KFC: Haters Gonna Hate, Use Them as Bait," WARC. Accessed at https://warc.com/content/article/apg/kfc -haters-gonna-hate-use-them-as-bait/127465.

11. Nathan McAlone, "Tons of People Lie About Being All Caught Up on TV Shows, According to Hulu," *Business Insider*, October 7, 2016. Accessed at https://www .businessinsider.com/hulu-research-people-lie-about-watching-tv-shows -2016-10.

Chapter Eight

1. Mary Meisenzahl, "Mark Zuckerberg Dominated People's Phones over the Decade. Here Are the 10 Most Downloaded Apps, Nearly Half of Which Facebook Owns," *Business Insider*, December 20, 2019. Accessed at https://www.businessinsider.com /most-downloaded-apps-of-decade-facebook-instagram-whatsapp-tiktok -snapchat-2019-12.

2. Keith Hawton, Ellen Townsend, Jonathan Deeks, Louis Appleby, David Gunnell, Olive Bennewith, and Jayne Cooper, "Effects of Legislation Restricting Pack Sizes of Paracetamol and Salicylate on Self Poisoning in the United Kingdom: Before and After Study," *BMJ* (*Clinical research ed.*) vol. 322,7296 (2001): 1203–7. doi:10.1136 /bmj.322.7296.1203.

3. Ingrid Lunden, "Amazon's Share of the US e-Commerce Market Is Now 49%, or 5% of All Retail Spend," Tech Crunch, July 13, 2018. Accessed at https://techcrunch .com/2018/07/13/amazons-share-of-the-us-e-commerce-market-is-now-49 -or-5-of-all-retail-spend/.

4. "Amazon - 23 Year Stock Price History | AMZN," Macrotrends. Accessed at https:// www.macrotrends.net/stocks/charts/AMZN/amazon-stock-price-history.

5. "Amazon Selling 'Just Walk Out' Frictionless Checkout Platform to Retailers," *Convenience Store News*, March 13, 2020. Accessed at https://csnews.com/amazon-selling-just-walk-out-frictionless-checkout-platform-retailers.

6. Alice Robb, "Americans Have Started Saying 'Queue.' Blame Netflix," *New Republic*, March 13, 2020. Accessed at https://newrepublic.com/article/116996/netflix-queue-and-history-british-word-america.

7. Minda Zetlin, "Blockbuster Could Have Bought Netflix for $50 Million, but the CEO Thought It Was a Joke," *Inc.*, September 20, 2019. Accessed at https://www.inc.com/minda-zetlin/netflix-blockbuster-meeting-marc-randolph-reed-hastings-john-antioco.html.

8. Robert Channick, "Despite Growth of Streaming, Redbox CEO Sees Future in DVD Rentals," *Chicago Tribune*, July 20, 2017. Accessed at https://www.chicagotribune.com/business/ct-galen-smith-redbox-exec-qa-0723-biz-20170720-story.html.

9. Barry Schwartz, "Is the Famous 'Paradox of Choice' a Myth?" *PBS News Hour*, January 29, 2014. Accessed at https://www.pbs.org/newshour/economy/is-the-famous-paradox-of-choic; Alina Tugend, "Too Many Choices: A Problem That Can Paralyze," *New York Times*, February 26, 2010. Accessed at https://www.nytimes.com/2010/02/27/your-money/27shortcuts.html.

10. Sarah Perez "Grocery Delivery Apps See Record Downloads Amid Coronavirus Outbreak," Tech Crunch, March 16, 2020. Accessed at https://techcrunch.com/2020/03/16/grocery-delivery-apps-see-record-downloads-amid-coronavirus-outbreak/.

11. A few months into the COVID crisis and the intense desire to bake your own bread has gone back all the way down to pre-COVID levels, according to Google Trends.

12. Naturally, when the economy dips, people may balk at the added cost of delivery, but by and large, once consumers adopt a habit that is intrinsically easier, it takes a great deal to shift them back to the more labor-intensive approach. Not a lot of folks went back to horses and buggies once they had access to a reliable, affordable "horseless carriage"!

Chapter Nine

1. These companies, who usually do some variant of "Marketing Mix Attribution," do often fall into the trap of just efficiency and overnight ROI. If you're not careful, you can "efficiency the brand to death," by moving all investment into what works for sales today, forgetting that you're also building a brand for the long term.

2. As described by Byron Sharp in *How Brands Grow*.

3. "Dear TV: We Love You. You're Perfect. Now Change. (But Not Too Much.)," *Ad Age*, April 18, 2016. Accessed at https://adage.com/article/media/future-tv-advertising/303565.

4. Lutz Jänke, "Emotions Are the Glue Holding Our Travel Memories Together," Swiss. Accessed at https://www.moments-that-last.com/en/article/67.

5. Shahram Heshmet, "Why Do We Remember Certain Things, but Forget Others," *Psychology Today*, October 8, 2015. Accessed at https://www.psychologytoday.com/us/blog/science-choice/201510/why-do-we-remember-certain-things-forget-others.

6. Sarah R. Lentz, "Love—What Is It Good For? A Lot, Says Evolutionary Psychology," *UT News*, August 3, 2018. Accessed at https://news.utexas.edu/2018/08/03/love -what-is-it-good-for/.

7. "Emotions and Memory," Psychologist World. Accessed at https://www .psychologistworld.com/emotion/emotion-memory-psychology.

Chapter Eleven

1. Charles Spence and Qian (Janice) Wang, "Sensory Expectations Elicited by the Sounds of Opening the Packaging and Pouring a Beverage," *Flavour* 4, 35 (2015). https://doi.org/10.1186/s13411-015-0044-y.

2. Janine Popick, "How Virgin Atlantic's Marketing Nails It," *Inc.*, April 12, 2013. Accessed at https://www.inc.com/janine-popick/how-virgin-atlantics-marketing -nails-it.html.

3. We can't move on from here without acknowledging Professor Jenni Romaniuk from the Ehrenberg-Bass Institute. Her work has helped to form the foundation of how we look at distinctiveness. She has personally taken the time to explain, debate, and explain again how she views the topic. The conversation got so engaging at one point that our team flew out to Chicago to meet her on her two-hour break between meetings to get a lesson in person from the professor herself.

4. Stuart Elliott, "Tropicana Discovers Some Buyers Are Passionate About Packaging," *New York Times*, February 22, 2009. Accessed at https://www.nytimes.com/2009 /02/23/business/media/23adcol.html.

5. "Maximize Your TV Advertising Effectiveness," Nielsen infographic, 2016. Accessed at https://www.nielsen.com/wp-content/uploads/sites/3/2019/04/tvbe -branding-best-practices-may-2016.pdf.

6. Ben Ice, "Survey Reveals the Most Recalled Ad on Australian TV: None," Australian Marketing Institute, July 11, 2017. Accessed at https://www.marketingmag.com.au /news-c/recalled-tv-ads/.

7. Simeon Goldstein, "Fairy Brings Back Classic Bottle to Celebrate 50th Birthday: Video," Packaging News, February 8, 2010. Accessed at https://www.packaging news.co.uk/news/materials/rigid-plastics/fairy-brings-back-classic-bottle-to -celebrate-50th-birthday-video-08-02-2010.

8. Bruce Horovitz, "No Bones About It: KFC Goes Boneless," *USA Today*, April 5, 2013. Accessed at https://www.usatoday.com/story/money/business/2013/04/05/kfc -kentucky-fried-chicken-boneless-fast-food-chicken/2011419/.

Chapter Twelve

1. Alexander Huls, "How Editor Jen Dean Created an M&M's Ad from 75 Years of Footage," *Pond5 Blog*, October 11, 2017. Accessed at https://blog.pond5.com/16171 -editor-jen-dean-created-mms-ad-75-years-footage/.

2. Lara O'Reilly, "How 6 Colorful Characters Propelled M&M's to Become America's Favorite Candy," *Business Insider*, March 26, 2016. Accessed at https://www.business insider.com/the-story-of-the-mms-characters-2016-3.

3. Will Burns, "Tiger Beer Proves Cause Marketing Can Be as Helpful to the Brand as It Is to the Cause," *Forbes*, March 30, 2017. Accessed at https://www.forbes.com /sites/willburns/2017/05/30/tiger-beer-proves-cause-marketing-can-be-as -helpful-to-the-brand-as-it-is-to-the-cause/#e69c5dd5cced.

4. Rebecca J. Ritzel, "The TWA Hotel, Design Icon from the Mad Men Era, Is Back in Business," *Air & Space*, October 2019. Accessed at https://www.airspacemag.com /airspacemag/trans-world-hotel-180973137/.

Further Reading

1. Rikke Friis Dam, "The Maya Principle: Design for the Future, but Balance It with Your Users' Present," Interaction Design Foundation, 2020. Accessed at https:// www.interaction-design.org/literature/article/design-for-the-future-but -balance-it-with-your-users-present.

Index

About the Authors

Greg Creed was born and educated in Australia before beginning his marketing career with Unilever, which took him from Sydney to London and New York. He then joined PepsiCo in their restaurant division, which was then spun into what we know as Yum! Brands today. He believes the job of a marketer is simple but not easy: to drive sales overnight and build the brand over time. Since retiring as the CEO of Yum! at the end of 2019, he has started a small "unconsulting" company, Creed UnCo, focused on helping companies with brand building, franchising, and culture and leadership.

Ken Muench was born and raised in Mexico City, and moved to the United States in the early 1990s to attend college and start a prolific career in marketing. He was a copywriter, creative director, and eventually director of strategic planning at multiple agencies before cofounding Collider Lab in 2015. Today, Collider Lab helps Yum! Brands—and a select group of external clients—connect their brands to emerging culture and set them up for success with the R.E.D. marketing approach.